Good Guys with Guns

Good Guys with Guns

The Appeal and Consequences of Concealed Carry

· ·

ANGELA STROUD

The University of North Carolina Press Chapel Hill

This book was published with the assistance of the Authors Fund of the
University of North Carolina Press
© 2015 The University of North Carolina Press
All rights reserved
Set in Charis and Lato by Westchester Publishing Services
Manufactured in the United States of America

The University of North Carolina Press has been a member of the Green
Press Initiative since 2003.

Library of Congress Cataloging-in-Publication Data

Names: Stroud, Angela, author.
Title: Good guys with guns : the appeal and consequences of concealed
    carry / Angela Stroud.
Description: Chapel Hill : University of North Carolina Press, [2016] |
    Includes bibliographical references and index.
Identifiers: LCCN 2015041169| ISBN 9781469627892 (pbk : alk. paper) |
    ISBN 9781469627908 (ebook)
Subjects: LCSH: Concealed carry of firearms—Social aspects—United
    States. | Firearms owners—United States—Attitudes. | Firearms—Social
    aspects—United States. | Firearms ownership—United States.
Classification: LCC HV7436 .S78 2016 | DDC 363.33—dc23
    LC record available at http://lccn.loc.gov/2015041169

Cover illustration courtesy of Northland College.

The only thing that stops a bad guy with a gun is a good guy with a gun.

—Wayne LaPierre, NRA executive vice president

I resumed staring at the gun. It occurred to me that this was the ultimate device for determining one's competence in the world. I bounced it in the palm of my hand, sniffed the steely muzzle. What does it mean to a person, beyond his sense of competence and well-being and personal worth, to carry a lethal weapon, to handle it well, be ready and willing to use it? A concealed lethal weapon. It was a secret, it was a second life, a second self, a dream, a spell, a plot, a delirium.

—Don DeLillo, *White Noise*

Contents

Figures and Table

Figures

Table

Acknowledgments

This research would not have been possible were it not for the generosity of the people who agreed to share their views and experiences with me, especially Bill and Mary, who allowed me into their training courses. Thanks to you all for your time, your honesty, and your trust.

I also appreciate the guidance and critiques offered by Mark Warr, Javier Auyero, David Kirk, and John Hartigan, and for the mentorship of Ben Carrington. I am deeply indebted to Christine Williams for supporting me during this research and in my time as a graduate student at the University of Texas. Those who have had the privilege of working with Christine know that she has extremely high expectations but that she will also help you figure out how to meet them. Christine, your belief in my work was what allowed me to persevere during some very challenging times, and I am sincerely grateful for all of your help, including providing research money that I spent at gun ranges!

The seeds of this research were planted very early, when I was an undergraduate at Southwestern University, and I am forever appreciative of Ed Kain, Dan Hilliard, Shannon Winnubst, and particularly Maria Lowe, who was the first to make me realize that I had a knack for sociology and who continues to support my work. I would also like to acknowledge my late grandparents, Doris and Audie Stroud, who made my attending Southwestern possible.

I would like to recognize my students, who are not only sources of inspiration but often my first audience. The chance to share ideas with you and to learn from you has made me a sharper thinker and a clearer communicator, and your enthusiasm and insights continue to be sources of inspiration. I am grateful to the amazing community of Northland College, a place that I am very lucky to have discovered and that I am happy to call home. My students and colleagues at Northland have pushed me to put social justice at the center of my sociological thinking, and for that I am a better scholar, teacher, and person. Thank you, Kevin Schanning and Les Aldritt, for the support that made finishing this book possible, and to Aby Lints for help with the references. To the amazing

Bob Gross: thank you for the beautiful cover (and on such short notice!), and to Brian Mrnak at Sports Hollow in Ashland, Wisconsin, thanks for the cover loaner!

Thank you to my editor Joe Parsons, all of the University of North Carolina Press staff who worked on this book, and the anonymous reviewers who critiqued it. Joe, your diligence and support kept this project moving along even when other life matters threatened to get in the way. Parts of chapters 2 and 4 appear in an article in *Gender & Society*, and I appreciate the guidance offered by editors Dana Britton and Joya Misra and the reviewers who critiqued that work.

It is impossible to imagine having arrived at this point without my graduate school crew, particularly Cati Connell, Megan Reid, and Corinne Reczek. You three were there in the earliest stages of this process and helped me figure out how to make it all happen. Thank you for the insights, the laughs, and all the love. Thanks to my parents, Michelle Kirby and David Stroud, who have always made me feel that I can do anything and whose unique blend of worldviews is found throughout the pages of this book. Thanks also to my stepdad Joe Kirby for teaching me to shoot and for giving me my first gun. My sisters, Lisa Hyche and Laura O'Dea, are two of the most important people in my life, and I am very lucky that they have always been in my corner. Thank you to Cynthia Belmont for your brilliant editing, incisive critique, and, most of all, unyielding support in everything. I am the luckiest person in the world.

This book is dedicated to my children, Mackenzie, Maddie, and Ryan, who have always inspired me to do what is right and just even when it is difficult. May you always seek the truth and let love be your guide.

I've had help along the way, but any mistakes are my own.

Good Guys with Guns

1 Introduction

· ·

I met John at his firearms training school located in a rural part of Central Texas where he and other instructors teach various safety and self-defense courses, from introductory pistol to SWAT tactics.[1] I was a couple of months into my research on concealed handgun licensing, and my enculturation into the worldview of license holders was well under way.[2] Though I started this project uncertain about why a person would feel the need to carry a firearm in public, by the morning John and I met, I had already heard enough stories about violent assaults and the horror of being helpless when confronted by an armed criminal that I was developing anxiety about the idea of victimization, and I was starting to see the appeal of carrying a handgun. This was happening despite my familiarity with the empirical evidence that clearly showed that violent crime rates were continuing a two-decade-long trend of steep decline and my deep reservations about what it would mean for our society to have an ever-growing cadre of armed citizens. Would we become increasingly suspicious of one another? How would basic social ties be affected? These questions loomed in the background as I interviewed John.

If proponents of concealed handgun licenses (CHLs) could handpick a spokesperson to promote their cause, John would be an excellent candidate. He is smart and articulate and speaks quickly and convincingly about why handgun licensing is effective social policy. For example, he explained that the likelihood of a police officer's being around when you need one is virtually zero: "It doesn't mean that they're bad people . . . [or] that their organization is a failure. It means that they have a limited number of officers, and we wouldn't want to live in a country where you have a police officer at your elbow twenty-four hours a day anyway. And most of the police officers would not want to work in an environment like that either. They're not interested in that. By definition that means that if you're going to be able to defend yourself against a violent attack from someone that has no justification for attacking you other than greed, malice, sexual, whatever, then, you've pretty much gotta be ready to take care of yourself." He continued, "Our joke is, 'It'll never happen to me' . . . is not a self-defense plan. But the vast majority of unarmed people, that's their self-defense plan. They say, 'Well why do you carry a gun? Nothing bad is ever gonna happen to me.' And I say, 'Well, let me give you some phone numbers. You know, let's talk to people that, yeah, they said that too. Right before something did. Or something happened to somebody they knew.'"

The likelihood that a person will become a victim of crime is a product of both the overall crime rate and whether that person falls into a "high risk" demographic (Koppel 1987). And while it is true that anyone can become a crime victim, it is also the case that the violent crime rate has dropped dramatically over the past few decades. For example, between 1993 and 2013 the violent victimization rate—which includes rape, sexual assault, robbery, aggravated assault, and simple assault—dropped from 79.8 to 23.2 victimizations per 1,000 people in the population who are twelve and older (Truman and Langton 2014). The homicide rate has experienced similarly steep declines and in recent years has reached lows last seen in the 1960s (Cooper and Smith 2011).[3] Factors that increase the odds that a person will be a victim of violent crime include sex (males are victimized more than females), race (blacks are victimized more than whites and Hispanics), and age (victimization is much higher for those between twelve and thirty-four than for those thirty-five and older; Truman, Langton, and Planty 2013).

As a forty-four-year-old white man who splits his time between a rural area with very low crime and a moderate-size city, John is not likely to be a victim of violent crime, and he knows it. But according to John, a firearm is needed not because a person is likely to become a crime victim but because of what he calls "low-probability, high-consequence" events. In other words, the only time that a CHL holder will use a gun is in the very unlikely event that his or her life is threatened and there is no other alternative: "The first rule of a gunfight is have a gun. And you can't be in a gunfight if you don't have one; all you can be in is a shooting."

John said there is much you can do to "increase your risk of being in a shooting," for example, "if you hang out with people who have criminal records" or "if you buy and sell narcotics," but it is also the case that you can avoid high-risk behaviors and still be at the wrong place at the wrong time. He likens this scenario to someone's having an unforeseen medical crisis: "My cousin dropped dead in front of her preschool class. [She] had a brain aneurism while she was teaching preschool. [She's] teaching, [her] eyes roll back in her head, boom! Hit the ground. Goodbye. No warning.

Nothing. That was it. Brain aneurism, never saw it coming, didn't know it was gonna happen." John sees this as an analogy for random acts of violent crime: "There are people, you know, I'm going about my day, I'm doing my thing, I'm at Luby's, WHAM! There's some nutbag who just drove through the [door], he's got a gun, he's shooting people. That's why I carry a concealed handgun. Because you can do everything right. Everything right. And still be at the wrong place at the wrong time."

John mentioned Luby's (a chain of cafeteria restaurants based in Texas) because of a mass shooting that occurred in Killeen in October 1991, when George Hennard drove his pickup truck through the restaurant's front windows armed with two 9mm handguns—a Glock-17 and a Ruger P-89—and at least six magazines of ammunition. Hennard walked through the restaurant and shot people at random, ultimately killing twenty-two. At the time it was the worst mass shooting in U.S. history.

Like similar stories that respondents refer to (e.g., Columbine, Virginia Tech), the Killeen incident captures the essence of how vulnerability functions for CHL holders: because we live in a society in which guns are readily available, at any time, any place, a person with a gun can decide to take your life. According to this perspective, the only safe response is to be armed in self-defense. To that end the CHL holders I interviewed argue that a gun is simply a tool. As John explained:

It's just part of the deal. You need a fire extinguisher to put out a fire, you need a seatbelt to keep you from flying out of your car in a car wreck, you know, you need a flashlight when it gets dark, and somebody tries to kill you, you need a gun. It's a tool for a job and a situation, in a low-probability, high-consequence situation, and if you're not wearing your seatbelt, you go flying out of your car and you die. If [your] kitchen catches on fire and you don't have a fire extinguisher, your house burns down. If it's dark and you need a flashlight and you don't have one, you can't see anything. If somebody tries to kill you and you don't have a gun, you're probably gonna die. It's pretty straightforward. . . . It's not this big deal. People get all wound up about guns being some magic thing that has magic powers to modify people's personalities. You know, it's a hammer, it's a flashlight, it's a fire extinguisher, it's a piece of gear, it's designed to do something, it's used for certain things at an appropriate place at an appropriate time. And you learn how to use it and you have it available,

and when you need it, you use it. . . . It's not as big a deal as
people make it out to be.

John presents a compelling explanation for why carrying a concealed firearm is a reasonable, even responsible self-defense tactic. Given such logic it is easy to find oneself imagining that there are no negative consequences to this social policy and that handgun licensing is simply a prudent response to potential victimization.

After approximately ninety minutes we were out of time, and on my way out John offered to show me the classrooms and firing ranges that make up his training facility. As we walked to the range, I felt lost in thoughts related to my own vulnerability. Like the unprepared people John had referenced, I did not have a self-defense plan or own a gun, and I considered whether I was failing in my duty to protect myself and my children from harm. I stared at the humanoid figures used for target practice and wondered how I would stop an assailant. Was I being irresponsible?

As John walked me to my car I managed to squeeze in one last question: I asked if he felt that gun rights are threatened in this country. Though he does not fear our government, he does believe that we might need guns to protect ourselves from the type of people our government produces, people he described as ineffectual, dependent, and reliant on criminal activity to satisfy their basic needs. He explained that Ayn Rand's books have had a significant impact on his way of thinking about human nature, and he believes that there are "contributors" who want to help make society a better place and "noncontributors" who only want to take from others. A friend of his, a police officer in an urban area, says that 5 percent of the population could disappear overnight and the only clue that they were gone would be that the crime rate would go down. While John did not claim this view as his own, and even seemed somewhat embarrassed while repeating it, the fact that he chose to share it anyway suggests at least a partial endorsement.

Listening to these comments I was instantly snapped back into awareness that carrying a firearm for self-defense is not simply a practice intended to guard against an abstract notion of indeterminate threat, and a firearm is not just like any other tool. It is a tool used to kill people, and to carry one with you is to be prepared to do that at any time. I was troubled by that reality and concerned that John's "noncontributors" comment was boilerplate culture-of-poverty rhetoric, which holds that at least some segment of the poor are likely to be criminal and that society would be better off if they disappeared. Contributors or not, we were talking about human beings. Yet as I reflect back on that day what strikes me most is that I drove away from the interview having been drawn into the logic of concealed carry. While I was concerned about how John and other respondents I had interviewed described the people they imagined as "bad guys," I was intoxicated by the rhetoric of the "good guy." I wanted to be prepared to protect myself and my family, and I wanted to have the power to respond to any threat we might face. My concern for the human costs of handgun licensing and the impacts on society were being replaced by a personal worry about victimization and a growing fear that I was vulnerable. Never had I wanted a gun more, and never had I come so close to mailing in my already completed application for a CHL.

In the research that follows I consider the social meanings of handgun licensing through an analysis of in-depth formal interviews that I conducted with nearly forty people who are licensed to carry guns in public and ethnographic data collected at gun ranges, a licensing course, and a women's handgun self-defense class. Whereas the participants I interviewed suggested that a concealed firearm is simply a tool for protection, I argue that it is much more. Caught up in a binary idea of "good guys" and "bad guys," they use their concealed firearms as part of a much larger discursive strategy that obscures dynamics of privilege and inequality operating via race, class, and gender. Their CHLs allow them not only to feel that they are safe in a world that they perceive is increasingly dangerous; their licenses also confirm that they are one of the good guys, a status that is about much more than not breaking the law.

The Push for CHLs in Texas

The shooting at the Luby's in 1991 was a pivotal moment in the push for CHL legislation in Texas. Not only was the shooting itself sensational, but one person who was most deeply affected had a very compelling story to tell about why private citizens should have the right to be armed. Once she realized what was happening, Suzanna Hupp, who was at the restaurant with her parents, reached for her purse and the .38 revolver that she had carried for most of her adult life. In her memoir recalling the event Hupp (2010, 38) writes, "Then it occurred to me with sudden and utter clarity that, just a few months earlier, I had made the stupidest decision of my life: my gun was not in my purse any longer!" There was no way for a private citizen to legally carry a concealed handgun in Texas in 1991, and because Hupp feared that a weapons charge could harm her thriving chiropractic practice, she had stopped carrying one. Her parents were among the people killed.

The Killeen shooting happened on the same day that Congress held debates on a national crime bill that would ban semi-automatic rifles, commonly referred to as "assault rifles," and high-capacity magazines for semi-automatic handguns (Barrett 2012). As news of the events spread, lawmakers on various sides of the issue used it as evidence to bolster their claims. Those in favor of the ban argued that Hennard would not have been able to kill so many people if his magazines had been limited to the standard ten rounds. For those opposed it did not matter how many bullets each magazine held because changing magazines on a semi-automatic handgun takes an experienced shooter a matter of seconds.

While Congress debated the national crime bill, debates at the state-level focused on whether individuals should have the right to carry concealed firearms. In the late 1980s and continuing through the 1990s, states throughout the United States started to loosen their restrictions on carrying concealed firearms (Wintemute 2006). In April 1993 the Texas House approved a bill that would allow Texans with a license to carry a handgun on their body either concealed or in the open. Those who opposed the measure argued that concealed weapons holders would only contribute to violent crime. Texas governor Ann Richards's spokesperson summarized the opposition to the bill as follows: "People who are scared, people who are frightened, people who are paranoid have absolutely no business having a gun" (Robison 1993a). Ron Wilson, a Democrat from Houston who sponsored the bill, responded to such sentiments by saying, "I don't live in a Norman Rockwell painting. I live in urban America. . . . Everybody is already on the street carrying guns, but it's the wrong folks" (Robison 1993a).

Though crime was generally on the decline during the 1980s, the violence associated with the buying, selling, and use of crack cocaine led to an increase in violent crime in urban areas (Reinarman and Levine 1997), while at the same time, semi-automatic handguns, which are much more lethal than revolvers because their magazines can hold many more rounds, became the weapons of choice for people involved in the drug trade (Barrett 2012). The combined effect of these two phenomena was an increase in homicides in urban areas. However, this increase in violence was not random; its primary perpetrators and its victims were young people directly involved with the drug trade (Wintemute 2006). Nevertheless the violent crime climate and high-profile mass shootings like the incident in Killeen contributed to the shifting legislative winds throughout the United States.

In June 1993 a concealed handgun licensing bill passed both houses of the Texas legislature. In front of television cameras, with a few dozen police officers at her side, Governor Richards vetoed the bill, saying, "I especially want to thank you for choosing to stand by me on this day, when we say 'no' to the amateur gunslingers who think somehow they are going to be braver and smarter with a gun in their hand" (Robison 1993b). Richards's opposition to the concealed handgun legislation drew the ire of pro-gun groups like the National Rifle Association (NRA), who financially backed her opponent, George W. Bush, in the next gubernatorial election. Bush, having promised to make CHLs a legislative priority, defeated Richards, and CHLs became legal in Texas in 1995 (South 1996).

The 1992 national crime bill failed to garner enough support to become law, but it was up for debate again in 1994, and most attention turned to the component of the bill known as "the Assault Weapons Ban." Hupp offered congressional testimony in opposition to the ban, presumably because her personal story would provide a compelling narrative that would justify the importance of firearms for self-defense. Since the shooting she had become a leading advocate for concealed handgun legislation (Hupp 2010). After explaining what happened the day her parents were killed, Hupp said, "I'm not really mad at the guy that did this. And I'm certainly not mad at the guns that did this. They didn't walk in there by themselves and pull their own triggers. The guy that did it was a lunatic. That's like being mad at a rabid dog. I'm mad at my legislators for legislating me out of the right to protect myself and my family."[4] In her final statement during the testimony Hupp said she was tired of hearing legislators say that assault rifles have no legitimate purposes for sport or hunting. Then she added, "People, that is not the point of the second amendment. . . . It's about our right . . . to protect ourselves from all of you guys up there." And with that she gestured at the committee.

The first shooting involving a license holder occurred just one month after CHLs became available. Gordon Hale and Kenny Tavai got into an altercation in Dallas after the vehicles the two men were driving brushed side mirrors. According to a witness, after both drivers stopped at a red light, Tavai walked up to Hale's window, reached into his vehicle, and started to punch Hale in the face. Hale pulled out his .40 caliber handgun and fatally shot Tavai once in the chest (Eskenazi and Gamboa 1996). Hale was arrested and charged with murder, but a grand jury failed to indict him because he acted in self-defense (Elizondo 1996).

The Tavai shooting seemed to confirm to those opposed to CHLs that licenses would encourage "vigilante justice" and increase violence (Eskenazi and Gamboa 1996), but there is no evidence to suggest that they do either of those things. In a summary of the effects of CHL laws in the United States, Garen J. Wintemute (2006) reports that there have been no consistent findings showing that CHLs increase crime, nor are there any studies that consistently show that they decrease it, despite the vocal claims of economist John Lott. In *More Guns, Less Crime* (1998), Lott argues that concealed firearm licensing is part of the reason the violent crime rate has declined so precipitously since the mid-1990s. But significantly his findings have been called into question by a large number of scholars who take issue with both his data and his conclusions (for a summary see Spitzer 2011). Notably no other researchers have been able to replicate his findings (Wellford, Pepper, and Petrie 2004), and most criminologists argue that the drop in violent crime is attributable to a range of factors, including the end of the crack boom and targeted policing (Wintemute 2006). Despite the dramatic drop in the crime rate over the past few decades, the rate of concealed handgun licensing has increased precipitously in recent years, and there are now over eight million people nationwide who have a permit to carry a concealed firearm (U.S. Government Accountability Office 2012). In Texas alone there were 825,957 people with an active concealed handgun license as of December 31, 2014 (Texas Department of Public Safety 2015), a figure that represents 4.81 percent of the population that is twenty-one and older.

In the first five years that they were available, the number of CHLs issued annually in Texas hovered around 50,000. As Figure 1 suggests, rates increased steadily from 2004 through 2008 and then shot up in 2009, when over 138,000 licenses were issued, a 61 percent increase from the previous year. Though 2010 saw a drop to just over 100,000, rates shot back up in 2011 and 2012. But no previous years come close to what happened in 2013 and 2014, when a total of 488,967 licenses were issued in just two years (Texas Department of Public Safety 1996–2015).

It was in the midst of the initial increase in 2008 that I first began this project. At the time, Texas news outlets were filled with stories about the surge in licensing that was overwhelming the Department of Public Safety (DPS), the state agency that manages CHLs, and licensing instructors re-

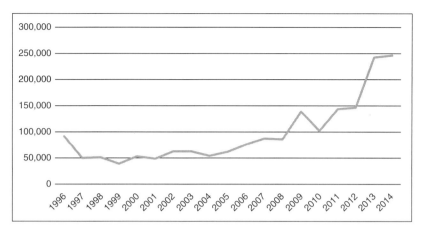

FIGURE 1 CHLs issued in Texas, 1996–2014. Source: Texas Department of Public Safety.

TABLE 1 CHLs issued by race in Texas, 1996–2014

Race	CHLs Issued 1996–2014 (%)	Texas Population Estimates 2010–2014 (%)
White	87.7	76.8
Black	6.2	12.7
Other	3.1	7.0
Asian	1.8	4.7
American Indian / Alaskan Native	0.3	1.2

Sources: Texas Department of Public Safety (1996–2015); U.S. Bureau of the Census (2010–2014).

ported that they too were struggling to keep up with demand. Intrigued by these reports, I looked into the publicly available data collected by the DPS and found that the agency tracks demographics by race, sex, and age of those people to whom licenses are issued, denied, and revoked. As I examined licensing for each year of the program's existence, it became clear that one group was driving most of the demand: men. Since the program's inception, 78 percent of CHLs have been issued to men and 22 percent to women. The data on race were also revealing, though unfortunately somewhat vague. The DPS tracks only six racial categories—white, black, Asian, American Indian / Alaskan Native, "other," and "multi-racial"—and provides no ethnic option for Hispanic or Latino. When no such category exists on forms, a large portion of this population, most of whom are officially defined as white, will select "other" (Swarns 2004); in a state with a 2013 Hispanic population of 38 percent, this is no small matter. One can only presume that "other" represents a large proportion of Hispanics given that it is the third largest category. Though these data are somewhat ambiguous, it is clear that the majority of CHL holders in Texas are white (even if many are also Hispanic) and that black and Asian license holders are severely underrepresented. And while gender is clearly significant, it is also notable that nearly twice as many white women have obtained CHLs than men in every other racial group combined.

Climate of Fear

Ostensibly people who obtain a concealed firearm do so because they are concerned about, maybe even afraid of crime. Fear of crime emerged as an area of focus in the 1970s, when researchers first realized that there is much greater fear of crime than actual crime, and it has since been studied from nearly every conceivable angle.[5] While much of the literature has been plagued by conceptual confusion and imprecise methodology, there is some consensus that fear of crime relates to emotional feelings of "alarm or dread caused by an awareness or expectation of danger" (Warr 2000, 453). Early research relied (often exclusively) on measuring fear by asking respondents, "Is there anywhere near where you live—that is, within a mile—where you would be afraid to walk alone at night?" For many years answers to this one question constituted the primary gauge of Americans' crime fears (Warr 2000, 457). Yet this question is so vague it is not clear precisely what it measures (Hale 1996). For example, analyses that rely on this question might exaggerate the extent to which walking at night induces fear because of crime or because of other reasons, like poor health or visibility (LaGrange and Ferraro 1989). Moreover the question is inadequate because it measures reactions to a specific activity and location and cannot account for whether people feel either safe or vulnerable in other public places or at home.

For more than twenty years Gallup has asked respondents whether they believe that there is more or less crime in the United States than the year before. Tracing responses to this question over time reveals that attitudes about crime have less to do with crime rates and more to do with feelings of general security. Over the course of the 1990s, as the economy boomed, most Americans believed that crime was falling, and it was; however, beginning in 2002, after the terrorist attacks of 9/11, sentiments changed dramatically, and the percentage of Americans who said crime was worse than the year before rose from 43 to 62 (Saad 2011). In 2009, when violent crime rates were at historic lows, 74 percent of respondents said that they believed crime was getting worse. These findings corroborate Lupton and Tulloch's (1999, 513) claim that attitudes about crime may function as a stand-in for other anxieties about social life: "People may become obsessed with crime and strategies for its avoidance because they feel that they can do something about this danger, unlike those underlying their other fears and worries." It is logical to assume that in 2009, while mired in a "Global War on Terror" and in the midst of a deep recession, large segments of the population felt insecure, and because of this they likely perceived that crime was on the rise, even though it was not. These feelings are characteristic of a "risk society," in which people are made anxious by the uncertainty in their lives and so are "drawn to discourses and practices which appear to offer the hope of order or control" (Holloway and Jefferson 1997, 259). According to Mary Douglas (1994, 30), "How much risk is a matter for experts, but [it] is taken for granted that the matter is ascertainable. Anyone who insists that there is a high degree of uncertainty is taken to be opting out of accountability." The notion that concealed firearms are required for "low-probability, high-consequence" events would suggest that CHLs may be indicative of a heightened risk society.

How risk and economic decline affect attitudes toward concealed handgun licensing is the subject of Jennifer Carlson's recent book *Citizen Protectors* (2015). She examines the case of Michigan, a state facing devastating economic hardship thanks largely to deindustrialization. Carlson argues that the citizen-protector role allows the predominant conceal carry demographic, men, to assert a version of masculinity that is compelling given that traditional ways of being a man (e.g., as the family breadwinner) have faded. Yet Texas has one of the strongest economies in the nation, and while no state was left untouched by the anxieties of the recession that became most evident in 2008, in areas like Houston licensing rates were high even when the economy was strong. My interviews suggest that at least in the case of Texas something beyond economic anxiety is afoot.

Americans and Guns: Attitudes and Ownership

In addition to attitudes about crime, any explanation of changes in licensing rates has to consider how larger social norms around guns have shifted over time. Surveys find that somewhere between 34 and 43 percent of Americans report that their household contains a firearm, a variability that makes it difficult to discern whether rates of ownership have declined significantly since the 1970s, when one national survey reported that 49 percent of households had at least one gun (Cohn et al. 2013).[6] Social scientists tend to agree that ownership rates are on the decline, and yet gun sales have remained strong, suggesting that already established gun owners drive much of the market (Tavernise and Gebeloff 2013). One clear social change that has happened is with respect to the public's attitudes. For example, while in 1959, 60 percent of the U.S. population thought that handguns should be banned, only 25 percent expressed that view in 2013 (Jones 2011; Saad 2013). According to Gallup, there is now more opposition to a *ban* on semi-automatic long guns known as "assault rifles" (53 percent) than there is support (43 percent), and in general Americans have become more "pro-gun," or at least more opposed to restrictions on guns, in recent years than ever before (J. M. Jones 2011).

Though public opinion has trended toward favoring general gun rights, in 2005 only 27 percent of Americans supported concealed firearm carry. In that year 17 percent of women and 37 percent of men said that private citizens should be allowed to carry firearms in public, and even among gun owners, 54 percent felt that concealed carry should be restricted to safety officials and citizens with a clear need (Jones 2005). Given the explosion in licensing rates that has occurred since this question was polled, it is likely that attitudes about concealed carry have changed, as more and more people are likely either to carry a firearm themselves or to know someone who does. In addition, over this same period new laws have continued to expand where permit holders can carry guns: in 2010 four states passed laws that make it legal for license holders to carry in bars (Gay 2010); federal legislation was amended to allow concealed firearms in national parks (O'Keefe 2010); some state legislatures have opened concealed carry to college campuses (though all but Utah have some restrictions on the practice); and even open carry has become more common.[7]

The normalization of carrying a concealed firearm likely has something to do with the increase in licensing rates, but there is also evidence that the spikes that happened in 2008 and 2012 were tied to the larger political climate surrounding guns in the United States. The year 2008 was something of a perfect storm for gun and ammunition sales. Not only was the country in a severe economic recession, but as that year's presidential campaign wore on, pro-gun groups, most notably the NRA, levied many of their resources in an attempt to defeat Barack Obama by rousing their supporters through various media. The NRA hosted gunbanobama.com, a website whose home page features the banner "OBAMA WOULD BE THE MOST ANTIGUN PRESIDENT IN AMERICAN HISTORY," and it regularly mailed political materials to members.

One highly effective way to disseminate anti-Obama rhetoric is through the lobby's monthly magazine, *American Rifleman*. With over one million subscribers, this "official journal" of the NRA plays an important role in constructing gun rights discourses. The magazine is largely devoted to advertisements, reviews of firearms and accessories, and up-to-date information on legislative actions and events relevant to gun owners, and so information could be considered the manifest function of *American Rifleman*. But guns and accessories are not the only things being sold on its pages; an analysis of its content reveals that its latent function is the construction of a vigilant and heavily armed gun owner who is ready to protect himself or herself from both criminals and the government.

The format of the magazine constructs these dual threats and holds them in tension, effectively playing one off the other for maximum effect. Each issue begins with a letter from the editor, followed by a section entitled "Armed Citizen," then a column by NRA executive vice president Wayne LaPierre called "Standing Guard," then the "President's Column," then featured articles. "Armed Citizen" relays stories of violent crimes thwarted by private citizens using guns, while the president and vice president typically devote their columns to warning readers about political threats to gun rights. For example, in the February 2009 edition of *American Rifleman*, (now former) NRA President John C. Sigler writes, "The coming years of the Obama-Biden administration will be the darkest in Second Amendment history. **Every law-abiding American gun owner must be ready.** We must be ready, willing and able to defend our rights at every turn and at every level, with all of our might, all of our hearts and all of our souls. Now is the time to act."

Another example comes from the March 2009 issue: "Everyone now knows the danger the Obama-Biden White House poses to the rights of law-abiding gun owners. We watched as President Barack Obama assembled his team from among the most anti-gun zealots to ever hold public office. With Hilary Clinton, Tom Daschle, and Eric Holder in the cabinet, and Rahm Emanuel as chief of staff, America's gun owners know the dangers we face and that our friends in Congress will be mightily challenged in their defense of America's beloved Second Amendment" (Sigler 2009b). The "beloved Second Amendment" is repeatedly used in articles that focus on threats to gun owners' rights, as are America's founding fathers, with words such as "freedom" and "liberty" peppered throughout.

Leading up to the 2012 election, *American Rifleman* was plastered with anti-Obama coverage. That year's February cover read, "2012: All or Nothing Election for the Second Amendment," and in his column LaPierre (2012) wrote, "If Obama is returned to the White House, if the pro-gun majority in the House of Representatives is reversed, and if Nancy Pelosi once again wraps her iron fist around the Speaker's gavel, gun owners will face the worst serial assault on our freedom ever." In the same issue NRA president David A. Keene (2012) wrote, "We have won the political and legal arguments in one forum after another over the last decade, but we cannot forget for even a minute that those hostile to our rights and the values we share are not about to give up and will continue to find ways to attack those rights. Enemies of the Second Amendment gather in our schools, in the media, and among the political elite." Given such rhetoric, it is no surprise that some gun owners might be reluctant to report whether their household contains a firearm.

In addition to the "real life stories" of self-defense in the "Armed Citizen" column, many of the reviews are for handguns and accessories that are designed for self-defense from criminal threats. This discursive framing is common in pro-gun discourse, a one-two punch of threats from above (in the form of government control) and below (in the form of criminal victimization). This two-pronged strategy not only ensures a motivated membership, it is also highly beneficial for the firearm and ammunition manufacturers who advertise on the pages of *American Rifleman*.[8] The NRA's rhetoric is often politically inflammatory, but it would not resonate with its members if it did not appeal to them, and according to social theorists, what makes it appealing is the underlying race, class, and gender meanings that such rhetoric conveys.

Gender, Race, and Guns

According to R. W. Connell (1995, 205), one of the keys to the gun lobby's success in terms of its political influence is that it is engaged in masculinity politics, "those mobilizations and struggles where the meaning of masculine gender is at issue and with it, men's position in gender relations." By utilizing masculine discourses like "security," "family values," and "individual freedom," the NRA works to control the meanings of guns, particularly in the wake of mass shootings, when public opposition to firearms often spikes. By utilizing such tropes, the gun lobby works to make masculinity "a principal theme" of gun debates rather than "taken for granted as background" (205). Scott Melzer (2009) builds a similar case; in his analysis of the NRA's history, its conventions, and its membership, Melzer found that the organization ties gun use with self-reliance, rugged individualism, and a strong work ethic, a constellation of traits that he refers to as "frontier masculinity." He writes that "guns and masculinity have long been inseparable" (30) thanks to mythologized narratives of the American frontier that are particularly appealing to working- and middle-class white men who, because of the feminist and civil rights movements, feel they no longer have a clearly defined place in U.S. society.

In his analysis of *American Rifleman*'s "Armed Citizen" column, Kevin O'Neill (2007) suggests that guns are constructed as powerful tools that allow "classically vulnerable" people—women, the elderly, and those who are disabled or in failing health—to achieve heroic masculinity by dominating criminals. He cites one story of a man whose children rushed into his room in the middle of the night to tell him that two men were breaking into their home. The father, who was disabled, grabbed a handgun, shot one of the intruders, and held him at gunpoint until the police arrived. O'Neill argues that these stories make readers feel empowered by guns, as they are able to achieve masculinity in defense of the innocent.

The literature on the NRA illustrates how this powerful lobby links gun use with what is known as "hegemonic masculinity." According to Connell (1995, 77), hegemonic masculinity is a "configuration of gender practice" that legitimizes patriarchy as idealized when culturally celebrated representations of masculinity are set in contrast to representations of women and marginalized men. The NRA constructs hegemonic masculinity through its discursive production of the ideal gun user: the real-life hero who defends the defenseless (O'Neill 2007) and cares deeply about "American virtues," particularly individual freedom (Melzer 2009) and family values (Connell 1995). These meanings not only compel NRA members to purchase firearms and support gun rights; they also "provide a cultural framework that may be materialized in daily practices and interactions," and thus represent what Connell and Messerschmidt (2005, 850) call a "regional" hegemonic masculinity. These representations become the frames that shape the possibilities for enacting idealized versions of masculinity in everyday life. What is unexamined is whether and how these meanings inform the ways that men think about CHLs and their own desires to be armed in public.

While men remain the primary gun-owning demographic in the United States, the NRA has worked tirelessly to promote women's gun use. One of the primary ways it has done so is through a self-defense program called Refuse to Be a Victim (Browder 2006; Smith and Smith 1995; Stange and Oyster 2000) that encourages women to take up firearms to protect themselves from criminals. An NRA-funded video captures the ethos of this campaign.[9] It starts with a scene that is emblematic of the type of public crime that women report fearing most: it is night, and a woman is walking alone through a parking garage when she senses that someone is lurking nearby. Suddenly there are footsteps in the distance. As she hurriedly tries to unlock her car, and just as she hears a man's voice, she drops her keys on the ground. To her relief it is only a coworker saying goodbye and not a potential perpetrator. A woman's voice plays over the scene: "Here's a situation we've all faced before—after work, on campus, and at the shopping mall—but what if it was a dangerous situation? Are we truly prepared?"

One woman who echoes the sentiments of the NRA is Paxton Quigley, among the most vocal and visible advocates of women's gun use. A onetime proponent of gun control, Quigley (2012) explains that her views on self-defense changed when a friend of hers was "attacked and viciously raped by a predator." Her best-selling book *Armed and Female* (1989) is filled with tales of women in harrowing situations who would have been violently victimized were it not for their ability to use a gun for self-defense. On her website Quigley (2012) reports that her mission is as follows: "If you're a woman, I want to encourage and inspire you to step out of character, abandon age-old bonds of male dependence, and break free from the powerlessness, fear and depression that has [sic] plagued our gender for so long."

Those who encourage women's gun use, including the NRA, have been criticized for playing on women's fear of crime, implying that women could "choose" not to be victims, and ignoring data suggesting that women might be more harmed by guns than protected by them (Blair and Hyatt 1995; Homsher 2001). Additionally, for many antigun feminists, promoting women's gun use is akin to encouraging women to be violent, a position that some have seen as counter to feminism's aims. Such criticisms were captured by a 1994 *Ms. Magazine* cover that featured a semi-automatic handgun with a title that asked, "Is This Power Feminism?" For the magazine's authors the answer was a resounding "No!" (Jones 1994).

While some feminists have been opposed to the idea of using guns in response to men's violence against women, pro-gun feminists believe that armed women represent a response to patriarchal definitions of women as weak, helpless, vulnerable, and reliant on men for protection (McCaughey 1997; Stange and Oyster 2000; Wolf 1994). These scholars argue that women should not wait for the link between violence and masculinity to change; instead women should learn to fight back, to disrupt the presumption that they are inherently vulnerable and physically weak or that women have "breakable, takeable bodies" (McCaughey 1997, 36). While a variety of self-defense strategies are available to women, those who advocate women's gun use insist that there is no better tool to equalize differences in size or strength between men and women than a firearm (Kelly 2004; Stange and Oyster 2000; Wolf 1994), and they dismiss the notion that guns are inherently problematic. For example, Stange and Oyster (2000, 44) write, "The gun is only the symbol of male power to the extent that we let it be. And as some feminists are finally beginning to realize, it can function as a particularly potent symbol of female resistance to male aggression." Proponents of this position explain that this is not a celebration of violence but a rejection of victimization (McCaughey 1997), and they insist that until the cultural construction of women's vulnerability to men is challenged, women will remain subject to patriarchal control. Moreover they argue that women must have the capacity to use violence if the rejection of violence is to have any meaning. This position is captured by Stange and Oyster (2000, 44) when they write, "The problem with so much feminist advocacy of nonviolent 'resistance': so long as women are perceived—and *perceive* themselves— as incapable of genuine aggressive action, nonviolence is not a strategy. It is merely the role culturally assigned to women." When women carry concealed firearms, they are potentially rejecting a dominant cultural discourse about their inherent vulnerability. And yet without critically analyzing the meanings they associate with the practice, it is impossible to know whether they are in fact disrupting patriarchal gender norms.

The existing literature on cultural discourses and guns focuses almost exclusively on gender, but race (and its intersection with gender) is also important to consider. Race has played a critical role in the development of gun policies throughout U.S. history: the first gun control laws emerged in the 1600s and were issued to keep firearms out of the hands of black slaves (Cramer 1999); one of the primary goals of the KKK in the post–Civil War South was to violently disarm newly freed blacks (Winkler 2011); and the contemporary gun control movement that began in the 1960s was in part a response to the fear induced in white Americans by images of armed Black Panthers. Prior to the 1960s it was legal to openly carry a firearm in the state of California; however, in 1967, as members of the Black Panthers Self-Defense Organization took up arms as a response to antiblack police brutality and armed black men were seen regularly in the news, California legislators sought to amend firearm laws to restrict gun carry in public (Leonardatos 1999). In supporting legislation that would make it illegal for members of the Black Panthers to be armed in public, California governor Ronald Reagan remarked, "There's no reason why on the street today a citizen should be carrying loaded weapons" (quoted in Leonardatos 1999, 972), a statement that no Republican, and few Democrats, would be willing to utter today.

It is no surprise that images of gun-wielding black men led to new laws against carrying guns in public given the pervasive racialization of crime in the United States, according to which the cultural image of the common criminal is a black man (Chiricos, McEntire, and Gertz 2001; Davis 2007; Russell-Brown 2009). This is a highly consequential construct that has profound effects on the lives of black men, and perhaps particularly so in an era when private citizens are carrying guns in public.

While the existing literature helps to explain the effectiveness of the gun lobby discourse and the cultural meanings of guns, it does not explain why people would want to be armed in public. Carrying a concealed firearm is ostensibly a simple matter of self-defense. But many social questions remain: Defense from what? From whom? How are threats conceptualized? Do men and women think of threat in the same way? Do people who are armed feel safer? What role does race play in employing CHLs as a response to risk? What does this form of self-defense say about how we conceptualize community? It was clear that new research was desperately needed to address these questions.

Current Research

Because I wanted to understand how cultural discourses inform the worldviews of people who obtain CHLs, I knew that I would need to rely on ethnographic methods. While in-depth interviews would allow me to hear from license holders why they want to be armed and how they imagine crime and self-defense, my participating in licensing courses and spending time at gun ranges would allow me to gain firsthand experience and ensure that I was competent enough at shooting to pass the CHL course that I intended to take. I had not fired a handgun since my stepfather taught me to shoot a .22 nearly twenty years prior to the start of this research, and so I took one ten-hour licensing course, attended a women's pistol course, and made regular trips to local gun ranges.

I first solicited participation for interviews by emailing CHL instructors whom I found online by searching for licensing courses. In the initial round of emails I contacted well over thirty people, and four agreed to be interviewed. After each interview I asked participants if they would be willing to share my contact information with their networks, and in total I interviewed thirty-six people, eleven of whom were instructors.[10] Thirty-four respondents had a CHL at the time of the interview; one woman was days away from attending her licensing course and had already taken a handgun self-defense course; and another woman had made plans to obtain a license in the near future and regularly carried a firearm at the time of the interview.

In this project I focus on people who are socially privileged. Nearly all respondents are white, the majority are men, almost all are heterosexual, and most are middle to upper-middle class (see appendix I for complete demographics).[11] While the best available evidence suggests that my sample mirrors the population of CHL holders in Texas, many voices are left out of this analysis. This is not intended to give undue weight to those whose views are already socially empowered; instead I use a critical perspective to better understand how "social categories that are not marked" (Sprague 2005, 188) play a central role in the reproduction of social inequality. That said, understanding the views and experiences of black and Latino license holders in Texas is an important area for future research.

Interviews lasted between one and two hours and were conducted at locations chosen by the respondents. Sites included a gun range, the respondent's home and office, coffee shops, restaurants, and a church. During the interviews research participants were first asked to describe their background experiences, including their earliest memories with guns, whether either of their parents was a gun user, and at what age they received their first gun. I then asked what motivated them to get a license and whether they have friends or acquaintances who are CHL holders. The third set of questions involved their firearm carrying practices, including whether they carry a gun every day, if they avoid places where carrying a gun is restricted, and if they have ever had to pull their gun from its holster. The final section included questions that asked participants their views on gun-free zones and gun rights. I digitally recorded and transcribed each interview, then read through the transcripts to identify themes. Additionally, after I completed each interview, I took time to record my impressions of the interview process, including my initial reactions to what I had heard. These memos were particularly useful in helping me to chart my evolving understanding of the dynamics that shape the worldviews of the people I interviewed, and they helped me to process the various ways my emotional reactions to concealed handgun licensing shifted over the course of this research.

Given that firearms are so politicized and aligned with conservative politics (Melzer 2009), I had some apprehension that my position as a graduate student at a university might make it difficult for me to establish contacts. One of my earliest respondents confirmed this hunch. I wrote in my solicitation email that one benefit of participating in this study was that respondents' insights would contribute to what people know about CHLs and the "ongoing debate over gun rights and concealed handgun licensing." One person, a man I call David, replied, "I would be pleased to participate in your study. I assure you that I have all of my teeth (some paid for), don't have an extra chromosome, or call every guy Bubba, or Dude. I do have a graduate degree (Master's), but I'm also a card-carrying Christian, as well as a card-carrying NRA/TSRA [Texas State Rifle Association] member. I hope that you, being a graduate student of the most liberal university in Texas can manage to be objective. Actually, I wasn't aware of an 'on-going debate.' " Given this response I wondered if I would ever be able to gain entrée into the world of CHLs.

Though his email was a passive-aggressive response, David agreed to meet me for an interview. Fortunately my second interview was with

Susan, who was very enthusiastic about participating and with whom I quickly developed a rapport. Susan informed me that David, who was an instructor at her licensing school, had warned her and others against participating in my study, and she said that she could not understand why he would be so concerned. While David and some other respondents were defensive and suspicious of my motives, others, like Susan, were warm and open and very willing to participate. Susan was happy to circulate my information to her wide network of CHL instructors and former students, and it soon became apparent to me that many of the people who contacted me were willing to participate because I had been identified as being "pro-gun" by Susan.

One of the more fruitful and compelling interviews I conducted happened when I approached the moderator of an online forum for CHL holders and asked if I could post a request for interviews. The moderator said that forum policy prohibited solicitations of any kind but that my research sounded interesting and that she would be happy to participate. A few weeks later Mary and I met at a café in the Houston area. Early in the interview she was terse and forceful in her responses, and she had an intensity about her that I found extremely intimidating. As the interview went on, there was a noticeable change in her demeanor, and she seemed to grow increasingly comfortable with my questions. By the end of our time together Mary seemed to trust me, at least somewhat. However, as we were wrapping up, she went back to the informed consent paperwork that she had read at the beginning and noted one point that she did not consent to. The form reads, "The data resulting from your participation may be made available to other researchers in the future for research purposes not detailed within this consent form." Mary said, "I refuse categorically to agree to that. Anything [I have said] needs to be completely brought to my attention. . . . I do not give consent to anybody else to use this but you."

While she had previously been defensive, this was the first time she had indicated the reason, and so I assured her that my intent was to fairly represent her views on CHLs. Mary said that she understood, but added, "You've got a tape recorder and you take two or three sentences, a phrase here, a phrase there, it's very easy to turn it around and make it sound [*pause*]. If you listen to what I say here, it sounds like I'm an incredibly paranoid person, [that] I think that they're going to come and try to kill me all the time and I need to be prepared, and that's not the case." I told Mary that many of the people I had contacted never responded and that

I felt that some people were reluctant to participate. She said, "Quite frankly, you live in Austin. You go to an Austin college. Austin is an incredibly liberal place. The concern with the conservative Second Amendment supporters is that . . . they might decide to label you as a liberal; therefore you're here to collect information to put out a book that may be slanted. [You might] have a hidden agenda. And that's the issue."

The extent to which all researchers have a "hidden agenda" has been a topic of some discussion among sociologists (Stacey 1988; Stein 2010). Interviews are not simply reported but analyzed, critiqued, and deconstructed for the ways they reinforce inequalities, and to that extent some research participants might feel that my agenda was hidden from their view. But given that nearly everyone I interviewed wanted to know if I was pro-gun and if I shot firearms, respondents seemed primarily concerned with whether or not I harbored antigun sentiments and if I was working on this project because I wanted to paint a negative picture of gun owners generally or perhaps CHL holders specifically. I told my respondents the truth about my views on what motivated my research: Though at the time I did not personally own a gun, I am not only unopposed to them, but I enjoy shooting, and in the years since these interviews concluded I've regularly shot firearms and am part of a trap shooting league. Truthfully the only reason I was not then a gun owner was because I hadn't been able to afford a gun. Moreover, and perhaps most important given my respondents' concerns, I agree with those who label themselves "pro-gun" that the Second Amendment guarantees an individual right to bear arms, and I do not share the position that some who are labeled "antigun" have that it is anachronistic, nor do I think that gun ownership is inherently problematic.

Given these caveats, I think that it is also important to acknowledge that there is a reason some are apprehensive, if not outright hostile, toward guns: they are a factor in a great many traumas and deaths in this country. There were 11,675 homicides and deaths by legal intervention, 21,175 suicides, 505 fatal accidents, and 84,258 nonfatal injuries with firearms in 2013 (Centers for Disease Control and Prevention 2015). The risk inherent in gun use was made clear in an interview with Ashley, thirty, a CHL instructor who helps her father run a gun range that he has owned for twenty years, over which time he has witnessed three deaths from two suicides and one accident. Ashley was at the range when the accident happened: "We had somebody mishandle their weapon, not in our CHL course, just out there, and drop it and go to grab it and he shot himself in the leg and he bled out." When I asked her if witnessing that incident ever made her question the safety of guns, she replied, "People die different ways every day. And it was tragic and it was awful and it was an accident. It was [the] mishandling of a weapon. And it was awful, I'm not going to lie. But it never for one second made me think, 'You know what, guns are wrong.' Because they're not. It was an accident and it could have happened a hundred other ways. Take guns out of the whole entire world and people are still going to die and people are still going to find ways to commit a crime without a gun. Because they did it before they had 'em and they're going to find a way now. So that's how I see it." When I asked her to respond to how antigun people might react to this story, she said:

> Guns aren't evil. The people that use them are. And the people that are out here trying to learn and educate themselves and legally obtain a weapon are not the people that are going to do harm with it. The people that are going to do harm with it are the people that are illegally getting these weapons; they are not going to get a CHL license; they are not going to learn how to use it. And I don't think that it's fair that they have [guns] and we don't. I want the right. I think that, I mean, it's, I'm sure you've heard it said a million times from other people: guns don't kill people, people kill people. And if they didn't have a gun, they would find something else to use for violence, be it a knife or, you know, anything. They can use a baseball bat and kill me, so it's, you know, it's not the gun, it's the person. And it's going to be anywhere. But as far as having your license, these people are good people because they're not criminals. They're going through all the right channels. That's just my opinion.

I heard variations on Ashley's view in nearly every interview I conducted for this project: as inanimate objects, guns are just as dangerous as anything else that can kill a person, including knives, cars, and even swimming pools, and thus the furor over guns is inherently irrational. Those opposed to guns argue that guns are not "just like any other tool"; they are tools crafted to kill. What other object could fatally wound a person, much less bystanders, simply by grabbing it incorrectly? And still, given the ubiquity of guns on a range, the fact that on Ashley's father's range there has been only one lethal accident and two other deaths in twenty years speaks to the reality that guns can be, and most often are, handled safely. Clearly deaths at gun ranges would not happen were it not for guns, and yet how many more people die in car accidents on their way to and from ranges than at them? The fact is that because of its destructive power, a loaded firearm has the potential to be incredibly dangerous, but it also can be handled safely. If one is willing to set aside the gun itself, questions of policy become much easier to address.

Still this does not mean that my analysis will leave all pro-gun advocates satisfied. In what follows I engage in a direct critique of concealed handgun licensing as policy, something that will likely be met with great resistance from those who believe that any infringement on gun rights is a step toward total government control and eventually an outright ban. I reject this view and, at the risk of being called naïve by some, believe that rights can be both guaranteed and regulated. That said, I agree with my respondents that the emphasis of the critique should be on people and not guns. This is not only because the United has an estimated 300 million firearms, an entrenched gun culture, a Supreme Court precedent that interprets the Second Amendment as an individual right, and a gun lobby that has effectively become a major player in national and state-level politics; it is also because what is most significant about guns is not that they exist but how they are used both materially and symbolically.

I first became interested in this topic not because I am opposed to guns but because I could not understand why a civilian would want to carry one in public. I had family members with CHLs who had explained their desires to be armed, but still I did not see their logic, and more than that, I wanted to understand the larger sociological underpinnings of the practice. When I told participants my views, it generally put them at ease, and when they asked me whether or not I would obtain a CHL and carry a firearm, I told them the truth about how I felt: that I did not feel the need to carry a gun in public and that I was personally ambivalent about the policy and worried about what an armed citizenry meant for our society. To my surprise many respondents said that they understood what I meant and that they too wished the world was not so dangerous that they felt the need to carry a gun to feel safe.

I feel confident that I ultimately came to a deep understanding of what motivates respondents' desires to be armed, and it is from that understanding that my analysis is built. One piece of data that I rely on in making the claims that follow is how my own perceptions of crime and vulnerability changed as my interviews mounted. While early in the research I was taken aback with the depth of vulnerability that respondents reported, as I heard more and more stories my responses began to change. When respondents explained real or anticipated victimization, moments of vulnerability, or scenarios in which they felt threatened, it was impossible not to feel anxious. Listening to respondents tell stories about being victimized—whether personally or in hypothetical events—had an effect on me. Though I entered into this project with a very minimal sense of vulnerability, as I delved deeper into data collection I developed a greater fear of crime than I had ever had before. And as I mentioned earlier, I started to see concealed handgun licensing as a logical self-defense tactic in a dangerous world, and I wondered if maybe, as some of my respondents suggested, I was being naïve and that without a gun I was putting myself and my children in danger. During the time that I was collecting data I would sometimes wake up in the middle of the night thinking that I had a heard a noise, and I would lie there with my heart racing, convinced that because I was unarmed there was nothing I could do. It was a feeling I had last had as a child, and yet here I was with children of my own and no way to protect them.

Kathleen Blee (1998, 382) says that "emotions evoked in the researcher in the process of collecting qualitative data can themselves be sources of useful data." Following Blee, I utilize my emotional responses not only to heighten my empathy for respondents but to better understand how fear operates in constructions of vulnerability and strategies for self-defense. Unlike Blee's respondents, who used fear to intimidate her and to control the research process, those I interviewed seemed worried about my inability to defend myself without a gun; I was offered free firearm self-defense and CHL courses by a number of people, and I had a strong sense that such offers were made not only to help with my research but also out of genuine concern for my safety.

Attention to emotion was as significant in the interview process as it was in those instances when I participated in shooting activities. Shooting a gun, both at the range and in the two classes that I took, represented "embodied knowledge" (Wacquant 1995) that allowed me to gain insight into the appeal of firearms for those who use guns for self-defense. The sense of power I felt when shooting was intoxicating, and I cannot think of another experience that leaves one feeling so completely capable of dominating another person; it is a power that feels like the opposite of vulnerability.

While there is no such thing as an objective study, I have done my best to fairly represent respondents' views and to thoroughly investigate what motivates their desires to be armed in public. And yet those who read this who support CHLs will likely take issue with some of the ways I analyze respondents' explanations. Turning to the tenets of sociology reminds me that it is my responsibility to be as fair as I can be, while at the same time critically analyzing my data. I agree with Arlene Stein (2010) that sociology is at its best when it deals with relevant social matters, refuses to shy away from contentious political issues, and engages readers in such a way that they might better understand the world. Though this endeavor is fraught with the potential for controversy, it is the job of the critical sociologist to face this challenge head-on, because, as Stein says, "sometimes controversy cannot, or should not, be avoided" (567).

In the chapters that follow I present the major findings from this research. In chapter 2 I focus on the interviews I conducted with men who have CHLs and explore the various ways gun use is linked with masculinity in American culture. What emerges most clearly from these interviews is that for many men, gun use is deeply tied to their sense of themselves as men. They identify getting married and becoming fathers as moments when their sense of security and need for greater self-defense changed, and their CHLs are an extension of this need, though whether they are always able to use their concealed firearms to protect their family is unclear. The older men I interviewed explained that as they have aged and their body has changed, they no longer feel capable of physically defending themselves as they could in their youth. Thus their CHLs are central to their sense of security, and they allow these men to reclaim the strength they valued when they were younger.

In chapter 3 I examine how women explain their gun use and their desires for concealed handgun licenses. Most of the women I interviewed learned to shoot from their father, husband, or boyfriend. This, in conjunction with cultural representations that mark guns as the purview of men, is likely why women associate guns with men and masculinity, even when they regularly use guns for target practice or for self-defense. The women I interviewed explain their gun use and CHLs as empowering because they are able to competently handle objects defined as "men's things." They also explain that carrying a concealed firearm makes them feel empowered because their guns reduce any size difference that may exist between women and men, something that is particularly relevant for women who have experienced victimization.

In chapter 4 I analyze how race intersects with gender in shaping how license holders perceive crime. Central to my argument is that the social construction of "bad guys" is as much about imagining criminals as it is developing a sense of oneself as good. Those I interviewed seem to feel that their "good guy" status should entitle them to greater access to public places with their firearms, and there is noticeable moral outrage over the constraints that exist for license holders in some establishments. Though the "good guy" construct hinges on being law-abiding, there are contradictions built into it that reveal the depth to which it is made possible because of how social status operates.

In chapter 5 I examine how respondents utilize moralized ideas about race and perceptions of cultural dysfunction in their understandings of the conditions that breed criminality. Throughout these explanations respondents emphasize personal responsibility, a discourse that masks privilege and reinforces systems of inequality in the United States. These meanings reach their apex for those who feel that a culture of dependency and a lack of self-reliance are steering society toward collapse.

As concealed handgun licensing rates continue to rise and as laws continue to expand where license holders can be armed, it is important that a sociological analysis shed light on the social dynamics that shape this practice. The implications of this form of self-defense extend beyond individual gun owners, and the risks associated with this practice are not limited to the inherent power of a loaded firearm. The vast majority of CHL holders will never need to draw their firearms in public. Thus what is most significant about CHLs and concealed firearms is not what happens in the moment a gun is drawn but in what they contribute to the cultural meaning systems that shape how we see ourselves and each other. In the pages that follow I examine what those meanings are and explore their impacts on society.

2 Men and Guns

· ·

To obtain a CHL in Texas, a person must complete a licensing course that includes both classroom and range instruction.[1] The course I attended was taught by Bill, a thirty-eight-year-old retired navy man with a love of firearms. As a software engineer with a comfortable salary, Bill emphasized that he does not teach CHL courses because he needs the money: "I get tired of seeing [people] learn the wrong way. I like to teach the right way."

Texas law requires all concealed handgun licensing courses to cover the following information: laws pertaining to weapons and use of deadly force; handgun use, proficiency, and safety; nonviolent dispute resolution; and the proper storage of firearms, with a focus on eliminating "the possibility of accidental injury to a child" (Texas Penal Code §411.188). Bill presented this material using PowerPoint slides and would often transition between topics by showing the class comical YouTube videos or engaging us with crime-specific scenarios. The entire time that Bill taught he was outfitted with what is known as an inside-the-waistband holster, a rig that allows a person to carry his or her firearm completely concealed. When Bill taught proper gun handling technique, including how to check around a doorway to assess a threatening situation, he replaced his real semi-automatic .45 with a red plastic replica.

After three hours, having completed the first half of the classroom instruction, we made our way to a nearby outdoor range where the shooting portion of the course would take place. That is where Derek, a white male who appeared to be in his late thirties, joined the class to recertify his CHL. At the time of this research those applying for renewal licenses in Texas were required to demonstrate shooting proficiency and to sit in for four hours of classroom instruction (continuing education is no longer required for renewals). Derek wore a military-style "drop leg holster" that attached to his belt and strapped around his upper thigh and was also wearing a tactical vest carrying extra magazines. Everything about his appearance suggested that he knew exactly what he was doing.

Leading up to the CHL course I had spent quite a bit of time at gun ranges, practicing and becoming more comfortable with shooting. Though

I still had the low-grade anxiety that is present any time I use a gun, I knew how to handle the Glock-19 on loan from the licensing school and was confident that I would have success consistently hitting near the center of the target. The same could not be said for the man who stood directly to my right. Roger, an African American in his late thirties or early forties, was visibly nervous about shooting. He had spent his career in the army, and yet he had trouble loading ammunition into his gun's magazine. He tried using a small tool called a magazine loader, which Bill openly chided him for, and still he struggled. With shaky hands Roger dropped rounds on the ground as Bill offered to help while playfully mocking the fact that a man in the army could not load his own gun. None of this helped Roger's confidence, which was unfortunate given that we were about to begin shooting.

The licensing test entails shooting twenty rounds at a distance of three yards from the target, twenty rounds from seven yards, and ten rounds from fifteen yards. Each shot within a twelve-inch ring around the center of the target (rings eight, nine, and center) is worth 5 points; shots within the number seven ring are worth 4 points; and any shot that misses the rings but hits the target is worth 3 points. The maximum score a shooter can receive is 250 points, and to pass the test a score of 175 or better is required. At twenty-four inches wide and forty-five inches tall, the target is not difficult to hit, and passing the test requires only a minimal degree of shooting competency.

When it came time to shoot, Roger was not very accurate. As we completed our shots at three yards, he openly questioned how he was going to hit the target at fifteen yards. "Where's the line at?" Roger asked as he anticipated moving back. Many of his shots hit outside the largest ring, and even at seven yards a few shots missed the target altogether. Occasionally he would look to his left at my target (which I was hitting rather consistently) and to his right at another shooter's target and remark on how poorly he was doing. He offered that the only firearm training he had received in the army was in basic training over sixteen years earlier, and even then he had only been trained to shoot M-16s. Later, as we stood around and waited for Bill to score our targets, I asked Roger what he did for the army. Almost apologetically he replied, "I'm an accountant."

I rode with Bill from the shooting range back to the prefabricated building where the classroom instruction would continue. As we drove he talked about Derek's appearance and mocked him for wearing tactical gear. "He looks like he was in the military or something," I offered.

Bill explained that Derek was in the Air Force Special Forces, a fact that he had gleaned from an emblem on Derek's vest. He said that it "says a lot" when a guy feels like he needs to dress like that on a shooting range.

After everyone arrived at the building and we settled into the classroom, Bill changed from an inside-the-waistband to an outside-the-waistband holster. Now his semi-automatic handgun was visible to us all.

Masculinity is a central organizing principle in society, and it is at the heart of the experiences described above. The fact that men are considered masculine to the extent that they can master "manhood acts" (Schrock and Schwalbe 2009) is likely why Roger felt anxious as he struggled to shoot. The ridicule leveled against him by Bill is typical among men, who often use putdowns as a way to shore up their own masculinity (Pascoe 2007). Meanwhile Bill's critique of the way Derek was dressed stemmed from a feeling that Derek was trying to prove something, and while Bill mocked this attempt to appear manly, his use of the outside-the-waistband holster when we returned to the classroom struck me as a similar strategy.

In this chapter I examine how concealed handgun licensing is tied to masculinity. First I review the literature on gender, firearms, and masculinity, then turn to an analysis of how men with CHLs explain their experiences with guns and their desires to be armed in public.

Masculinity Theory

As a binary concept, one of the most fundamental and commonsense ideas about gender is that men and women are "opposites." Traits like strength, courage, and aggression are presumed to be innate in men, while "feminine characteristics" (e.g., nurturance, emotionality, passivity) are presumed to be natural in females. Though these attributes are often explained as the result of biology, sociologists of gender argue that they are instead socially constructed, the result of agreed-upon meanings rather than inevitable truths. By reinforcing expectations of how men and women should act and then employing a variety of strategies to ensure that they uphold those standards, various institutions and individuals coerce people into embodying gender norms. As a process and a product of ongoing coercion, gender is not a stable identity and instead must be accomplished over and again through daily interaction (West and Zimmerman 1987).

The need to constantly prove oneself as sufficiently masculine means that many men experience a "chronic uncertainty" about gender that compels them to seek ways to ensure that they measure up to cultural standards of manhood (Kimmel 1996). Men are expected to be successful, competent, strong, athletic, virile, and, most important, in control. According to Michael Schwalbe (2014, 59), control is "the defining quality of a masculine self," and so to be considered masculine one must "be seen as capable of exerting control over things, people, thoughts, and emotions." One way that men can demonstrate they are capable of exerting control is through "manhood acts," those behaviors that have the effect of "signifying—with or without conscious awareness—that one possesses the capacities to make things happen and to resist being dominated by others" (Schrock and Schwalbe 2009, 280). Manhood acts allow men to prove to themselves and to others that they are "real men."

One of the most basic ways that dominance and control are achieved is through violence, and so it is no wonder that in American culture, which defines itself largely via masculine achievements (Kimmel 1996), violence is a central element. Ritualized violence is a celebrated aspect of sports and a prominent narrative device in action films and video games (Donovan 2010; Goldstein 2005; Messner 1992), but despite its ubiquity, there is a certain amount of social ambivalence about violence. For example, while "head-ringing hits" were once highly valued in football, troubling evidence regarding the permanent physical and neurological damage caused by such blows has resulted in efforts to reform the rules of the game (O'Connor 2011). In addition, highly publicized school shootings by adolescent boys have compelled some to question the cultural endorsement of violence in media (Mifflin 1999). Media are a site of much critical analysis because of the ways they facilitate the spread of cultural meanings. Media representations are part of the discursive formation of any subject position, and so they are the material with which we learn how to "do gender" successfully.

The reality that media play a large role in how we imagine ourselves and the world is, of course, not lost on industries that use various forms of marketing to compel consumers to buy their products. According to Joan Burbick (2007, 13), gun manufacturers have always had the challenge of convincing consumers that "the gun—a weapon designed to kill—[is] a morally acceptable product." The gun as a moral weapon has been facilitated by its prominence in stories of the Wild West and in television and films. In the early days of television, westerns linked guns with heroic masculinity when male lead characters routinely saved the day (Mitchell 1998); contemporary representations have taken on a decidedly more militarized and muscular form. Beginning in the 1980s images of heroism have revolved around "hard bodies"—men who have massive muscles and huge firearms (Jeffords 1994)—a link that has become so naturalized that biceps are colloquially referred to as "guns." According to James Gibson (1994), representations of muscular, militarized masculinity emerged as a cathartic response to the U.S. defeat in Vietnam and as an answer to what some saw as the weak foreign policy of the Carter administration. This trope is perhaps best exemplified by the *Rambo* series. Gibson argues that these images were part of a larger "New War" ethos in American culture that was characterized by a constellation of cultural meanings around physical toughness, aggression, and militarism.

The latest development in cultural productions that link heroic masculinity with firearms is video games. The first-person shooter (FPS) games that have proliferated during the late 1990s and throughout the 2000s allow users to insert themselves into the dramas of the New War ethos. FPS games take the perspective of the person who is playing, using on-screen animation that portrays arms extended with weapon in hand as the player navigates the game's terrain. The player is typically the hero of the narrative, who wins by accomplishing an elaborate mission. Most FPS games are structured around complex and detailed narratives of war (e.g., *Call of Duty*), postapocalyptic scenarios (e.g., *Halo*), or both. According to one analysis of FPS games, the narratives usually revolve around "saving the world, restoring humanity, and fighting the forces of evil" (Hartmann and Vorderer 2010, 110). Unlike the films that Gibson analyzes, FPS games "permit gamers to see themselves on screen as the noble hero. . . . Here, the *player* of the game *is* the story" (Power 2007, 285); in this way video games represent an interactive experience with the New War ethos. First-person shooter games exemplify how the fantasy of using guns to fight "bad guys" is not only an acceptable form of violence in U.S. culture, it is celebrated.

The distinction between good guys and bad guys is central to how violence is evaluated. Part of what defines a good guy is that he follows the rules and uses violence only when necessary, while bad guys are those who refuse to follow rules and who seem to take pleasure in violence for violence's sake. Thus the social construction of the good guy is one example of hegemonic masculinity—that version of masculinity that represents "the currently most honored way of being a man" (Connell and Messer-schmidt 2005, 832). Hegemonic masculinity emerges through contrasts between masculinity and femininity and among various forms of masculinity. Good guys are good to the extent that they are able to distinguish themselves not only from bad guys but also from other versions of masculinity that do not measure up to the ideal. Femininity is central to how hegemonic masculinity operates, not only because women serve as props that allow men to establish masculine senses of self (Connell 1995) but also because feminized men operate as foils against which "real men" can establish their masculinity. Given its central role in American culture, the good guy is the ultimate masculine ideal.

Gun Use in Real Life

While the gun lobby and popular representations routinely suggest that heroes can use guns to save the vulnerable, most of the research on the gendered meanings of firearms in real life have focused on the commission of violent crimes and on what Connell (1995) might label "subordinate" or "marginal" masculinities. If hegemonic masculinity represents those traits that are most culturally valued in men, marginalized and subordinate masculinities are those that are culturally disparaged (Connell 1995). Subordinate men are subjected to ridicule for being either gay or too feminine (e.g., Pascoe 2007), while marginal men fail to live up to hegemonic ideals because of their race and/or class status (e.g., Wing-field 2009).

One way dominance is exerted and masculinity is achieved in U.S. culture is through social status. Messerschmidt (1993) argues that race and social class structure opportunities for boys and men such that those who lack the resources needed to be seen as masculine through legitimate means (e.g., a high-status job) may resort to crime and violence. It is because of the link between social dominance and masculinity that men and boys perpetrate most criminal activity, including violent assaults (Britton 2011). Nearly all of the school shootings in the United States have been committed by boys and young men who "had tales of being harassed—specifically gay-baited—for inadequate gender performance" (Kimmel and Mahler 2003, 1440). By using firearms to commit acts of violence, these boys attempted to move from margin to center, from being the wimp who was picked on to the aggressor who dominated and controlled others. Stretesky and Pogrebin (2007) interviewed gang members serving prison time for violent crimes and found that the reputations of both the gang and the individual gang member were determined by their ability to defend their honor and to be seen as masculine, and the primary way this was accomplished was by using firearms: "Guns provide gang members with a sense of power" and "help gang members project a tough image" (90). Because guns are lethal, they imbue their users with the capacity to control others and thus are highly effective tools for achieving masculinity, particularly for men with few other resources. But what about men who are privileged? What role do guns play in their pursuit of masculinity? And how is carrying one in public shaped by gender? I now turn to an analysis of interviews with men who have CHLs in order to address these questions.

Guns as Men's Things

While demographic data on gun ownership are notoriously difficult to gather, the most recent figures suggest that in the United States 46 percent of men and 23 percent of women own guns (Saad 2011). To understand how gender shapes people's desires to become licensed to carry a gun in public, it is important first to investigate the various factors that make gun ownership a male-dominated phenomenon.

Fathers, Sons, and Guns

Seven of the twenty men I interviewed were introduced to guns while hunting with their father when they were young. What is interesting about these interviews is both the fondness with which they recall their early experiences and the gendered framing they use to relay their stories. For example, Mike, thirty-six, described the centrality of hunting in his childhood and how the rural town in Mississippi where he grew up would shut down on opening day of deer season: "When we're talking about a six-year-old hunting, it's really a six-year-old going out and shooting, you know, birds. Just anything that was moving around. [It's] kind of priming for real hunting, is the way I looked at it." He continued, "I remember going on my first deer hunt with my dad, sitting on a power line cut-through. [I] didn't see anything that day. I think I carried my BB gun along and he had his rifle." Eventually Mike was introduced to a .22 rifle, and somewhere around the age of ten his father gave him a .410 shotgun. He recalled the first time he shot his uncle's .357 revolver, and how the force of his father's 12-gauge shotgun knocked him over. The rich details that Mike used to describe hunting with his father and the ease with which he told me the story suggest that he thought about and perhaps told this story often. It struck me how male-dominant Mike's experiences with hunting had been. When I asked if his sister was ever involved in such activities, he seemed a bit taken aback: "Honestly, I don't remember about my sister. That's a good question. I'll have to ask her that."

Likewise George, forty, discussed how he and his father would hunt together when he was a child. His sister came along when she was young, but then "she drifted apart, doing girl stuff." George told a story similar to Mike's, about the first time he shot a 12-gauge shotgun, around age seven: "BOOM! . . . I fell on my back. I was a little kid. . . . I knew that if I complained about it [my father] wouldn't let me shoot anymore till next year. So I said, 'Okay, give me another one.' And that was it. I was hooked after that." George described the initial experience as painful and loud, but he "sucked it up" and continued on. For a time he and his father weren't close. However, his father has started to invite him to go hunting again, and they use the activity to bond. When I asked George if his mom or wife ever hunt, he said that his mom went once, but because it was raining and cold she was "miserable." "[My wife] says that's my deal. That gives me my opportunity to hang out with the guys or whatever."

These hunting stories, relayed with emotional tenderness, are about male-centered experiences with firearms. Hunting rifles were regularly talked about as symbols of these times, made especially poignant when passed down from grandfathers and fathers. This was true for Mike, who had a long and painful falling-out with his father after his parents divorced. When Mike was in college, his father was diagnosed with late-stage cancer. Mike explained, "We reconciled to the best that we could. You know, not knowing my dad, reconciling with him, with a guy who doesn't express emotions or talk about feelings . . . is a difficult thing. But I think we reconciled." When Mike asked his father for something that he could have to remember him by, he was given his prized .30-06 deer rifle: "And I was really proud that he gave it to me. This is Dad's deer rifle. You know? I took it back home, and even though I hadn't been deer hunting much at the time, I felt this kind of connection to my childhood and hunting and Dad and all that stuff." In this way firearms signify a connection between sons and fathers, something that was also on display when Mike proudly showed me a photo of his infant son at the deer lease on which he hunts.

According to the men I interviewed, hunting provides men with an opportunity to spend time with their fathers and relate to them in ways that they may not be able to otherwise. When Mike said that his father was not one to talk about emotions, he conveyed this as a loss, something that interfered with their ability to have a relationship. Patriarchal gender norms make it difficult for men to express tender emotions (Connell 1995), but hunting allows for a masculine way to establish and nurture relationships, and so for some men hunting rifles come to symbolize their emotional connection to their male relatives.[2]

Though this pastime certainly could be shared with women and girls, this was not common among the people I interviewed. None of the respondents openly forbade girls or women from inclusion; instead hunting is marked as a "manhood act" through its discursive construction as something that men do. Joseph, forty-four, said that when his daughter was young, she would hunt with him and did so until about the age of five: "And now, she's a girl." While this explanation suggests that Joseph thinks there is something about being a girl that makes hunting unappealing, such a construction does not preclude all women and girls from participating. He said that he recently took his granddaughter hunting: "[She] loves to shoot guns. Yeah, I took her out to the deer lease, just me and her. We spent the night and had a campfire. You know, the whole nine yards." Though girls and women can occasionally join in, hunting is defined as masculine. This was reinforced by Joseph's wife, Anne, who was present during my interview with him and said that she does not hunt because the weather is often bad and there are no restrooms at the deer lease. Anne explained, "[Hunting is] his thing. You know. So I'm not opposed to it. If he's goin' hunting, I'm goin' shopping." Rather than hunting Anne would prefer to do something that is decidedly feminine. This sort of gender framing was common throughout the interviews: though women and girls are sometimes invited to hunt, it is marked as a man's domain; when women and girls choose not to hunt or otherwise shoot guns, gender is used to explain their lack of interest, further defining this as a manhood act.

Learning to Shoot in Masculine Institutions

Of the twenty men I interviewed, six had served time in the military and three were retired police officers (Leo and Chris did both). By contrast, only one of the sixteen women I interviewed was at one time a police officer, and none had ever served in the military. The military and police are both masculinist institutions,[3] places wherein the logic of the organization is defined by masculinity. For this reason and because being a soldier or a police officer is among the most culturally honored ways to be a man in the United States, men are much more likely than women to enter into these fields. Participation in these institutions includes learning to handle firearms (though, as Roger's experience suggests, this does not guarantee competency), and so it is an important component in some men's socialization into gun use.

Leo, fifty-two, said that because he is from New York City and his family is from Puerto Rico, two places with fairly strict gun policies, he had never fired a gun prior to his experience with basic training in the army. When he was first learning to shoot, he found it to be "pretty scary." He said, "I mean, uh, because the drill sergeants want you to understand, you know, how deadly the weapons are and they scare the bejesus out of you, and when you shoot that thing—I had never fired a weapon— and you know the gunpowder smoke and everything else. I thought it was gonna blow up in my face! But after I shot, you know, forty, fifty rounds down-range, you know, then the opposite was true. [Then they have to] control these guys from shooting their weapons. It was a lot of fun." The masculine draw of the military and police work for Leo was clear when he explained what he enjoyed about both careers: "I believe it's just in my character. I just enjoy law enforcement, military, anything that had to do with that kind of warrior spirit, you know, handgun kind of stuff."

Experience in the military and with the police is significant in shaping men's gun use beyond merely providing exposure to firearms. According to those I interviewed, it also shapes their worldviews such that they see potential threat as ubiquitous. For example, Joseph, who worked as an undercover police officer for one year, said that his time as a cop changed how he feels about people. He elaborated: "It changes you, like I said, the way you view people, the way you view society. Uh, the way you carry yourself. To this day I like sitting with something solid behind me. You know, where I can see everything that's goin' on. I'm real observant over everything." His experiences are not simply based on fantasies of potential violence; as a police officer he was shot twice. His desire to carry a gun is hardly surprising.

Another prominent institution that socializes boys by providing firearms experience is the Boy Scouts of America. Like Leo, the first extensive shooting that Paul, thirty-four, ever did was in basic training, but it was not the first time he had ever handled a gun; that happened when he was a Boy Scout. Paul initially said that there were not any guns in his house when he was a kid but then clarified: "Actually I think my dad had one, but it was nothing I ever saw in the house. I think it was [because] my mom didn't like guns." He remembered first shooting a firearm around the age of ten or twelve as a Boy Scout. He and a group of younger boys shot five rounds with a .22 rifle at a paper target, while older Scouts tried to shoot out the flame of a lit candle.

Though only two of my respondents described shooting as Boy Scouts, the organization is likely the first introduction to guns for many American boys. The NRA is very involved in encouraging and supporting the Boy Scouts, as is evidenced in the following passage from *American Rifleman*:

> Of the millions of boys who have proudly worn the BSA [Boy Scouts of America] uniform, uncounted numbers (including these authors and the editor-in-chief of this magazine) were given the opportunity to handle and shoot their first guns during Scouting-sponsored events. NRA training counselors, certified instructors and range safety officers today provide safe and educational environments for Scouts to learn firearm safety and be introduced into the shooting sports at hundreds of BSA summer camps and range-day activities. The NRA Foundation has provided 1,468 grants totaling $4.9 million to local Scout councils, camps and troops to acquire training materials and equipment and to establish camp range programs across the country. NRA staffers participate in the National Jamborees to provide tens of thousands of Scouts an opportunity to experience firearm use and learn how to safely handle and care for firearms. (Schreier and Horak 2010)

One of the NRA's missions is to promote the shooting sports (hunting, target practice, etc.), so on the one hand, the NRA-BSA relationship is unremarkable. However, this organizational connection is important when one considers the larger discursive framing of gun use and masculinity by these two groups.

By teaching sports, camping, and civic participation to boys, the BSA is engaged in producing an idealized image of what boys should be, an image that is tied to the NRA's representation of the ideal gun user in its deployment of mythic themes of masculinity and American virtue.

Though only two respondents' first experiences with firearms happened when they were in Boy Scouts, the organization plays an important role in the larger discursive framing of masculinity and firearms in the United States. Tellingly, marksmanship is not an activity that Girl Scouts of America promotes.

The Barbie for Men

In addition to hunting and male-dominant institutions, the framing of guns as masculine also occurs in the context of consumerism, where they are commodified as "manly" objects. In many cases in my interviews, guns were discussed as "men's toys" and as having intrinsic masculine appeal. Richard, thirty-eight, discussed his desire to purchase an AR-15 rifle, one of the military-style black rifles that were illegal under the assault rifle ban that lapsed in 2004. Richard spoke at some length about how he loves to purchase guns that can be accessorized. Some of the more popular firearms are sold in such high quantities that there is a large market of options that can be used to customize them. Richard called the AR-15 the "Barbie for men. It's just that I can buy stuff for it, still increase my use out of it, without buying a whole new gun." His Barbie analogy emphasizes that firearm use is, at least in part, fun for Richard, and his interest in being a gun owner is not simply about self-defense.

Paul is one of the eleven respondents who said that he carries a firearm with him whenever possible, and he explained that as soon as he gets dressed, his gun goes on his hip. Because anyone who carries has to use a gun that is small enough to be concealed, I asked if he ever carries a larger, higher caliber gun, for example if he is driving in an area of town that he perceives to be unsafe. Paul said, "[No]. I mean I have others that I could carry and I will carry at times just because I think they're, I don't know, a little more fun. [*Laughs.*]" He followed up by saying, "I went out with a buddy of mine last weekend. . . . I hadn't shown him yet. So I decided to carry that one instead of the normal one. It gets to the point, it's kind of like women with purses—they like to show off what they get." As in Richard's Barbie comment, Paul suggests that part of the appeal of guns is that they are fun to buy and fun to show to friends. Though shopping is marked as a feminine activity, shopping for guns is masculine. While most of my respondents describe guns as "tools of self-defense," they are not simply utilitarian; they are also consumer objects and "men's toys."

While hunting culture, masculinist institutions, and the commodification of guns as manly consumer objects illuminate why so many more men than women own guns, they do not explain why men are much more likely to obtain CHLs than are women. To address that issue, I now turn to an analysis of how men describe their desire to be armed in public.

Wanting a CHL

According to my interviews, conceptions of vulnerability and physical strength are key to understanding the gendered implications of concealed handgun licensing. While many of the men I interviewed said they did not feel vulnerable in their youth, as they have aged they have begun to feel a need to be armed in self-defense. In addition their becoming fathers and husbands compels them to want to be armed in public. Throughout their explanations contradictions and paradoxes suggest that the social construction of vulnerability and safety is as much about cultural ideals as it is about pragmatic concerns for safety.

The Body and Victimization

The body is central to how masculinity is communicated to others, because "to be fully, appropriately masculine, a male person must exhibit physical control of his space and be able to act on objects and bodies in it" (Crawley, Foley, and Shehan 2008, 59). Most of the men who were younger than forty explained that they rarely if ever felt physically vulnerable. When I asked Mike if he had ever felt threatened, he said, "Nothing really jumps out at me. I'm probably a little bigger than average. Average height for a male here in America is like five-nine, last time I checked. I'm six foot. I've got a pretty good build. So I think maybe physical appearance might keep some guys away from me [and] maybe they'd pick on somebody smaller." Because Mike knows that his body communicates to other men that he is capable of fighting back, he assumes they are not likely to see him as a potential victim. This sentiment was echoed by Joseph when he described how his physicality likely deters potential assailants: "You learn how to carry yourself to where you don't look like a victim. I'm six-two, 275, 280, you know. Somebody's gonna have to be really desperate." Mike and Joseph assume that their physically imposing bodies are the reason they have not been targeted by criminals, but then, why carry a gun?

Steven, thirty, decided to obtain a CHL because of his work as a criminal prosecutor. Early in his career he handled mostly petty drug crimes; when his office prosecuted an aggressive and threatening member of a white supremacist gang, everyone involved with the case received threats, and Steven decided it was time to look into obtaining a permit to carry a gun. Under Texas law anyone who works as a judge or prosecutor is able to carry a concealed firearm if a licensed firearm instructor submits a sworn affidavit attesting to his or her ability to competently handle a handgun. The justification for this policy is evident in stories Steven told about being confronted in public by people he has prosecuted.[4]

Steven, like Mike and Joseph, has above-average height and an athletic build, but his feelings about the importance of physical strength extend beyond his own body: "Frankly, I know the cops that patrol this area. If somebody's breaking into my home, I want a big dude to show up at my house to protect us. I know the cops that are coming out of the academies now are small girls. And again, I don't mean anything sexist by this, but from a practical perspective, if somebody's breaking into my house, I don't want that five-foot-four guy rolling up to my house, you know. . . . Oh, and there's a lot of overweight cops too. It's just, they're not going to be able to protect you, you know?" Steven has a clear image of the body type needed to protect others from harm—tall, strong, and athletic—and he believes that despite their training, various weapons, the force of the law, and access to backup, the police might be unreliable protectors if their bodies do not convey that they are physically capable of dominating a perpetrator.

While these men say that a strong and imposing body is critical if one is to be an adequate defender, my interview with Mark provides a stark example of the body's limits. Mark stands six feet, ten inches tall and looks as though he weighs close to 300 pounds. Because of his size he never felt particularly vulnerable and said that it was not until he had a job as head of security in a nightclub that he realized how unsafe he might be. One night he had to escort a man out of the club who was threatening to fight with another patron: "I told him he had to leave. He got real irritated, but he huffed off. And so I was leading him . . . out, and as he left, he kind of made a motion, because he was wearing a button-up shirt, made a motion to his back. And I saw [a gun]. I absolutely did see one. And it scared the bejesus out of me." Mark said, "At that point, that was the first time I kind of realized my vulnerability." Even though he is a very large man who is trained in self-defense, and despite the fact that he had a gun on him at the time, the presence of a firearm in the waistband of a threatening person made Mark's size and physicality irrelevant. If he had drawn his firearm before Mark could reach his own weapon, the smaller man could have harmed him.

That guns are widely available has fundamentally altered how some men think about control and domination. When I asked Paul if he had ever been in a situation in which he felt vulnerable and did not have a gun on him, he explained, "Only as like a younger kid. You know. I've gotten jumped before, gotten beat up, gotten in fights before and stuff like that. That's when I was younger, when I was a kid, and people didn't carry guns. You know, a fight was a fight. Nowadays you get in a fight and somebody wants to take it to another extreme or level, you know. If kids were just out there fighting with fists, okay, let's fight. I mean the guy that I got in a fight with kind of became a friend of mine after the fact because I was a small guy, he was a big guy, we got in a fight and I held my own. He respected that. It was over with. Nowadays it doesn't seem like people fight with just their fists. They fight with other things and . . . you have to worry about what you have to defend yourself with." In other words, because anyone might be carrying a gun and because it is imperative that one not be dominated, the only sure protection is to be armed.

The capacity to dominate makes men feel secure as it allows them to maintain a feeling of control over themselves and others, a central component of masculinity (Schwalbe 2014). An athletic body and above-average height convey toughness and invulnerability and provide men with some confidence that criminals might keep their distance. Yet they cannot be sure. Nevertheless few respondents younger than forty said that they need a gun primarily to defend themselves and instead focused on their need to protect others who are vulnerable (a point to which I will return). However, five of the twelve respondents forty and older explained that age factored into why they have a CHL.

Like many respondents, Jeff cannot carry his gun at work. When I asked him how that makes him feel, he replied, "Vulnerable. [*Laughs.*] As I'm being reminded, like today at my orthopedist, trying to get my knee fixed, I'm not as young as I used to be. And [*pause*] I don't, I don't want to have to dance with somebody if they want to do me violence." Jeff said that with a gun he does not feel this sense of vulnerability and instead feels relaxed knowing that he has "a superior ability to deal with a situation harshly if I have to." He tells the following story: "Years ago I was practicing martial arts regularly. And a friend of mine at the office . . . a good friend of mine was just always real aggressive. And he had his usual fifteen pots of coffee that day and got vulgar like he always did, and I think . . . he said, 'I'll kick your ass' or something like that. I just turned around and smiled at him. And he said, 'Oh man, I'm sorry. I didn't mean it. I was just joking.' I said, 'I know. I know you were joking, don't worry about it.' [*Laughs.*] Then we laughed it off. And he was very visibly shaken. I wasn't gonna do anything to him, but he knew and I knew that I could've. No big deal." Jeff felt proud that his officemate feared him, and though he is older now and not able to do martial arts, carrying a firearm gives him the same sense of confidence. His firearm supplies him with a virility that his aging body has surrendered. He feels "calm and relaxed" when he's carrying a gun; if someone threatens him, he can just smile back rather than worrying about how to handle the situation.

Gil, sixty-six, lives in a major metropolitan city in the Southwest and said that he carries a firearm because "I refuse to be a victim. I refuse to put myself in the position where someone can exercise that kind of control over me." Gil relayed a story about a time when he felt threatened as he left a sporting arena: "We were goin' into the parking ramp to get our vehicle. And there were a bunch of [*long pause*] young [*pause*] punks." He struggled to find the words to describe the group of people he was approaching: "It was pretty uncomfortable for about five minutes, until I was certain that they were goin' somewhere else and not to us." When I asked if the group of people were being hostile toward him, he replied, "Well . . . let's just say I was uncomfortable." And after a long pause, "I think we've all had that experience in a public place." Because sports arenas are gun-free zones, Gil could not carry his gun and had left it in his car. When I asked him how his behavior would have been different if he had had his gun on him, he said that he would have been "more confident that I can take care of myself. You know, at my age, I'm not gonna win many kung fu fights with an assailant. [*Laughs.*] And, you know, thirty-four years ago if someone wanted to mix it up, I probably would've been okay taking my chances. But you get to a certain age and you've got some problems. You know, dealing on a physical level. And you don't run as fast. [*Laughs.*] You know what I mean?" He then said, "You know the old saying, Don't piss off an old guy because he'll probably just kill ya? [*Laughs.*]" This joke was an abrupt and awkward response to his admission that age has hampered his physical abilities, and I believe that Gil used it to salvage his masculinity by conveying that though getting older has taken its toll, if provoked he could still rise to the challenge.

Another example of how firearms can compensate for lost capacities as bodies age comes from Larry, a goateed, tall, stout, fifty four year old who arrived on a Harley motorcycle and was wearing a black bandana and black leather vest. Throughout the interview Larry projected a very tough, almost threatening persona. When he told me that he carried a gun long before he had a CHL, I asked him if that was because he had experienced a violent incident or if it was because of a generalized fear that something could happen. Larry quickly dismissed the notion that he feared violent crime. Instead, he said, he's realistic: "Most people have this delusion that the world's this warm happy place, and for most of them, it is. But that's only because nothing's happened to them yet." Similar to the New War ethos that Gibson (1994) studied, the worldview that Larry has constructed is a perpetual struggle between forces of good and evil, and this justifies his tough, aggressive, thoroughly masculine self-presentation. Later in the interview I asked him if he had ever felt physically threatened when he was unarmed. Again Larry dismissed the idea that he would feel threatened. He explained that this is because of his military training in hand-to-hand combat: "If I've got a stake or a pool cue, I will own your ass. As far as not having anything? When I was a little bit younger and in a little bit better shape, I was comfortable with up to three people. So, no, I didn't particularly feel threatened. If worse gets to worst, I can grab one person, they will scream like a little girl before it's all over with and the other two people will not want to get that close." In this moment, and in many others during the interview, Larry wanted to make it clear to me that he is not afraid and that he is confident he can dominate other men. He is both willing to engage in violence and capable of domination, traits deeply tied to masculinity (Messner 1992; Messerschmidt 2000). However, he also admitted, though subtly, that growing older has taken a toll on his body.

Since Larry was so quick to dismiss suggestions that he might feel vulnerable or threatened, and because he feels that he can dominate other men without a gun, I asked him, "So then why do you carry [a gun]?" He responded, "Because you never know," and proceeded to tell a story about a time when he went into a convenience store and thought he might have to draw his firearm. A homeless man was causing problems: "Somebody had called, you know, the manager, complaining about him for whatever reason. The manager told him, he said, 'Look, you need to leave.' And basically the guy went off on him. And there was a little old black lady there, probably like 473 years old, with her cane, and he started screaming about her, about her being the one who bitched to the manager about him, it was all her fault, and, you know. [He] walked down to the aisle where the kitchen knives were. [I thought he might] come back and kill her and start in on the manager. I'm sittin' here watching this, thinkin', 'Well, this is gonna get good. Let's see if he comes back with a knife.' It ended up, he left." When I asked him how he would have responded, he said, "I would've shot him." By claiming that his gun is primarily needed to defend others, Larry has resolved the fundamental tension at play for men who carry a firearm: although it is a useful tool for self-defense, it is also an admission of potential vulnerability. While Larry denies this aspect of carrying, he is clearly motivated by a desire to prevent being dominated at the hands of another man.

Michael Kimmel (1996, 6) has argued that "manhood is less about the drive for domination and more about the fear of others dominating us, having power or control over us." While some of the younger men take solace in knowing that their build likely keeps others from seeing them as a target, some of the older men have lost this sense of security and now view themselves as less dominant than they were before. By carrying a gun they are able to recoup the sense of strength that stems from having an ability to fight back, a critical component of hegemonic masculinity. Unlike subordinate men who are unable or unwilling to fight, "real men" are able and ready to defend themselves. It is striking how elaborate the fantasies of potential domination can be: Larry describes an imaginary fight scene with a group of three men; Gil wishes that he had been armed when a group of young men, who did not physically threaten him, walked by him in a parking garage; and Jeff uses a gun to essentially recapture a kung-fu warrior fantasy. For these men guns are symbols of virility, and thus carrying one allows them to defend themselves not only from criminals but also from failed masculinity. This helps to explain the appeal of concealed firearms for some men: not that they are communicating to others their ability to dominate them but that they are reassuring themselves that they will not be victims.

But younger men carry guns too. And while they do not feel they are likely to be targeted by criminals, they are nevertheless concerned that they might not be able to fight back against an assailant. This is particularly true among those men who believe that criminals are likely to be armed and that a person with a gun is stronger than even the most physically imposing of bodies. Despite John Lott's (1998) contentious findings that more guns equal less crime, it is instead likely that given the masculine imperative to ensure that one is able to resist domination, more guns might only equal more guns

Good Fathers, Good Husbands

The vast majority of the men I interviewed are married, and ten have children living at home; nearly all of these men explained that they obtained a CHL so they could protect their families. Adam, thirty-six, said that he first bought a gun around the age of twenty-one because, having just finished college, he could only afford to live in "lower-income neighborhoods where there's more crime and there's more shootings and violence." Adam described one such neighborhood as "a bad part of Houston" and said that he used his gun only for protection in his home and was never very serious about self-defense. This changed when he and his wife were expecting a child: "[As a dad] I think my role is that I have to protect my family. That's my number one duty as a dad: to provide . . . food, shelter, and protection for my wife and my child. I mean that's what being a dad is." I asked Adam if that is a role he is trying to learn or if it's one that a man automatically assumes when he gets married. He responded:

> I think you automatically assume it when you get married. And then especially when you have a kid. And I don't know if that's my belief or it's just the way I grew up or whatever. But you know, when you get married, you're supposed to do certain things. You know, you have roles. And I know that in today's society [*pause*] a lot of people like to think, well, men and women, they're the same and, you know, the women work and so do the men and all that stuff. Which, to some extent, I agree. But there's other certain inherent parts of being a man and being a woman that you have certain roles. I can't have a baby! You know, physically I can't have a baby and physically I'm stronger than my wife. And it's just up to me to protect her, in every situation. And if, you know, if we were ever attacked or accosted or something, then, then it's up to me to protect her until she can, you know, be safe.

Adam became very animated regarding what he termed "his role" in his family and seemed exasperated by the suggestion that men and women are equals in all senses. He sees his wife and child as dependent upon him for their safety, and by rooting his argument in bodily differences, he makes this construct seem natural and inevitable, particularly insofar as he compares physical strength and child bearing.

While the idea that bodily strength means it is a man's job to protect his family is a commonsense notion in the culture, notably such meanings exist alongside explanations that women should carry firearms because their guns would make them physically equal to any man intent on hurting them. This is what is meant when guns are referred to as equalizers, something that I address at length in chapter 3. But of course not all men are equally strong, and so guns could serve the same function for men. This is particularly true for those men who are not physically large or imposing (as is true of Adam), and yet guns were almost never referred to as equalizers for men. Instead the need for an equalizer was displaced onto women, as in the following quote from Richard, who, though claiming to love CHLs because they "level the playing field," uses a woman he knows who carries a concealed firearm to make his case: "She's this tiny little thing, nobody probably has any idea she's packing. That's what I love about the law. To me it's an equalizer. Why? If I had a criminal intent on my mind I have no idea if someone's packing a gun. And I hope everyone thinks of that when they try to commit a crime."

Guns could also equalize dynamics between husbands and wives. Despite her smaller size, Adam's wife could just as easily occupy the role of family defender—a possibility that seems logical given her disproportionate time spent with their children. The reason she is not the family protector has nothing to do with an inability to handle firearms; Adam admitted that his wife knew more than he did about hunting and shooting guns when they first met. In fact, though he initially attributed his desire to obtain a CHL to becoming a father, then later said that it was because of Obama's election, he also casually dropped a third explanation for why he wanted a license: "Oh, my wife had one. So, she, you know, it's kind of like, okay, your wife has one but you don't. You need to get one."

Because at various points in the interview Adam offered three different explanations for obtaining a CHL, one might question whether any of his justifications can be taken seriously. Did he initially forget why he wanted a license but later remember? If so, does that mean that his final explanation (Obama's election) is the *true* reason he wanted a license? Does the fact that he mentioned his wife's having one merely as an aside signal that this was not a core part of his desire to be armed but was instead a peripheral concern? A critical analysis suggests that Adam's seemingly conflicting responses are held together by a single thread: all three are explained by the imperative for him to live up to cultural standards of manhood.

Mark, the very tall man described earlier, is married with two small children. Mark said that when he and his wife were expecting their first child, he developed a deep-seated need to ensure that his family was protected: "You know, I've got a newborn child that is relying on me to not only protect him but to protect myself and his mother." As his perspective shifted toward a focus on defending his family, Mark not only obtained a CHL, he also pursued advanced training in handgun self-defense tactics and now carries a gun everywhere he goes—including the gym and his own home—whether or not it is legal. Like Adam, becoming a father was a transitional moment for how Mark thinks about vulnerability and self-defense.

Though Mark said that he carries a gun to protect his family, he spends much of his time apart from them, and so he would love for his wife to carry a firearm: "If something happens to me, you know, if I get shot, she can take it and use it. If I'm not there. If she's by herself." He elaborated by saying, "I can't be with [my kids] twenty-four hours a day. She can't be either, but you know, she's more . . . likely to be there than I am." In this explanation Mark wants his wife to be armed not because she would also become a family defender but because in his absence, his wife and children are vulnerable. Most of the other married men I interviewed said that they wished their wives would obtain a CHL, but in contrast to how they see their role as a father, they do not see their wives as "natural protectors." Moreover their wives' refusal to be armed further emphasizes that it is a man's job to protect his family.

When I asked Mark if he is ever stressed about his wife's safety when he is not with her, he replied, "No, I mean . . . she's a good girl. She can take care of herself. [*Laughs.*] But you know, it's been in the back of my mind always. You . . . gotta kinda balance the practicality versus the, the uh [*long pause*] oh, what's the word? The paranoia." There is a disconnection between how Mark explains his need for a CHL—because crime can happen to anyone, anywhere—and his general comfort with the fact that his wife does not carry a gun. His contradictory response underscores how, in addition to simply being a tool for self-defense, Mark's CHL signifies that he is a good father and husband.

Another instance in which the "father as protector" role becomes clear is when men travel without their families. For example, Jeff carries a firearm with him whenever he can, but his wife has no interest in firearms, a fact that "bothers [him] greatly." Jeff said that as a woman, his wife needs "that equalizer," and he suggests that she is naïve about safety. This is particularly worrisome to Jeff when he goes out of town, and so before he leaves, he quizzes her about the location of the gun safe and its combination. When I asked him if he tries to convince his wife to think about using a gun if needed, he said, "We had to review. Yeah. She's just [*pause*] she's not me." Even though he knows that she will not use the guns, Jeff reviews where and how they are stored, which serves to remind his wife not only that she is vulnerable but that she is particularly vulnerable without him around. When his wife rejects his insistence that access to a firearm is necessary, she is also rejecting the terms around which Jeff's role is built. This represents a moment when women's resistance to these constructs is clear. While the men I interviewed have developed a sense of their own masculinity vis-à-vis their otherwise vulnerable wives, this does not mean that their wives necessarily consent or that they personally contribute to this construct.

Richard, who is married with two young sons, said that while his wife does not have much interest in guns and has no interest in getting a CHL, she does occasionally resort to reaching for the bedside gun when he is out of town: "I occasionally test my wife to make sure she remembers [the safe combination]. Cause I know she gets scared, because I've gone out of town like on a huntin' trip and come back and that gun is sitting on the night stand. I said, 'Why's the gun there?' She goes, 'I thought I heard something.' So she gets the gun out; she knows how to use it; she knows how to get in the safe." Though they may only be concerned about their wives' safety, when men test their wives about the gun safe combination or remind them where the guns are kept, they also reinforce the social construction that without men, women are vulnerable. When they are out of town, a gun by the bedside serves as a symbol of both the absent husband and the vulnerability of being a woman alone.

Paradoxically, having a CHL does not actually enable a man to defend his family. In fact these men recognize that their wives are more likely than they are to be in a position to need to use a gun to defend themselves or their children. This contradiction suggests that while carrying a concealed gun may symbolize the role of father and husband, it may not actually translate into an ability to protect loved ones from harm. Though they may never be in a position to carry out heroic fantasies of masculine bravery, in imagining that their wives and children are dependent upon them for protection (whether or not this is actually true), the men I interviewed are positioning themselves as brave leaders of their families; thus a CHL is a very useful symbol that allows men to construct hegemonic masculinity. In many respects it is an ideal symbol because it signifies to them that they are good fathers and husbands even when they are away from their families.

Can a Victim Be a Man?

No one wants to be a victim of violent crime. But the way gender operates in discourses of victimization suggests that many men believe that masculinity and victimhood are fundamentally incompatible. This does not mean that men are required to be aggressors, but it does suggest that to preserve their masculinity, some men may be willing to go to great lengths to resist becoming a victim. Gil made this distinction when he said, "You know, none of us want to be victims. [It's] not that any of us are cowboys or going out there looking for a fight, but nobody wants to be a victim." I discuss the connection between femininity, women, and victimization in chapter 3, but here it is important to analyze how masculinity factors into victim discourse.

When I asked Paul to respond to the idea that one reaction to being mugged or robbed could be to let criminals take what they want, he replied, "But see, people aren't happy with just your stuff. You know. I don't know what's going through somebody's head. If I give them five dollars, are they happy? Give 'em five hundred dollars, are they happy and gonna leave me alone? Or do they just want everything and [to] take my life? I have no idea what's going through that person's head. So why not just stop it? End it right there. You want something from me, I don't want to give it to you, and you've threatened some means of taking it from me. All right, well, I have this means to prevent that. Now, obviously, we've come to a situation. Are you going to advance or are you going to retreat? Your fight-or-flight reflexes are, you know, going to kick in. I've already shown you that I'm willing to fight. Are you gonna fight? Or are you gonna try to flight? . . . But I didn't just sit there and roll over and say 'Please don't kill me. I hope you don't kill me.'" Phrases such as "sit there and roll over" or the commonly used "bend over and take it" work to feminize anyone who is dominated by another man, and they do so through sexualized discourses of violence. Because a violent crime is an act of domination, many men are compelled to use whatever is at their disposal to ensure that they will not be made subordinate to another man and thus symbolically turned into a woman.

The lengths to which some men say they will go to avoid becoming a victim was most evident in my interview with Joseph. When I asked him to explain the point at which he would know he needed to use his firearm, he said, "When the threat becomes intimate. To where I see it in his eyes that he's gonna use it. There's really, there's no other way to describe it. . . . You just have to know. You can see it in people's eyes. . . . If he's just comin' in here to [rob the place] but he starts telling people to get on the ground and I start to see him going around behind the counter, you know, his intentions are more than just taking the money. You see what I'm saying?" Joseph's understanding of criminal behavior is in part a product of the year he spent as a police officer. As he continued, the significance that he places on control and his absolute rejection of victimization were evident: "He points the firearm at me, then, yes, we're gonna have trouble. If you're gonna point a gun at me, you better be ready to use it. . . . I'm gonna do whatever I can do to get him out of here. Simple as that. Until I feel that he's not gonna leave or his intentions are wrong. Because, it's like I've always told her, and she knows this: that if we're gonna die?" At this point his wife, Lisa, interjected, "We're gonna die his way." "We're gonna die my way," Joseph affirmed. "He's gonna shoot me," Lisa explained. Joseph continued, "Not his way, we're gonna die my way. Cause I'm not gonna go down, I'm not gonna be a victim. You know, he might beat me to death with my gun, but it's gonna be an empty gun. It's gonna be completely empty. You're not gonna find no shells left in my gun. [*Laughs.*]"

Joseph's description of what he imagines doing in the event of a violent encounter is chilling. He will not let another man have control over either him or his wife, who in this context seems only to operate as an extension of himself. He will make the decision about how they die, not she and certainly not someone who is intent on killing them. The phrase "like I've always told her" and the fact that Lisa already knew what Joseph was going to say suggest that this is a rehearsed idea and not one that he spontaneously thought of as we discussed the unlikely event that someone would try to rob the coffee shop where we sat. Lest it seem like Joseph is a sociopath, my sense from our interview was that he is a genuinely nice person who is in love with his wife and who only ever thinks about using violence to defend against victimization. His fantasy of how he would respond if someone tried to rob the coffee shop fits within the larger cultural narrative of what we expect from heroic men. He has an image of what bad guys might do, including not only robbing the place but also violently victimizing his wife. As a good husband, a good guy, he has the courage, the willingness, and the capacity to respond.

So what is a good guy in this context? He is someone who is intent on defending the defenseless, standing up to criminals, and doing whatever is necessary to protect those around him. But he is also someone who is so intent on ensuring that his image of himself as a "real man" remains intact that he will not only fight to the death, but he will also decide whether and how his wife dies in the process.

Masculinity and the Appeal of CHLs

These interviews suggest that guns are associated with masculinity for reasons that go far beyond the reductionist notion that guns are masculine and thus men like guns. Rather than any sort of natural affinity between men and guns, there exists a relationship between firearms and masculinity that is circulated in the media, maintained by traditions, and lived out in men's everyday lives. Many of the men I interviewed were first exposed to guns as children through hunting with their fathers. What stands out in these descriptions is how deeply meaningful such experiences are in father-son relationships. These men do not say that they exclude women from hunting; women seem simply to be uninterested in the activity, preoccupied by more feminine pursuits. Nevertheless the gendered boundaries around hunting help to mark it as a "manhood act," and as such, participation marks males as "real men" (Schwalbe 2014). Like all manhood acts, there is nothing inevitable about this association, and it must be re-created as gendered to maintain its significance.

The institutional influence of the military, police, and Boy Scouts is another way that the guns-as-masculine association is forged. The cultural traits associated with masculinity—courage, bravery, strength, loyalty, and so on—are the same ones that are celebrated as critical to success in these milieux, and these are also places wherein boys and men are socialized to become gun users. The framing of gun use and masculinity that the BSA is engaged in is very similar to that which the NRA produces, an organization itself committed to discursively linking idealized masculinity and guns (Connell 1995; Melzer 2009; O'Neill 2007).

Given this connection, it is not surprising that the NRA is so heavily invested in the Boy Scouts.

In addition to the central place that they occupy in traditionally male-centered activities, firearms are marked as masculine when men describe them as "men's toys." While shopping is often viewed as a feminine activity, guns are objects that men can take pleasure in consuming and showing off to other men. Again women could just as easily participate in this pleasure, yet given how deeply guns are associated with masculinity, they are likely to experience various tensions if they do so (something I discuss in chapter 3).

What these findings reveal is that men are more likely than women to be gun users because firearms allow men to access masculinity, but this does not explain what would compel some of them to want a license to carry a gun in public. The men I interviewed have elaborate fantasies of potential violence at the hands of other men. As they age, some begin to see themselves as less capable of self-defense, and because the body's capacity for aggression and violence is central to what it means to be masculine (Crawley, Foley, and Shehan 2008), some older men feel that their masculinity is diminished. According to Kimmel (2010, 120), this gets to the root of men's fear: a fear that others might "unmask us, emasculate us, reveal to us and the world that we do not measure up, that we are not real men." With a concealed handgun, the capacity for aggression and domination is restored. As Jeff explained, this can boost a man's sense of confidence, as he is able to regain access to the muscular version of masculinity that is celebrated in American culture. According to my analysis of these interviews, some men are compelled to be armed in public in order to defend their wives and children. Ironically, although men say they need a gun to defend their family, they are often away from home and thus might be unable to carry out their role of the defender should the need arise. Men who say it is their job to defend their family because they are physically stronger than their wives are among the same people who say that women need guns because they are equalizers. These contradictions suggest that handguns function as props for doing masculinity by asserting the father/husband as protector, and so having a CHL is a material practice that sustains a man's belief in essential gender differences by enabling him to fantasize about being the defender of his family. One consequence is that this heightens the extent to which women are presumed to be vulnerable and in need of protection by the men in their

lives, something that, as I discuss in chapter 3, has potentially dire consequences for women

It is clear from these interviews that one of the explanations for the
disproportionate rate of handgun licensing among men is that they are
responding to the gendered construction of victimization. Because they
feminize victims and see it as impossible that someone could be a victim
and still be a man, they feel that they must have the capacity to be armed
to defend themselves. This is especially important because they believe
that most other men, particularly those who intend to commit crimes, are
likely armed and thus capable of domination.

While these explanations of how CHLs and masculinity are linked explain the appeal of carrying firearms for some men, they do not explain
the increase in licensing rates that has occurred over the past decade.
However, there are clues embedded in this analysis that might offer some
hints for the increase. The first is that the normalization of concealed
carry may leave men feeling increasingly vulnerable as they presume that
more and more people around them are armed and capable of dominating them. Texas' recent open carry law may only deepen this desire, as a
gun holder's capacity to dominate and control others is now able to be on
full display. In addition, as men learn that people in their networks are
seeking licenses to be armed, they may feel compelled to keep up with
the standards of masculinity defined by this manhood act. Whatever the
reason, masculinity offers only one part of the explanation for why CHLs
have become such an appealing form of self-defense. To understand the
larger gendered significance of concealed carry, I now turn to interviews
with women who are licensed to carry guns in public.

3 Refuse to Be a Victim?

Femininity, Guns, and Victimization

· ·

Lisa is a forty-four-year-old CHL holder and gun rights activist. Though guns play an important role in her life now, she was not raised in a home with firearms. Originally from California, Lisa explained that when she was five, she and her family moved to Texas, where she quickly became immersed in the state's gun culture: nearly every kid owned a BB gun, most trucks had a rifle on a gun rack, and sleepovers were at kids' homes where mounted animal trophies hung on the walls. Lisa was always fascinated by firearms, but her first opportunity to fire a gun happened as an adult when a man she was dating asked if she would like to shoot with him: "He had property so we just, you know, set up a target, and he was like, 'You just need to get comfortable.' . . . And so we started with a .22, and then we would go to the range and work our way up."

CHLs became available to Texas residents in 1996, and in that year Lisa's boyfriend gave her a gift certificate to a licensing course for her birthday. According to Lisa, he told her, "You need to go do this. You need to go protect yourself. I don't want you traveling without it." Friends laughed at the gift: "Everyone was like, 'Oh, really romantic!' And I was like, no, think about it, it was really romantic! You know, he wanted me to be able to take care of myself . . . when I was out and about."

It took six months of regular practice for Lisa to feel comfortable enough to go through with getting a CHL: "Of course, once I got it, I wanted to go shopping." She and her boyfriend went to a gun show and found the gun that she eventually named Annie: "She's a Colt 1911, government-issued .45. And she's beautiful. She's custom." Lisa talked about "Annie" like a glowing parent: "We were shopping, and I fell in love with her, and I just think she's, I mean, very girly, I know, but she's pretty."

Lisa's story is representative of many of the accounts that I heard when interviewing women with CHLs in Texas. Lisa was taught to use a gun by a boyfriend, who also encouraged her to purchase her own firearm and to carry it with her for protection. Presumably this concern for Lisa's safety is tied to cultural constructions of women's vulnerability, but in being armed Lisa is rejecting the notion that women are inherently vulnerable or reliant on men for protection. What does it mean when women obtain CHLs and carry firearms for self-defense? What are the implications for how we understand women's vulnerability? Moreover how do women like Lisa balance the cultural imperative that they perform femininity while also carrying a gun, an act that in chapter 2 I argued is tied to masculinity? In this chapter I utilize interviews with women in Texas who have CHLs in examining how gender shapes their motivations to obtain licenses to carry guns in public. As my interviews will show, while carrying a gun has the potential to undermine patriarchal definitions of women as vulnerable and in need of men's protection, for many women this potential is undermined by the ways they actually use their guns.

Women, Gender, and Guns

In chapter 2 I explained that CHL use by men is facilitated by a combination of cultural processes that include media representations of guns as masculine, ritualized access to firearms, and ideas about appropriate behavior for men and boys. Men's gun use is thereby socially constructed, though it is often presumed to be a natural byproduct of their innate desires. Women occupy very different social locations than men, and vastly different cultural meaning systems are used to explain women's behavior. Thus when considering the cultural meanings that shape women's CHL use, it is important to examine how ideas about gender impact everything from how they gain access to guns to cultural perceptions of their vulnerability.

From Sigourney Weaver in the *Alien* series to the character Lara Croft in *Tomb Raider*, armed heroines have enjoyed some visibility in American culture, though to a much lesser degree than have men (Kelly 2004). Laura Browder (2006, 1) argues that images of "iconic women with guns have challenged and yet reinforced the masculinist ideal of America—that guns are inextricably tied to both masculinity and American identity." For example, the most well-known woman shooter in American history, Annie Oakley, did little to upend the link between guns and masculinity and instead reinforced it by crafting a normatively feminine persona through her "ladylike appearance" and "highly genteel" brand of shooting (89). By contrast, women who have used guns in ways that allowed them to embody masculinity and thus defy patriarchal gender norms— as did female gangsters of the 1930s and political radicals in the 1960s and 1970s—were subjected to ridicule and public scorn, much more so than men who occupied the same sorts of roles. According to Browder, what makes women's gun use threatening is its potential to undermine patriarchy. She writes, "Our fascination with the armed woman is an expression of our societal ambivalence about women's equality with men: we are titillated, but we are afraid" (232). What is it about women's gun use that is so threatening to patriarchy?

The Social Construction of Women's Vulnerability

The capacity for guns to upend patriarchy lies in their ability to alter dynamics of vulnerability and victimization that are tied to the way violence is gendered. As I described in chapter 2, patriarchal gender norms operate as a binary construct according to which femininity and masculinity are defined in opposition: that which is masculine is by definition not feminine, and vice versa. Though strength and the capacity for aggression are valued in men, feminine women are encouraged in American culture to be passive, meek, and soft, leaving them ill-equipped to deal with violent crime. This is compounded by beliefs about men's and women's bodies: the "typical woman" is imagined as weak, small, and vulnerable to rape, whereas the "typical man" is thought to be large and strong, and his body is seen as a potential "tool of sexual violence" (Hollander 2001, 84). Such ideas translate into women's "perceived vulnerability" and men's "perceived dangerousness," placing women in the paradoxical position of both fearing men and relying on them for protection (Hollander 2001). Importantly the "passive woman" represents an idealized version of femininity that is dependent upon race and class; the cultural image of the sympathetic victim is most commonly that of a white woman (Madriz 1997), while black women are imagined as insufficiently feminine because they are "too tough" and unwilling to be reliant on men (Collins 2000). Particularly in underserved urban areas black women who are subjected to violence cannot afford to adopt the role of the "passive victim," as using violence is sometimes a necessary strategy for survival (N. Jones 2009; Miller 2008).

It is critical to focus on women's vulnerability as a social construction rather than an empirically supported fact because while women report fearing violent crime at much higher rates than do men (Ferraro 1996; Warr 1984), they are much less likely to be victimized.[1] This gap between fear and actual victimization is known as "the gender paradox" and has been the focus of a great deal of research. Studies consistently find that the threat of sexual assault drives women's fear of crime, leading Mark Warr (1984, 700) to conclude that for women "fear of crime *is* fear of rape." Women have good reason to fear rape: they are much more likely to be sexually assaulted than are men—18.3 percent compared to 1.4 percent (Black et al. 2011). But in terms of how sex crimes typically unfold, cultural perceptions often do not match the realities. For example, while most discourses about women's vulnerability, including measures of their crime fears, focus on "stranger danger" (Stanko 1995), 51 percent of rapes are perpetrated by an intimate partner and 40.8 percent by an acquaintance (Black et al. 2011). In addition, as Jocelyn Hollander (2001, 95) explains, there is a "widespread misconception that sexual assaults are motivated by victim's attractiveness," creating the false impression that rape is primarily a sexual act rather than one of domination and control. Tellingly, as women age they begin to see themselves as less likely targets of sexual assault, and their fear of crime lessens (Franklin and Franklin 2009).

While some scholars have argued that the gender paradox is the result of problems with methodology rather than an accurate reflection of men's and women's fear of crime,[2] studies that suggest men actually fear crime as much as women do might underestimate the way gender shapes how people experience and imagine vulnerability. As these scholars suggest, men may be "doing masculinity" when they deny feeling afraid of crime; however, due to cultural definitions of manhood, many men may actually see themselves as not being particularly victimizable, despite crime statistics. Conversely, because the very definition of what it means to be a woman is to be seen as a potential victim, women are regularly encouraged to guard against what is constructed as the ubiquitous threat of male aggression (Hollander 2001). For example, women are often told to take precautions to protect themselves, such as not walking alone, avoiding male-dominated spaces, and asking men they know to escort them to their cars, steps that in fact serve as everyday reminders that they are under the constant threat of violence (Madriz 1997; Stanko 1995).

As I argued in chapter 2, though violence is sometimes used against women in order to affirm masculine dominance, men's *defending* women against violence can also be used to reinforce patriarchy. When men say that women are weak, in need of protection, and incapable of self-defense, they are positioning women as their dependents. Given such characterizations, it is no wonder that women are much less likely than men to own guns and obtain CHLs. As R. W. Connell (1995, 83) explains, "Patriarchal definitions of femininity (dependence, fearfulness) amount to a cultural disarmament that may be quite as effective as the physical kind." The very definition of femininity in a patriarchal culture means that women are unlikely to take their defense into their own hands. Given the extent to which fear of crime and the threat of male violence operate as tools of patriarchal control in women's lives, what potential might carrying firearms have for disrupting feelings of vulnerability for women? How do women with CHLs explain victimization and self-defense? In the rest of this chapter I analyze interviews with women in Texas who have CHLs in order to understand how gender shapes their desire to carry a gun in public.

How Is Gun Use Gendered?

Any analysis of the gendered meanings of concealed handgun licensing must grapple with a central question: Why do so few women own and use guns? According to one study, exposure to guns in childhood predicts adult gun ownership more than any other variable (Cook and Ludwig 1998), suggesting either that women are not socialized to use guns as children or that something happens to women as they get older that reduces the likelihood that they will own firearms as adults. Though interviews with women who have CHLs cannot explain why fewer women than men own guns, they can shed light on the gender dynamics that frame women's gun use.

Becoming a Gun User

While the men I interviewed learned to use guns from their father or through participation in Boy Scouts or in the military (some had all three experiences), the women in this study had far fewer institutionalized opportunities to learn to shoot. Nevertheless most report that they were reared in homes where guns were present, and nearly all were taught to shoot as children.

Ruth, fifty-three, is the only respondent who was raised in a home with guns but was not taught to shoot as a child: "[My father] never showed them to me, never did anything. . . . I guess, since I was . . . an only child [and] since I was a girl, my dad never really talked to me about [them]." Though she is not sure why her father failed to teach her how to shoot, it may be that he thought of guns as men's things: "When I grew up and got married and had sons and he was getting old, he gave [a gun] to them." Unlike Ruth, most of my respondents had some shooting experience as kids, even if only with BB guns.

Nevertheless, most of the women I interviewed grew up believing that guns were men's objects. One reason for this is that the household guns almost always belonged to and were used by their father, while their mother rarely—and in many cases never—used guns. And it was not just their fathers' guns that were in the home; as in Ruth's family, it was common for guns to be passed down from fathers to sons or grandfathers to grandsons. For example, when I asked Krysti, thirty-seven, when she first saw a gun, she said, "Oh, goodness. I don't remember not seeing guns." Her father had a wide variety of firearms, some of which "were passed down from his father to him and from his father's father to him."

Hunting is one of the primary contexts in which people are socialized into gun culture, and for those I interviewed it is a predominantly male endeavor. Jackie, fifty-three, is among the women who did not grow up with guns. Her paternal grandfather moved from Sicily to the outskirts of Pittsburgh, and according to her family, the only people who had guns were the "mafioso" or the police: "Good guys didn't have guns. Cops had guns and bad guys had guns, and that was it. So, my dad . . . didn't consider the possibility that having a gun could be a good thing." The first time Jackie saw one was when she was invited on a hunting trip with her college boyfriend's family, an experience that was filled with what she termed "macho" gun use; the men on the trip were the only ones who handled the firearms. She explained that the attitude was "Oh, you don't have to handle them. It will be okay. We'll take care of them for you." Similar sentiments shaped her next experience, when at the age of twenty-three she married her first husband, a gun owner who sometimes hunted. Though she had a "mild interest" in learning to shoot, Jackie explained that "the women stayed in the kitchen and the guys went out and shot the guns. It was a very chauvinistic kind of arrangement."

It was rare for the women I interviewed to describe the gun-using men in their lives as chauvinistic; however, it was very common for both women and men in this study to take for granted the notion that guns are predominantly used by men. Molly, thirty-six, explained that as kids, she and her sisters (one of whom was also interviewed for this project) were always around guns: "I would join my dad bird hunting [though] I wouldn't actually shoot. I didn't ever like the loud noises, and the guns really scared me. But I would go with my dad and my uncles while they hunted." When I asked if her mom ever hunted, she said, "I don't remember her with a shotgun. But she was out with us. . . . We'd all go together. But I don't know that I specifically remember her with a shotgun shooting doves and birds and stuff." While many of the men I interviewed hunted with their father when they were young and then became hunters as teens and adults, this was far less common for the women.

The one exception is Caroline, who is sixty-seven and lives outside Houston. Her father is a retired air force colonel, and the self-described "military brat" moved regularly as a child. When asked if she recalls the first time she ever saw a gun, Caroline said, "I can't ever remember a time that we didn't have guns in the home." She hunted with a gun when she was very young and learned to shoot a shotgun around the age of six or seven. Caroline's story of learning to shoot is much like those relayed by some of the men I interviewed: the gun was so strong and she was so small that it knocked her over. I asked if the experience scared her, and she replied, "No. Dad said, 'It will probably knock you down,' and it did. So [I] got up, dusted off, and tried it again."

Though Caroline remembers that it was her father who taught her to use a gun, both of her parents were capable shooters, and she told one story that illustrated the pleasure she took in her mother's marksmanship: "We went to Germany right after the war. . . . It was a very dangerous place to be for Americans. My dad was provost martial, and we had a home and everyone [near us] was robbed. My mother could shoot from the hip better than anybody I ever knew. The maid would hold up a bamboo pole and touch cherries, and mother would quick-draw and shoot the cherries off the tree. The Germans lined up around and watched [my mother] shoot and we were never robbed." Later, when they lived in Wyoming, her mother was a hunting guide and the whole family hunted pronghorn, moose, deer, bears, and elk—an animal that Caroline said was too beautiful for her to shoot.

Similarly both of Catherine's parents regularly shot guns, though neither of them hunted. She was given a BB gun around the age of seven and participated in shooting accuracy competitions between the ages of eleven and fourteen. When I asked Catherine, thirty-five, who taught her to shoot, she explained, "My dad, my grandfathers, my mom." She said that "everybody" was into shooting, but then clarified, "[Not] my grandmothers, neither of them, they were both terrified of guns. But my mom and dad were both really into it." Catherine's story—in which "everybody" in a family excludes all but one woman—exemplifies the fact that women's gun use is the exception rather than the rule. Unlike Catherine and Caroline, typically when respondents reported that their mother used guns, it was a tacked-on comment, suggesting that the experience was rare. For example, Mary, fifty-three, said there were rifles and shotguns in her home when she was a child and they belonged to her father. When I asked if her mother ever shot the guns, she said, "She has shot, yes."

When women explained how they learned to shoot, most recalled being taught by their father as children; however, because most women did not use guns during adolescence or as young adults, they often had to relearn to shoot when they were older. In nearly all cases they learned how to use guns from husbands or boyfriends. Molly described how she and her husband would go to his friend's ranch: "The guys would go hunting and, you know, girlfriends were welcome. And we would target practice . . . when they were done or whatever. [My husband] had a gun and I hadn't shot much . . . so he decided it was time to start showing me."

While women have access to guns and are often invited along on trips where they are used, guns are most commonly owned and controlled by men. Most women interviewed made no mention of the significance of firearms' being marked as "men's things," but this is the larger context in which their gendered meanings should be understood, as it operates as a commonsense background assumption framing how people interpret gun use. Those with whom I spoke for this study said that while men are more likely to use guns and to have experience with them, in the interest of safety both men and women should know how to handle firearms. And yet, given how firearms are gendered, it is not surprising that some women are initially reluctant to shoot. Respondents' descriptions of gun use contain subtle suggestions that men are "natural" gun users while women are not. For instance, when I asked Krysti if her mom uses guns, she explained, "No. But we want to get her out there . . . because my dad travels a lot and she's home by herself. I would just like her to be able to, if she had to, be able to use it. . . . I don't think she has the confidence." On the question of whether her mom might come around to the idea, she said, "I think with the prodding of me and my dad getting her to finally just get out there. Just saying, 'So you're getting in the car and we're going to the range today! You know, after you get your hair done.' [*Laughs*.]" This sort of casual gendered framing was embedded in nearly every interview.

The notion that shooting is masculine was reinforced even by those women who work to encourage women's gun use. Susan, thirty-three, a CHL instructor who owns a firearms training and handgun licensing school with her husband, told me a story about a woman whose husband had tried to get his wife to learn how to shoot, but she simply refused. One of the times that Susan was working at a gun show, the man brought his wife to Susan's table on the pretense of looking at a shirt he thought she might like. Their conversation convinced the woman to try out a pistol class. "She was very reluctant to come," but ultimately she took multiple shooting courses, became a CHL holder, and now "she's all about her guns." Slowly drawing out her words for emphasis, Susan explained, "She understands it now."

According to Susan, it is common for women to express reluctance about learning to shoot for self-defense: "Yeah, I get a lot of ladies that [in a high-pitched voice] 'Oh, I'm afraid of guns' or 'I don't know anything about guns.'" Given the mocking tone that Susan used to explain such views, it was clear that she finds this perspective contemptible. She suggested that some women "think that it's a gender thing that guns are for men and that women who do carry guns are, you know, . . . overly butch or, you know, whatever." Susan's ridicule of femininity inadvertently reinforces the masculinity of gun culture. Lisa, who said that some people seem shocked when they find out that she carries a concealed firearm, shows how it can feel for a feminine woman to function as a gun user. Lisa likes that she might "take the stigma off" or challenge "stereotypes" that others might have about CHL holders: "I mean, not that I don't wear my boots, not that I, you know, can't get down and dirty just as anybody else. But I mean, look at me. I've got cute little flip flops on, you know. I'm a girl!" Like the men discussed in chapter 2, the women I interviewed reinforce the perception that gun use is expected of men and that it is novel, though encouraged and celebrated, when done by women. This gets to the heart of how discourse operates: guns are so thoroughly constructed as masculine and as men's things that it is very difficult for women to comfortably occupy the position of feminine gun user.

One answer to this dilemma for gun manufacturers has been the creation of guns with pink accessories. While pink accessories might be appealing to some women, these feminizing embellishments inadvertently reinscribe the notion that "normal guns," "real guns" are for men and novelty guns are for women. Thus, paradoxically, pink gun grips are part of the discursive formation whereby guns are defined as masculine.

Scary Guns and Doing Gender

In addition to guns' generally being marked as "men's things," the gendering of firearms certainly involves the fact that they are intimidating. This is not to suggest that men are more likely than women to use guns because they are less likely to be intimidated by them; rather it is important to analyze how gender frames men's and women's conceptions of their emotional responses to learning to shoot. Because this sample consists of gun owners, it is not surprising that few say they find guns intimidating. Nevertheless a small number of men and women interviewed for this project admitted that learning to shoot handguns was an anxiety-inducing experience; their narratives capture an additional way in which gender influences men's and women's gun use.

One respondent who had a strong emotional reaction to learning how to use a handgun is Allison, thirty-five, who was not raised in a home with guns but decided to learn to shoot when she started dating Catherine (also interviewed for this study). Allison felt that since Catherine carried a firearm regularly, it would behoove her to know how to use it. She said that the first time she shot a gun was "probably about two years ago. And I had never shot one before. In fact the first time I actually shot it, I had tears running down my face." When I asked her what caused that response, she replied, "I think it was overwhelming. I think it was frightening. I think it was unfamiliar, and I think it was just a combination of all those that really just kind of freaked me out for a second. You know, I think I just have always had a fear of firearms. I don't know why. I can't even rationalize it. I think it's just the power of it. I think it's like the first time you get behind the wheel of a car, you know, most of us recognize the magnitude of what we're about to do. About the possible repercussions associated with it."

Rachel, forty-one, had a similarly strong reaction when she learned to shoot. Though she had grown up in a home with guns and had used BB guns and air rifles as a child, Rachel first shot a handgun around the age of thirty-five, when she and her husband, a former "military man" who was a member of Special Forces, moved to a house in a rural area. Her husband felt that it was important that she learn how to shoot because of the wildlife in the area and because "he travels quite a bit and he wanted me to be able to protect myself." Describing what it was like the first time she fired a handgun, Rachel said, "I thought, 'My God these things are so loud! Why do people like this?' And that was with all the hearing protection I could have. I do the double thing, the things that go in the ears and the big old muffin things that go over the ears. And I thought, 'Phew! This is terrible!'"

Rachel's and Allison's descriptions of learning to shoot handguns should not be read as evidence that women are unlikely to enjoy shooting because guns are scary and loud. Instead it is important to consider how feelings about firearms are shaped by cultural beliefs about gender, including which emotions are permissible for men and women to express. Allison and Rachel were both intimidated by guns and initially did not enjoy shooting, but over time, and with a lot of practice, both women became more comfortable with handguns, and each now has a CHL.

Mike provides a telling contrast. Mike first contemplated getting a handgun for self-defense after the terrorist attacks on September 11, 2001. He said, "I was always a long gun guy. Matter of fact, I was always just a hunting guy." He saw no use for handguns or semi-automatic rifles like AR-15s, but after 9/11 he decided he wanted a handgun. Knowing nothing about them, Mike asked an experienced friend to show him how to use a Glock he had purchased. He described how uncomfortable the experience of learning to fire a handgun was: "So we [shot] and I sucked! I was nervous. It was so strange because I grew up around guns. I've had a gun in my hand since I was six, you know? You put a handgun in my hand and . . . I got [pause] jittery! There's just something about, there's this stigma about handguns: 'Ooh they're dangerous! They'll kill you!' You know? So I was really . . . trying to figure out how this thing works. And to a certain extent that's good. Because that kind of a [pause] nervous energy? [pause] keeps you aware, you know. As I've gotten more experienced in handguns, I would not say that I've gotten lax in the safety, but I don't have that same nervousness about it. I know this thing can kill you. And I still have a respect for it. But not the same as I did before." As with Allison and Rachel, Mike's lack of familiarity with handguns meant that he was anxious about learning to shoot.

Throughout our interview Mike was very talkative and bordered on emotional at times; his eyes misted over when he recalled his feelings about 9/11 and his memories of his deceased father. There was nothing about our interview that suggested he is overly concerned with concealing his emotions in order to conform to cultural ideals about masculinity.

But while his experience parallels Rachel's and Allison's, the difference in how he relayed his anxiety speaks to the larger gendered meanings that shape firearm use: "I hate seeing stories about people who were sitting there, just cleaning their guns, and they take a round in the forehead and they're gone. Cause that's just dumb. And I don't wanna [*pause*], I don't wanna die being dumb, you know?" Whereas Allison and Rachel explained their anxiety as rooted in the power of the gun, Mike summed up his reaction in a quintessentially masculine way: accidentally shooting himself in the head would be a humiliating display of incompetence.

Guns as Empowering

Though some women are initially intimidated by firearms, nearly every woman interviewed for this study agrees on one thing: guns are empowering. According to my analysis, there are three sources of this empowerment: (1) because guns are marked as men's things, women are often proud of their shooting ability; (2) because guns are "equalizers" that reduce the significance of body size between men and women, they make women feel less victimizable; and (3) for those women who have been victimized, guns can restore their sense of themselves as strong. In the following sections I analyze how women utilize empowerment discourses to explain their CHL use.

The Joy of Shooting

Because cultural meanings associate guns with men, women who are competent shooters often take great pride in their ability. For example, Molly, who was taught to shoot by her husband on a hunting trip, said that learning to shoot was "very empowering. I didn't think that I would be good at it. And I actually out-shot my husband that day. And so I [thought], 'Wow! Hey I can do this! I can control a handgun and not be quite as intimidated.'" This was a common sentiment among the women I interviewed, many of whom were surprised by how capable they were as shooters and by how much they enjoyed shooting guns.

Lisa did not seem surprised that she was a good shot, but she did describe the fun that she had in becoming a proficient shooter when she explained, "Once I picked up a gun and shot, I was hooked. I mean, the first time I put that .22 in my hand and he was like, 'See if you can hit that target.' And it was the challenge. And I was like, 'I'll show you I can hit that target. And where else do you want me to hit it?!' You know? And so for me, it was very much a challenge of being able to master the gun, if you will. Master the sight, the direction, knowing, being in control of placing that bullet and being in control of the gun." Though mastering an activity is something that men and women might both enjoy, the gendered implications of shooting well are evident when women explain the significance of their abilities. Lisa later admitted that part of the appeal of learning to shoot and obtaining a CHL was that it made her different from other types of women: "And then there was just a little bit of the ego. Hey, I'm a girl, and I carry [a gun], you bet!"

Mary received extensive handgun training in the year she spent as a member of the California Highway Patrol and is now a semiretired firearms trainer and competitive shooter. When I asked her to describe what it was like to learn how to shoot, she said, "It was very empowering and a lot of fun. It was something that I did well. I enjoyed doing. I had excellent instruction, and so it was, it was empowering." Mary compared learning to shoot to learning how to drive a car: "Any time you take any piece of machinery and . . . you learn to use it properly . . . it gives you a sense of accomplishment." Though Mary's explanation of learning to shoot is not overtly about gender, the sense of accomplishment she felt is likely tied to the fact that others may not have expected her to master firearms, a point that emerged when she explained why she was drawn to law enforcement. She said she enjoyed becoming a law enforcement officer "because I could. And people didn't think I could because I'm a small woman. And it interests me; I like law enforcement anyway. And I could, and I did and I set the height minimum. They can't claim that they can't hire anybody who's not five foot or taller because I made it." Mary was clearly very proud of her trailblazing legacy.

The women I interviewed evince pride in shooting, and this operates as empowerment because it defies cultural constructions of gender that lead most women to believe they are unlikely to be good at what are purportedly men's activities. This is particularly significant given that in a patriarchal culture "men's activities" are highly valued and worthy of mastery, while "women's activities" are not. In contrast the men I interviewed seemed to assume they were supposed to be able shooters and to have the technical knowhow to competently handle firearms, an assumption that has a paradoxical consequence: women are often considered better shooters than men, something that I heard the first time I visited a gun range, in the firearms courses that I attended for this project, and in interviews with CHL instructors. When I asked those who made this claim to explain why this is the case, they reported that men often assume they know what they are doing with firearms even if they do not, whereas women, who make no claims to know anything about guns when they do not, are more apt to listen to instruction.

Guns as Equalizers

As was briefly mentioned in chapter 2, advocates for CHL use argue that concealed handguns are superior to all other forms of self-defense because they can "level the playing field" between people of unequal body size. This is what is meant when guns are referred to as "equalizers." Mary succinctly explained this view when she said, "Guns are empowering, especially handguns, because they give you the means to put everybody on a level playing field. It doesn't matter if there's a six-foot-two guy who weighs two hundred and plus pounds coming at me or whether it's a five-foot-one scrawny kid coming at me. With a firearm, and I can use it appropriately, I am equal to them in size if I needed to defend myself." Mary said that she rarely finds herself in situations where she feels threatened: "If there's one thing I'm good at, I'm really good at intimidating people." I certainly found this to be true. Until Mary felt confident that she could trust my motives, she was overtly intimidating, terse, and forceful early in the interview. Later she admitted that she was "screening" me to determine whether or not she felt comfortable giving my contact information to her extensive network of CHL holders.

Despite her capacity to intimidate others, Mary acknowledged that without a firearm, she would still be at risk of physical harm. She said, "I'm a small woman, I don't have the strength. I don't have the size. Even if I had a lot of strength, I don't have the size to do battle. Although I can take down a six-foot guy with my bare hands, it's not a problem, I can do that. But I would probably get hurt in the process. And those things being all considered, it's so much nicer to have other means to fall back on, other things that you can do." With a handgun Mary does not have to consider whether she is weaker than a potential assailant. Her firearm makes any physical differences between herself and others irrelevant.

According to the women I interviewed, having an equalizer means they can go places and do things they might not otherwise be willing to because they believe they are inherently vulnerable to potential victimization. June, a sixty-seven-year-old widow, always carries her gun with her when she takes long-distance road trips to visit her grandchildren out of state. Likewise Lisa said that she has had several jobs that required that she drive long distances: "Driving to and from Austin or to and from Dallas, there have been times where I have . . . gotten tired, so I will pull off to a rest stop. You know, turn off the car, put it in park, lay my seat back, but Annie's in my lap, in her case, with the case open. And I'm totally comfortable taking my twenty-minute catnap so I can get back on the road safely." Lisa described this freedom that a gun gives her as feeling "hugely empowering."

Ashley, thirty, captured the connection between beliefs about gender, bodies, victimization, and the desire to carry a handgun when she said, "If something happens and I am alone, my husband will not always be there, and someone will not always be there to protect me." Later she elaborated, "I'm a woman alone. I'm not a large woman. Someone may see me as easy [to] overpower and [will do] whatever they [want]. I want to be able to protect myself." The combination of Ashley's size and her being a woman means that she sees herself as a potential target of (presumably sexualized) violence at the hands of men. It is clear from her description that she is primarily concerned with the risk of being attacked by a stranger. She also points to the paradox of gendered discourses of vulnerability identified by Hollander (2001): women are taught both to fear men and to rely on them for protection. Ashley believes that either she must be protected by someone (her husband) or she needs a gun.

Importantly women's carrying a gun does nothing to fundamentally alter their view that they are inherently vulnerable to men. For example, when I told Allison that one of my areas of interest with this project was exploring the different ways men and women think about self-defense, she said, "Yeah, we definitely live our lives differently than men do. We have to." "In what ways?" I asked. "Well, just because, because we're, I hate to say it, but we are, we're weaker. We're physically weaker. We need something to level off the fight [*pause*] should there ever be one." When I asked her what role firearms play in this dynamic, she explained, "If a man wants to bash my head in . . . there's very little I can do about that, physically. I can try, and I may win. But if I have a firearm, then I have a little bit of a better chance of surviving. Hopefully. You never know." Allison's explanation supports the notion that women's bodies are inevitably vulnerable to male aggression. Though she thinks that she might have a chance to fight off a man who is intent on hurting her, she is more confident—while seemingly still uncertain—about her chances for survival if she is armed. The idea that there is "very little" that she could do to defend herself from a man because of average physical differences dramatically inflates the extent to which women are weak vis-à-vis men.

While cultural discourses about gender create a strict divide between men's and women's bodies that reinforces the idea that women are always vulnerable to men (Crawley, Foley, and Shehan 2008; Hollander 2001, 2009), the empirical evidence makes clear that even without guns, women are most often successful at fending off physical assaults (Clay-Warner 2002; Ullman 2007). Nevertheless the women I interviewed suggested that the only way they have a chance to defend themselves from what they believe is the ubiquitous threat of male aggression is to be armed; this is considered a fact of life that women must learn to deal with. Some women experience this realization as fear, while to others "that's just the way it is." When women carry firearms, they carry with them the capacity to forcefully respond to potential victimization, and this may mitigate the sense of perpetual vulnerability that women are socialized to feel from a very young age. While every woman I interviewed explained that guns reduce feelings of vulnerability, this was most poignant for those who had been victimized by crime.

Carrying a Gun after Victimization

For the majority of my respondents, carrying a concealed handgun is not motivated by a previous experience with violent crime. Not so for Caroline and Catherine.

Caroline told me that her first personal protection gun was a .38 that she bought when she was twenty-five and living in Washington, D.C. I asked her if she intended it for use in the home, and with a matter-of-fact directness she said, "I was abducted and raped and I had a gun after that." I was stunned by her frankness and said, "I can't imagine how life-changing that experience would be." She said, "[It was a] big change. But I was very cautious. You know, I recovered. They offered nothing back then for you. I did work with the police to attempt to catch the guy and . . ." She paused, and then, with her voice trailing off, said, "I just always had a gun after that." Caroline never again went without a gun, despite the fact that it was a criminal offense in Washington, D.C. I asked her if prior to that experience she had ever thought about self-defense. She said, "I lived in Wyoming and Idaho, kind of a simple [life]. We lived out on the ranch . . . or on a military base. I don't think there was danger. . . . There was no concept of danger there. But you go into Washington and Virginia, there's a real concept of danger." During our interview it became clear that Caroline had always seen herself as a strong woman, and though the trauma of rape might have made her decide that she was more vulnerable than she had previously thought, carrying a gun restored her sense of strength.

The consequences of this transformation were very clear in a story she told about a time when she used her gun to defend a stranger in public. It was during the time that she lived outside of Washington: "I was dressed for a party in a silk dress, [and I] had long blonde hair down the middle of my back." As she walked down a street in three-inch high heels, she saw a man try to steal an older woman's purse: "[She was] a little old lady, and she was probably my age now. [*Laughs.*] But to me, she was a million years old." The man did not simply take the woman's purse; Caroline described how he pushed the woman down and "stomped her" with his foot. Furious at what she was witnessing, Caroline "chased that sucker six blocks in full high heels and caught him and arrested him." After I had turned off my tape recorder, she repeated this story and said that the man, lying on the ground with a gun pointed at him, told her he knew she wasn't going to shoot him. She responded, "I'll shoot one ball off at a time and you'll probably bleed to death before the cops get here." Caroline laughed as she told this story, and there was evident joy in her eyes. She did not shoot the man, but she did hold him at gunpoint until the police arrived. The judge decided not to charge her with a weapons crime, and he even gave her his business card in case she ever needed help with a gun possession charge. A year later she was stopped by the police while driving, the gun was found, and a call to the judge helped Caroline avoid a charge. This story is clearly very meaningful to how Caroline saw herself when she was younger. She was unable to fight off the man who raped her, but she was able to fight back against another woman's attacker, and she credits this to being empowered by her firearm.

Though Caroline regularly carried a gun without a permit, she first decided to get a CHL a few years ago while experiencing a lengthy recovery from a badly broken leg that required surgery. She also has arthritis that is so severe she has had surgery to straighten her hands, and she describes herself as "slightly crippled." While recovering from surgery she was dependent on others' help, and she was not able to leave the house by herself. A postsurgery outing to the local mall was the first time she realized that she was more vulnerable than she used to be: "This was my first excursion out by myself [after surgery]. I was so thrilled to be out!" When she entered the mall, there was a "Mexican gang at the door and I heard a very strange whistle.[3] And I thought, 'Oops.' And I got to the door and they were kind of circling. And the whistle was to point me out. And so I spent hours in the mall. And when I came to the door, there was the whistle and every head turned of that group. And then I realized: I have no control over this." She elaborated, "I knew that whistle was about me, instantly. [I] turned around, and of course there stands a whole gang." Caroline found a police officer to help her out to her car. It was shortly after that experience that she decided to become licensed to carry a concealed handgun.

In chapter 2 I argued that as men age and their bodies change, they begin to see themselves as vulnerable, particularly men who in their youth valued strength and an ability to fight. Caroline's description of being aware of her vulnerability is very similar. She said, "You know, as I've gotten older, like I ran somebody down six blocks [*laughs*] when I was young; I was a pretty strong gal. I'm not that way anymore. . . . I couldn't run a mouse down, much less a thief! I'm fully aware of that." I asked Caroline if her awareness of the difference between her youthful strength and what she sees as her present vulnerability compels her to want to carry a gun. She said, "Absolutely! But I carried when I was young. So who knows."

Caroline's example illuminates the social constructedness of gender: there is nothing inevitable about how gender norms shape self-concept. Reared on farms and in the outdoors and having parents who were both shooters—including a mother whom she proudly saw as intimidating to potential criminals—Caroline was a woman who did not feel vulnerable; she saw herself as strong and capable of self-defense. Despite this self-concept, she was targeted by a man who chose to physically attack and violently victimize her; she was made into a victim, though she had never seen herself as one before. She said that it took time for her to recover emotionally, but she eventually did, and it seems that carrying a firearm was a central component that allowed her to recover her sense of self. In terms of her own self-concept, she has "refused to be a victim."

Later in our interview Caroline and I discussed her plans for home safety. There was a time when she always had a gun readily accessible in her home, but she no longer does: "I felt like it made me nervous all the time. I couldn't relax. I felt like I needed a safe zone. And so I choose my house to be my safe zone. And if it's not, well, that's just life." She contrasted this view with that of a friend who is always armed with multiple guns. Caroline laughed heartily as she described her friend: "She's a woman about my age and at least seventy-five pounds overweight and five-foot-two and she is sure the whole world is out to rape her. I told her that at our age, we came off the high-risk list!" Then Caroline explained, "I know that I am not being stalked by everybody in the world. [*Laughs.*] And I like that feeling. But I do like the feeling that I might have some control. And so that's the reason I got the CHL." In this moment Caroline identified the main difference in how men and women experience aging: women perceive that they are safer as they grow older because they are less likely to be seen as objects of sexual violence, while men feel more vulnerable because they are no longer able to physically dominate other men.

Unlike Caroline, the other woman I interviewed who had experience with victimization took some time to decide to obtain a gun. Catherine was reared in a rural area near a medium-size city in Texas, and though she grew up with guns, stopped shooting when she moved away to college. Shortly after graduating she bought a house that was in need of major repairs. During the renovation the contractor she hired got into significant legal trouble, tied in part to his attempts to cash his clients' checks at check-cashing businesses, a practice that Catherine said is illegal. She put a hold on the check she had given him, and soon there were "thuggish guys showing up at my house demanding money. When I'd leave my house people would follow me." At one point "he dropped nine guys off on my lawn . . . and told them that I was the reason that they weren't getting paid. And that they should get paid however they saw fit." Catherine was hosting a party at the time, and fortunately her guests outnumbered the men, but events like this left her emotionally strained, and she did not sleep well for months. In addition to threatening her with sexual violence and stalking her, the contractor did an estimated $67,000 worth of damage to her home. Though she still owns the property, she cannot afford to fix it, and it remains uninhabitable. Catherine said the expense of having a mortgage on a house that she cannot live in has left her "flat broke" and that the financial strains of the situation pushed her and her girlfriend, Allison, to discuss moving in together. During this time Catherine struggled with whether or not to buy a gun for personal protection: "I wanted to have one for a long time in that experience, but I still didn't really know what to do. I was so lost. I was so used to not having one, and I didn't own one. I don't know. I didn't think that I could shoot somebody, so I figured it was useless." Finally, after much consideration, Catherine decided to obtain a license when she and Allison began living together: "That was kind of where I drew the line. I didn't want to not have a gun when I had brought this mess with me. I didn't want anybody doing anything to Allison because they were after me."

Catherine's experience with victimization has left her forever changed, an impact that she said even friends and family have noticed. Though she was initially uncertain about whether she wanted to carry a gun, she is very clear on the sense of empowerment that carrying a firearm has given her. When she was being stalked and harassed, she was panicked and anxious and rarely felt safe: "All situations [were] more frightening." In contrast, "I feel much more comforted knowing that I'm armed when I go places, because if nothing else, I have a way out."

These interviews suggest that like other forms of self-defense, CHLs have the potential to reduce feelings of helplessness and increase feelings of empowerment (Hollander 2004). Both Caroline and Catherine saw themselves as strong and capable of self-defense prior to their experiences with victimization, but being victimized fundamentally upended their self-perceptions, and they felt vulnerable for the first time in their lives. With guns these women have been able to reclaim their strength and sense of self.

Armed Women: Family Defenders?

While three of the women interviewed for this study are single, ten are married heterosexuals and three are partnered lesbians. As is true for the men in chapter 2, relationship status plays an important role in how women view their concealed firearm use, and yet this operates very differently for women than it does for men. Whereas sixteen of the eighteen married men I interviewed have wives who do not have a CHL, only two of the married women in this sample have a CHL while their husbands do not. Earlier I argued that men use their CHLs to enact the role of family protector because it allows them to embody hegemonic masculinity. In this section I ask how women relate to the family protector role and analyze the ways that gender shapes this dynamic. My analysis suggests that women almost never see themselves as responsible for the protection of their families, something that is most clearly revealed when they explain their gun-carrying practices.

Molly likes to have a gun when she drives long distances, especially when her children are with her. She described her motivation as a "'mama bear protecting her cubs' feeling"—a feeling that is shared by all four of the women in my sample who have children living at home. However, Molly said that if her husband is carrying his gun, "I don't mind not having mine. Again, when we have the kids, I do feel better when I know that one of us has a gun." Though they do not have a formal arrangement about who will be armed when they travel, Molly's husband carries more regularly than she does, and in fact she identified traveling without her husband as her primary motive for having a CHL.

A similar dynamic exists between Wendy, age fifty, and her husband, Matt, forty-six. Wendy and I had arranged to meet at a coffee shop on a Friday evening. She arrived with Matt and asked if it would be okay if he sat with us during the interview. The couple had contemplated getting CHLs since moving from California to Texas in 2004, but it was not a financial priority until the 2008 election, when they both felt that gun rights were threatened by the election of Barack Obama.[4]

Wendy grew up in the Houston area and said that she has always had a great deal of awareness about crime and victimization: "I've always been that kind of person. So it was nice to be able to take advantage of the legalities, and getting the handgun [was] the next step." Though she is very comfortable with her handgun and enjoyed learning about self-defense in the CHL course, Wendy admitted that she does not carry her firearm regularly: "Do I always carry? Not always, and, you know, I've come under fire from the ones that say, you know, 'Carry twenty-four–seven or guess right.' You know, maybe I'm not guessing right sometimes. But sometimes I just don't feel like I'm in a situation where I would need it. I think I've always been more worried about defense at home than defense out." Then Wendy looked at Matt, laughed, and said, "And I very seldom go anywhere without you. I don't know how that works."

Later in our interview Wendy explained that she felt safe in her town and rarely carried a gun in public "until they had an attack at Wal-Mart about a mile from my building at one in the afternoon. And that's made me kind of rethink my security a little bit. . . . [Now] I probably carry more often out than I did. Especially if I'm going to be by myself. Not so much when I'm with [Matt], and I don't know why that it is. I don't know if it's 'the man will protect me' kind of thing or what. [*Laughs.*]" Wendy seemed somewhat embarrassed that she inconsistently carries a firearm and that she relies on Matt for her defense. Later, when our discussion turned to home defense, the couple said that should a break-in occur while they are in their bedroom, Wendy will call 911 and Matt will investigate the situation. Thus both inside and outside of their home, Wendy sees Matt, and it was clear that Matt sees himself, as the primary defender of the family.

Like Wendy, Susan also relies on her husband in this respect. When I asked Susan if there are any places where she is able to relax and let down her guard, she said, "I do that more so when I'm with my husband. Because I know that he's always thinking of it, more so than I'm thinking of it. So like when I'm on my own, sometimes I'll forget [my gun], but I find myself being more aware of where I'm at. But when I'm with my husband I do let my guard down because I know that he's thinking about it for both of us." Because they both carry guns and are trained in self-defense, I asked Susan if she is ever in charge of being on guard so that her husband can relax. She said no: "That's just who he is."

The only married women in my sample who said they do not rely on their husband for defense are Caroline and Jackie (whose husbands do not have CHLs) and Ruth and Mary (self-described "twenty-four–seven carriers"). Though Mary does not rely on her husband for protection, she explained, "The only time I truly let my guard down is when my husband is close or when I'm sleeping and I have no choice." In explaining why she feels comfortable in these instances, Mary said, "He's better than I am." She elaborated, "He's faster, he's more accurate, he's more aware, he's a far better sheepdog than I am. So, yes, I can, I can relax around him. And that's great. The nice thing is we can trade off. If I see . . . he's tired, I can be a little more alert. When we're sleeping at night, when he goes to sleep he's a pretty sound sleeper, he can sleep through most anything. I allow myself to be a lighter sleeper. I allow myself to wake up and pay attention to things when I hear them. So if there's something I can do to give him the relief, I do. If we're traveling and I see he's tired, I'm a little more alert. So we trade off." Mary's narrative suggests that though her husband is the primary defender of the family, she is capable of playing that role and willing to if need be, but only as his backup.

Though few respondents articulated why men are necessarily the family defenders, Mary offered an explanation that is rooted in what she believes to be innate gender differences. When I told her that one of the women I had interviewed said that she had had to come to terms with the idea that her life is more valuable than that of someone trying to victimize her, Mary said:

Absolutely. But look at where men and women are, though. Men are by nature the protector and provider for their home. By nature, by God, they were made warriors. Women were made nurturers. We give life, we nurture life. Women have a huge, huge natural inborn hard-wiring to overcome to get to that point to where we would be warriors. We're only capable, with very few that are not, of being a warrior on the drop of the dime without any thought when it comes to protecting our young. That, most women have no problem. They will live, die, bite, scratch, whatever it takes to protect their young. That they will do. But when it comes to themselves? They don't have that sense of worth. They don't. And what I tell those women is, 'Okay, fine, you are willing to die for your young, but are you willing to live for them? If you are willing to say "I'm not going to take a life to protect myself," you've given up your life for your children, and they won't have you. Wouldn't it be better to live for them? That takes a lot more courage.' And some women, they go, 'Ah! I've never thought of that!' And they have their moment of seeing their worth.

In addition to being a competitive shooter, Mary teaches women's-only CHL and handgun self-defense courses and regularly works to promote women's firearm use. Through encouraging women to be armed against violent victimization by emphasizing that as mothers they would be letting their children down if they were killed, she is utilizing patriarchal gender discourses rather than dismantling them. Such framing might be effective at getting women into her classes, but it also contributes to cultural discourses that minimize women's inherent worth as human beings by tying their value exclusively to the maternal role.

The three partnered lesbians interviewed for this study offer interesting insights into how gender shapes the role of the family defender. Catherine and Allison are both licensed, and they have different views on carrying a gun in public. Catherine said, "I'm a lot more into carrying. I carry more often. But that could just be because [Allison] recently got her permit. She just recently carried for the first time like last week. I think. And normally I guess she knows that I have a gun, so she doesn't carry, but that drives me crazy! Because I'm afraid that something will happen to her, you know, when we're not around each other. But she just got a new carry pistol this weekend, so maybe she'll start carrying that." As a "twenty-four–seven carrier" who says that if she is dressed, she likely has a firearm on her, Catherine does not like the fact that Allison does not regularly carry. Allison said that she really likes the added security of having a gun in the home—she stores her gun in her bedside table for easy access—but generally does not feel the need to be armed in public. Though she cannot have a firearm in her car when at work, she always has it in her glove box when she is not at work. When I asked what motivates her to carry a firearm in her car she said, "Because it gives [Catherine] peace of mind."

When I told Allison that many of the men I interviewed reported a need to protect their families from harm, she said that she feels the same way: "I mean, we're a small family, but we're a family. And even the dogs, I don't want anything to happen to the dogs. I don't know if I'd take a human life over the dogs, but if there's a person that is entering the house, yeah, I've got a responsibility to [Catherine]." Catherine is more experienced with shooting and has a stronger desire to regularly be armed, but Allison feels they share an equal responsibility for each other's defense. (This shared responsibility is partly what motivated Allison to obtain a CHL.)

The other partnered lesbian interviewed for this study is Cindy, thirty-nine, who has been carrying a pistol regularly since she was seventeen, well before CHLs were legally available. Cindy's partner, Erica, who was present for the interview, was raised in an adamantly antigun household and credits this early socialization for her present-day attitude toward guns: she has no interest in shooting them or relying on one for self-defense. In general Erica is not worried about victimization, whereas Cindy is extremely cautious and concerned about crime, as exemplified in her use of a house alarm. Not only is the alarm set every night, but Cindy also sets it when she leaves for work in the morning because Erica is often home alone during the day and Cindy is concerned for her safety. Cindy said, "Because I know she's not going to have the gun next to her all the time. You know, if somebody knocks on the door in the middle of the afternoon, well, if I'm home and alone a lot of times I'll have a gun with me." In contrast, Erica said, "If somebody's at our door, I look, but I don't yell at them through the door asking them who they are or what they want." Cindy responded, "She'll help the guy that's lost, and I'm like, that's the perfect way that they could get you!"

Interviews with lesbians who have CHLs shed light on how gender shapes the construction of the family defender role. At first blush it seems that Catherine and Cindy are family defenders, just like the men I interviewed. However, there are some marked differences that are important to understand. Those men who said they need a gun to defend their wives and children largely minimized their own vulnerability and instead described their obtaining a CHL as being motivated chiefly by the need to protect others. This is not the case for Cindy and Catherine, both of whom are very clearly worried about self-defense as well as the defense of their loved ones. This is likely because they are not operating within a compulsory gender binary. Allison, who was always cautious about crime anyway, feels that she should learn about guns so that she can do for Catherine what Catherine does for her: be prepared to defend her should the need arise. This sort of reciprocity does not exist for the heterosexuals in this study.

Cindy and Erica's example also sheds light on the gendered nature of the family protector role, but for different reasons. Whereas Cindy, the CHL holder in her household, is admittedly terrified of crime, the men I interviewed never admit to fear; they never say they are scared that their wives will be harmed in their absence. Perhaps this is because they do not experience (or admit to experiencing) their vulnerability as fear, or perhaps it is because, as family defenders, confronting the fact that their partners are vulnerable in their absence would undermine their ability to carry out their roles as good husbands and fathers.

Caroline and Jackie are both married to men who have no interest in carrying a concealed firearm. My interview with Caroline happened in her home with her husband, Hank, present. When I asked him if he had ever had any interest in obtaining a CHL, he said that though he was raised around guns and used to hunt, he does not want to carry a gun in public. Caroline offered a reason: "He says he would never kill anybody." "No, I couldn't, I don't think," Hank replied. Caroline said, "Well, I admire you for telling me that. I couldn't imagine why he wasn't taking the course, and he told me, and it's not ever been a problem since." Though Caroline admires her husband for being honest, she certainly cannot relate to his feelings about being unarmed: "I could shoot somebody without remorse. I know that sounds terrible. But if someone was threatening my life or my children or grandchildren, it would not keep me awake to take care of that."

Jackie decided to take a women's-only firearm class in order to become better acquainted with her husband's firearms. She sees that experience as a turning point in fueling her interest in owning her own firearm and subsequently attending a CHL course. She said that she is motivated mainly by the fact that she and her family regularly drive from a city in Texas to Memphis to visit her sister-in-law. Jackie said, "I don't want to take my kids up there; I don't want to be driving around up there without being able to protect ourselves. Again, going back to the [idea]: Don't mess with my kids or you're going to have a she-tiger on your hands!" Though Jackie carries a gun in order to defend herself and her children, she said, "I asked my husband if he wanted to get one and he said flat out, 'No.'" According to Jackie, her husband does not want to have to worry about having a gun on him: "So he would just as soon not have it on. I don't think it's logical, but that's his opinion and it's firmly held. And it's one of those ones where you go, 'Yes, dear.'" Jackie's explanation of her husband's reticence to be armed is nearly identical to those of the husbands I interviewed whose wives were uninterested in carrying a gun: she feels that her husband is being irrational, but it is his choice to be so.

Though Mary believes that husbands are more likely to be armed than wives because of innate characteristics, I would suggest that these dynamics revolve principally around cultural beliefs about men and women. As I argued in chapter 2, cultural discourses construct notions of the good father and good husband that include the responsibility to protect one's family from harm. These constructs are easy extensions of masculinity; they entail bravery, strength, and courage, and because they fit so well with the expectations for men in our culture, it likely feels natural for husbands to occupy the role of the family defender. Tellingly, when married women are licensed to carry firearms and their husbands are not, the women do not explain that they are protecting their husbands. It is also noteworthy that those women who have children living at home often explained their firearm use via analogies such as the "mama bear protecting her cubs." I would suggest that they must rely on such analogies because since women are viewed as inherently victimizable, there is no existing cultural frame within which to explain a woman's aggressively fighting for her own survival. When Jackie says that if you mess with her kids, you'll "have a she-tiger on your hands," she is utilizing a discourse through which she can understand being a fighter rather than a victim: as a mother, she will fight to the death to protect her children. In this way the "she-tiger" discourse bears some resemblance to the "good father" trope, but unlike men, women are seen as being capable of aggressively fighting back only when their children's lives are at stake. This analysis also identifies one of the ways that patriarchy operates: children are dependent upon their parents for protection, and many married women are dependent upon their husband, but never is a man dependent upon his wife, even when she is armed and he is not.

Femininity and the Limits of Empowerment

Interviews with women who have CHLs reveal the extent to which gun use is seen as a "manhood act," even among women gun owners and advocates for women's gun use. Because our culture compels people to successfully enact gender norms (West and Zimmerman 1987), it is no wonder that women are much less likely than men ever to become gun users at all, much less CHL holders. Nevertheless interviews with women who do become licensed suggest that they feel empowered by their gun use and their ability to carry firearms in public. Not only does their mastery of a culturally defined "manhood act" allow them to revel in their competency, but when women obtain licenses and carry firearms, they believe they have the capacity to respond to violent crime and to defend themselves from men who might be stronger than they are, men who might use their strength to exert their dominance. Armed women can take steps to "refuse to be a victim," as the NRA suggests, and thus concealed handgun licensing represents a bold response to the social construction of women as inherently vulnerable to male aggression.

However, interviews with women who have CHLs suggest that obtaining a license does very little to fundamentally upend the notion that women have "breakable, takeable bodies" (McCaughey 1997, 36). While women may feel less vulnerable when they have a firearm, what happens when they are unarmed? What resources might women draw upon to feel empowered in spaces where guns are banned? Additionally, like Susan, Wendy, and Molly, women who are married to men who have CHLs often choose not to carry a gun when they are with their husbands, further entrenching the role of the family defender as one occupied by men. This is profoundly consequential as the defender role exists vis-à-vis dependent others who are construed as vulnerable and victimizable. In other words, the good husband as defender relies on the discursive construction of a potential victim. Were women to occupy the family defender role, there would have to be some acknowledgment that women are also capable of control, that husbands could also be victims, and that men and women are both vulnerable to violent crime. In fact the empirical evidence makes clear that it is men, not women, who are most likely to be crime victims. So long as women's victimization is seen as uniquely tragic, and to the extent that women are seen as more likely than men to be victims, not only is the social construction of women's vulnerability strengthened—and women's fear of crime deepened—but the link between men as physically dominant and women as reliant upon them for protection is legitimized. This dynamic reinforces the notion that men are physically superior to women and can, if they choose, have physical control over them.

This is particularly significant given that women are at much greater risk of violence at the hands of men they know than from strangers. Between 1980 and 2008, 41.5 percent of murdered women were killed by a current or former husband or boyfriend; 30 percent were killed by an acquaintance; and 16.7 percent were killed by a family member. Only 12 percent of women who were murdered during this time span were killed by a stranger (Cooper and Smith 2011). In 2010, 64 percent of violent victimizations of women were perpetrated by someone the victim knew (Truman 2011). Violence against women is much more likely to result in homicide when a gun is available. According to one study, there is a threefold increase in the odds that a woman will be killed in her home if a gun is present, and women killed by intimate partners are seven times more likely to live in homes with guns than those who do not (Bailey et al. 1997). And any woman who might want to obtain a license to carry a firearm because of the fear of random public shootings should recognize that between 1999 and 2013, there were nearly twice as many mass shootings that occurred within families than of the public type that respondents describe could happen in schools or other workplaces (Krouse and Richardson 2015).[5]

I do not present this evidence in order to suggest that Susan, Wendy, or the other interviewees who rely on their husbands for defense are likely to be harmed by them, nor am I suggesting that these women are contributing to violence against women. However, their reliance on their husbands stems from and reinforces a cultural meaning system in which men's aggressiveness and women's vulnerability are made to seem natural and inevitable, when in fact they are social constructions—products of agreed-upon meanings about how men and women should be. The man as protector requires the woman as victim, and while this dynamic might comfort some women, it nevertheless reinforces patriarchal gender norms that men are *supposed to be* in control of themselves and those around them. As too many women well know violence is one way some men try to regain control when they feel it has been lost.

4   Good Guys and Bad Guys

· ·

While in previous chapters I focused on the relationship between gender and self-concept in motivating license holders to carry guns, another key part of the explanation involves how they view criminals. Mary said that her desire to carry a gun is an extension of a long-held belief that her life is more valuable than that of someone intent on hurting her: "It's just [that] I've never not seen myself as a valuable person. And I've never had any problems seeing bad guys as not valuable. Some more so maybe than others. But that's the way it is. Some people just need killing. [*Laughs*.]" When I asked Mary to elaborate on what she thinks motivates criminals, she said she believes that some people are "just innately bad," then she continued:

> My decision is not to kill somebody. But if their decision is to kill me, well, if I get a chance, I'm going to kill them first. . . . It's just a mind-set. It's the way you get. There are, if you will, there are sheep, sheepdogs, and wolves. Sheep is the vast majority of the people. They just go around in a herd, and they go around munching the grass all day long. That's what they do. They're not good, they're not bad, they're part of society and [you] gotta love 'em, because they keep society going. Then there are the sheepdogs. They're always going around protecting the sheep because it's in their nature. They're the heroes; they're the ones that do what has to be done. They're the ones who see the raccoon that's obviously got rabies and nobody really wants to shoot anything and kill it, but they're the ones who go and get the gun and shoot it. They're that kind of a person. And they will do it. And so they're the good guys. They're your police officers. They're the ones who usually run around with the CHL. And then there are the wolves. And the wolves are the bad guys. They're predators, that's what they are. It doesn't mean that it makes them [*sigh*; *pause*] something that should just plain be exterminated. I think that an effort should be made to help them see the errors of their

ways if possible. But there are some wolves that are such a
predator that all you can do is shoot them

Mary's explanation is a harsh commentary on what she sees as human
nature, and yet it is representative of the "good guys" versus "bad guys"
discourse that was core to many of the interviews I conducted for this
study. What is critical to examine is how these categories are imagined
in real life. As metaphorical abstractions, it seems as though "sheepdogs"
and "wolves" could be anyone. But, as has already become clear, the "good
guy" status relies on the social construction of gendered ideals. In this
chapter I examine how race and class shape perceptions of good guys and
bad guys through an analysis of how respondents imagine criminals and
how they see themselves in contrast.

The Social Construction of Crime

On its face, crime might seem like an objective fact that is best measured
by whether or not a law is violated, but like all other facets of social life,
crime is a social construction. What is defined as criminal and what solutions are offered to remedy those crimes are the products of cultural
meanings (Griswold 1994). And, as critical criminologists argue, power
dynamics shaped by race, class, and gender determine who is considered
a likely threat and who a likely victim (Madriz 1997).

Earlier I analyzed how the men I interviewed draw upon discourses of
the ideal gun user propagated by groups like the NRA in order to make
sense of their desire for a concealed handgun, and I suggested that hegemonic masculinity is central to how men understand their gun use. This
chapter extends that discussion by analyzing how race and class intersect
with gender in the "good guy" construct. Race and class are central to
hegemonic masculinity (Connell and Messerschmidt 2005) but have been
virtually ignored in research on guns. This elision is significant particularly because the image of the ideal gun user that is constructed by the
NRA emerges alongside controlling images of black masculinity that
frame black males as "threats to white society" (Collins 2006, 75). I explore how racialized discourses related to crime and self-defense shape
the meanings around gun use in the production of good guys and bad
guys.

Just as beliefs about gender shape the way men and women are treated in society, "commonsense" ideas about race "provide the rules for perceiving and dealing with the Other in a racialized society" (Bonilla-Silva 2001, 44). This happens through the process of racial formation whereby meanings are created about different racial groups that are structurally situated around competing interests (Omi and Winant 1994). Though racialization provides all people with a "commonsense understanding" of race, it is most significant because of how it privileges whites and oppresses people of color (Bonilla-Silva 2001).

One of the most persistent ideas that white Americans hold about black Americans is the association of blackness with crime (Feagin 2010; Madriz 1997; Russell-Brown 2009). According to Joe Feagin (2010, 105), "Much social science and other research shows that many whites automatically connect black Americans as a group with crime, while they do not easily associate whites as a group with crime." More specifically white Americans tend to believe that black *men* are criminals. For example, perception of a neighborhood's crime problem is tied more to the percentage of its population of young black males than to any other factor, regardless of the area's actual crime rate (Quillian and Pager 2001). This association has led Kathryn Russell-Brown (2009, 3) to coin the term "criminalblackman," a concept that identifies the social reality that "the picture that comes to mind when most of us think about crime is the picture of a young black man."

The postindustrial economic vacuum that existed in American inner cities in the 1970s and 1980s contributed to a burgeoning drug trade, particularly in crack cocaine (Reinarman and Levine 1997). The combined effects of the drug itself and the violence associated with its use and dealing further marginalized black Americans (Reiman and Leighton 2010; Wintemute 2006), who already were socially abandoned by racist housing policies, racial residential segregation, and deindustrialization (Peterson and Krivo 2010). But the most consequential development of the crack era was the War on Drugs, a multifaceted government policy that included huge increases in policing, a prison construction boom, and the implementation of federal mandatory minimum sentences for even minor first-time drug possession offenses (Alexander 2012; Reinarman and Levine 1997). These draconian measures have devastated many black communities. Part of the ideological machinery that justified the War on

Drugs was representations of black criminality in media, from news to films to rap music that persistently linked black men with violence (Russell-Brown 2009). Tellingly these representations of blackness were largely shaped by white politicians' interests (Reinarman and Levine 1997) and white consumer tastes (Collins 2006). For example, the profitability of hardcore gangsta rap in hip-hop was driven primarily by white male consumers who were drawn to lyrics that "turned the blighted conditions of ghetto poverty into an oasis of adolescent fantasy and popular entertainment" (Watkins 2005, 46).

One consequence of these representations is that the black male as criminal has become a "controlling image" of blackness in the white imagination (Collins 2006). In other words, white Americans tend to associate all black men with the potential for criminality and violence, regardless of criminal history or socioeconomic standing (Anderson 2008). These characterizations are a form of gendered racism according to which black men are seen by whites as "threats to white women, prone to criminal behavior, and especially violent" (Wingfield 2009, 10). Given such controlling images, the meanings associated with gun use by black men are very different from those associated with the ideal gun user promoted by the NRA. For example, in an analysis of the media outcry over black NBA players' gun ownership, David J. Leonard (2010, 257) writes that in the hands of black athletes, "guns merely become a signifier of the danger, the lack of discipline, and purported pathology of black athletes."

There are many consequences of controlling images of black men as criminals. For example, black drivers are much more likely than white drivers to be stopped for minor traffic violations and to have their vehicles searched, a phenomenon known as "driving while black" (Russell-Brown 2009). For many years New York City police have utilized a tactic known as "stop and frisk" in which they stop, question, and frisk people who have not committed any crimes (because of legal challenges, the NYPD has officially put an end to this policy). There were over 680,000 such incidents in 2011, and 87 percent of those stopped were black and/or Latino (Taylor 2012). In addition to having disproportionate levels of contact with the police, black and Latino men are more likely to be sentenced and convicted and to receive harsher sentences than white men, even for the same crimes and with similar criminal histories (Reiman and Leighton 2010). And as events in 2014 and 2015 revealed, black men are much more likely than any other demographic to be shot and killed by police officers and armed private citizens, even when they are unarmed.

Race is a "fundamentally relational concept" (Desmond and Emirbayer 2010, 38), and yet whiteness is often invisible to whites because it operates as a commonsense, background assumption against which other racial meanings are produced. This is what is meant by the notion that whiteness is hegemonic (Lewis 2004). Whiteness is often identifiable only when failed versions emerge at the intersection of race and class, for example, with terms like "redneck" and "hillbilly" (Hartigan 2005). While it is not always visible, whiteness almost always operates as "subtext," particularly when people attempt to make sense of inequality by invoking "color blindness" (Bonilla-Silva 2001; Lewis 2004). One way to consider the centrality of whiteness in discussions of crime is to ask whether crime is thought of as problematic for its consequences to black people and black communities or as a matter of the fear that it induces in whites. Considering the policies that can be implemented as a result of the perceptions of white middle-class Americans, there is perhaps nothing more dangerous to black communities than white anxiety. Thus the role of whiteness in racialized perceptions of threat must be central.

Amanda Lewis (2004, 637) says that while black Americans are profiled as criminal, white Americans experience a form of racial profiling as "innocent, even in the face of evidence to the contrary." And yet the very meanings of whiteness make it difficult to empirically prove this reality. Thus the "innocent white" makes sense as a theoretical construct vis-à-vis the criminalblackman, but the specific ways it is constituted and the various consequences of its existence are unclear.

In the rest of this chapter I utilize a critical race perspective to examine how the CHL holders I interviewed understand crime and their desires to be armed in public. I pay particular attention to how respondents construct a sense of self and other through racialized perceptions of crime and vulnerability. I not only analyze moments when respondents specifically use racialized language; I also note where race is discursively constructed, even in the absence of this language.

Race, Class, and the Good Guy

One of the main points that the CHL instructors I interviewed emphasized is that license holders constitute a special class of citizen. This claim is tied to the licensing process, which, at least in Texas, is expensive and proves that license holders do not have a criminal record. Susan explained, "The point of the concealed carry is you're having more people going through stringent background checks, knowing that they're out there carrying legally. These are the cream of the crop of our community. It should make you feel better. Because then the bad guys know that there's more of the good guys carrying that know better, that know the law, that are stand-up people that aren't gonna tolerate ill behavior." David, a sixty-six-year-old CHL instructor, stated many times during our interview that he "puts a lot of faith" in the background check because it ensures that applicants will be denied a license if they have ever committed a felony, if they have committed a class A or B misdemeanor in the previous five years, or if they have ever been convicted of disorderly conduct or domestic violence. Jack, a forty-six-year-old CHL instructor with advanced firearm training, who blamed Hurricane Katrina evacuees from New Orleans for what he perceives to be a steady increase in violent crime in Texas, said, "That's always a point that I make with my clients, is that we're the good guys."

In addition to the legal restrictions that prevent people with a criminal history from obtaining a CHL, it is a costly endeavor. Some respondents in this study mentioned that they put off getting a CHL until they could afford one. In Texas CHL courses typically cost between $60 and $100, and the state fee is $140. Though he does not directly connect this to the cost of the course, David celebrates the fact that most of his students are college-educated professionals: "Fortunately I don't see too many, what you might consider bubba types coming to class. Yesterday I taught a class, I had five. I had one pastor. The other four were high-tech individuals. . . . Everybody's college-educated." When I asked David to elaborate on what he means by "bubba types" he said, "If it's somebody that shows me . . . they have a lot of racial prejudice . . . or . . . if something in our conversation would lead you to believe that maybe they have the mind-set that they need to go form a militia." In using such constructs David is distancing himself and his students from poor whites, people onto whom he can displace racial prejudice and antisocial behavior. His class bias was evident when he suggested that his students are good candidates to carry a gun in public in part because they are professionals and college-educated. David uses "bubba types" to construct a preferred middle-class whiteness by marking "failed whiteness" (Hartigan 2005), a framing intended to legitimize CHLs as a whole.

John said, "What I expect you're gonna find is a recurring theme that our behavior patterns are different from the criminal class." Whereas criminals think, "What can I steal, rob? How can I get paid today?," CHL holders are professional and upstanding. John elaborated, "It's more people that are established in their careers and their lives and their family and their community. Guys that are Boy Scout pack leaders and . . . soccer and baseball [coaches], and they're PTA members. What I tell people is, you know, my students are the kind of people that are gonna pull over if there's a car accident on the highway. They're gonna pull over and see if they can help. They're not just gonna drive by. They're the ones that have the first-aid kits in their car, the ones that are gonna stop and render aid, the ones that are volunteer fire department members. They are the ones that are out there being an active member of the community, contributing and doing what they can." John's explanation of the types of people who get CHLs makes it clear that he sees them primarily as *men* who are good citizens. The good guy is literally a guy; masculinity is hegemonic in these accounts, as it operates as a common-sense assumption that frames how CHL holders are imagined.

Because he sees those with a license in such a positive light, John said that it "irritates" him that there are laws that restrict where CHL holders can carry their gun: "It's a personality issue. If you're mentally and emotionally squared away to where you can handle it, then it doesn't really matter where you are or what you're doing or who you're around." Like John, most of the people I interviewed suggest that the licensing process creates a pool of good citizens who should not have to disarm in gun-free zones. Most respondents scoffed at the notion that there is such a thing as "gun-free" because, to paraphrase Bill, "bad guys don't read signs." For example, when I asked Adam his views on gun-free zones, he said, "I think it's kind of a joke. Because when you're posting a gun-free zone in a school, well then, who's gonna have the guns in the school? The bad guys, the guys who are, you know, bringing them there illegally anyway. Right? I mean people who don't go buy their guns and register them and get a concealed handgun license. Just guys who are . . . for lack of a better word, bad guys, right?"

Both Gil and Barbara have printed business cards to hand out to store owners who prohibit guns in their establishments. The cards state (among other things) that, as a CHL holder, the person passing out the card has no criminal history or mental illness and asks, "Can you say that about your *other* customers?" (see figure 2). Interestingly Gil and Barbara both say they have never actually handed the cards to anyone who operates a business in a building that is "posted." Neither respondent said they would be willing to be confrontational with a store owner, but they heartily

I have noticed your sign and will respect your wishes by taking my business elsewhere.
I only shop where I can carry.

As a Citizen with a concealed handgun license, I:
- Have no felony convictions.
- Have never been convicted of domestic violence.
- Have no history of mental illness or drug addiction.
- Have passed a background check and have my fingerprints on file with the Authorities.
- Have passed mandatory training in both the use of a firearm and the applicable law.

Can you say that about your other customers?

FIGURE 2 "No Gun, No Money" card. This is an example of the cards that some CHL holders have printed to distribute to businesses that post signs making it illegal to carry a gun on their premises. Reprinted by permission of Nebraska Shooters (nebraskashooters.com/unfriendly).

agree with the sentiments of the card and cannot fathom why they would be prohibited from carrying their guns into gun-free zones.

When CHL holders attempt to justify why they should have the right to carry a firearm in public, they often rely on the licensing process as proof that they are not criminals and thus will not use their firearms illegally. In this discourse CHL holders contrast themselves to a criminal other against whom their goodness and moral right are established, a construct that leaves them baffled by business owners who do not permit armed good guys on their premises. Susan explained her perspective on gun-free zones as follows: "I feel that everybody knows that nobody in there is armed, so that would be a good place to come and do something. You know, like Taco Cabana that has the big 'no gun' sign. We don't go sit inside Taco Cabana, because basically it's telling everybody, 'Nobody in here should have guns, so come on in and rob us.'" Susan said that although such signs are well-intentioned, "they don't realize the message they're sending to the bad guys. They're telling the good guys, 'We don't want your business,' and they're telling the bad guys, 'Come on in and rob us cause it's easy pickings.'"

While some respondents said they respect a business's right to refuse service to anyone and do not see gun restrictions as a reason not to shop at an establishment, others will not support businesses that refuse to honor their right to carry in public. An example of this latter view comes from Mike, who told me about a time when he was shopping for an anniversary present for his wife. He stopped at a jewelry store and noticed as he approached its entrance that it was posted with a "30.06 sign," indicating that firearms are not allowed on the premises. Mike went back to his truck to put his gun in his console and entered the store. He said:

> [I] went in and I looked at what they had. And I went, "This is really nice, I like this. It's exactly what I'm lookin' for. You guys have a sign on the front door that says that I don't have the right to defend myself. And you're in Texas. [Laughs.] What are your thoughts on that?" And the lady, she actually engaged me in conversation and said, "Well, you know, that's a corporate policy? Uh . . . and up until like two weeks ago?" She said, "We always had armed security at the front." Oh, well, I can understand why a corporate office would make that decision if you're gonna pay for armed security. So why did the armed security leave? She said, "Uh, it was too much of an expense." I said, "But the sign's still up. So now you've got an open target here with *all* this jewelry. No armed guard and no armed citizen to defend against a robber." She said, "Huh? I guess. Okay." "Well, if you ever get that policy changed, I'll buy this ring. In the meantime I appreciate you talkin'." And I bought it from somewhere else. Even though they had the best price and the best-looking band. I'm not gonna support a company that's gonna strip me of my ability to defend myself.

Though Mike explained that the gun-free zone policy is problematic because he cannot defend himself while in public, he chose to disarm and reenter the store to engage with an employee about the store's policy. Some of the people I interviewed who are very concerned about crime will simply carry their firearm into places that are posted, even if in doing so they are breaking the law. But as Mike did, some decide instead to engage with a larger struggle over their right to carry firearms in public, protest statements that are an attempt to make sure that their views are well-known in the hopes that gun-free establishments will change their policies. Given that these resistance actions sometimes include strategically disarming to make a point, they should be read as layered and as containing meanings beyond simple fear for one's safety. Mike's outrage over his inability to be legally armed is a product of his feeling entitled to carry a gun in any and all spaces, something that is tied to his belief that he is an ideal candidate to protect himself and others from an armed robber.

A few of the people I interviewed said they are not put off by businesses that post gun-free signs, but most respondents say they refuse to shop in such establishments, and some are actively involved in working to get businesses to change their policies through letter-writing campaigns and boycotts. Because they see themselves as good guys, some CHL holders believe they *should* be armed and that, when armed, they *should* have access to any public or private spaces.

When Good Guys Carry Illegally

While most respondents emphasized that CHL holders are different from other people because they insist on doing things "by the book," a handful of the people I interviewed admitted to carrying their firearms illegally, something that clashed with their suggestion that bad guys are bad in part because they illegally carry guns. This contradiction points to the significance of privilege in the social construction of bad guys. Mike, who was adamant about the distinctions between criminals and CHL holders, said, "I'm a very 'do it legally' kind of guy. Which I think that most CHL guys are." Mike explained that if people are willing to go through the hassle of a CHL course, they are likely law-abiding: "You don't get people to sit through this . . . friggin' class and pay all that money and go to the range and show that you can shoot reasonably well from people who don't have a respect for the law. Those people, they're gonna carry whether they have this or not." Later Mike also said that he does not carry in gun-free zones.

Though early in the interview he explained that there is a firm distinction between lawbreakers and law abiders, when describing places where he cannot carry his firearm Mike said, "Work won't let me, and, you know, because I follow the law and follow the rules as much as possible, I don't carry at work. There [were] two times that I did. What happened? Something happened about five years ago, [and] I brought my gun with me to work [for] two days in a briefcase." Mike also admits that according to the employee handbook, it is against company policy for him to have a gun in his truck when he is at work, but because he feels the need to be protected during his commute, he knowingly breaks the law.[1] At once Mike insists that he is law-abiding while also admitting to breaking the law, a contradiction that is important not because he actually has criminal intent but because of what it reveals about how privilege operates: by defining himself as a good guy, Mike is able to explain away his illegal behavior and to rationalize why his actions are reasonable.

Another example comes from Krysti, who regularly carried a gun before obtaining a CHL. When I asked her if she knew that without a CHL she had been carrying the firearm illegally, she said yes and seemed embarrassed by this fact. I told her that she was not the first person I had interviewed who had admitted to carrying a gun without a license and so she need not feel bad. Krysti laughed and said that she didn't feel bad and that if she had been caught, she would have claimed that she didn't realize it was illegal. In a high-pitched voice she said, "I'd be like, 'Oops! I didn't know you had to have a license!'" It seemed clear that Krysti assumed that as a woman she could claim ignorance about the law. Significantly, she apparently took for granted that she would be presumed innocent and naïve and not counted among those criminals who carry guns illegally.

When I asked Krysti if she had known that she was breaking the law, she said, "Yeah, I did know. I didn't care. My thought was, 'Yes, I need a license; I'm supposed to have a license. But my safety is [my] priority.'" Because she had carried a firearm illegally before obtaining a CHL, I asked her why she would go through the trouble of getting a license. Krysti said, "Because it's the law. Everyone should obey the law." "Were you worried about getting caught?" I asked. Krysti responded, "No. You have to give 'em a reason to get caught."

All the respondents who admitted to carrying a gun illegally were white, and all either explicitly explained or implied that the only time they could ever be caught with a gun is if they had to use it to defend themselves.[2] In this way they are able to rely on the fact that whiteness does not carry the stigma of criminality that people of color especially men—endure. They are not likely to be stopped and frisked as they navigate their daily lives. Because they are most often imagined as victims and not perpetrators (Madriz 1997), white women might feel particularly free to break gun laws, as they may assume that police officers will not presume they are armed. One advantage of white privilege is that because white people are assumed to follow the law, they are less likely to be surveilled and thus they are less likely to be caught when they do commit crimes.

Perceptions of Threat in Public Spaces

One of the reasons in-depth interviews and participant observation proved so critical to this project is that these methods allowed me to get beyond the commonly used rhetoric circulated by the gun lobby and well-known to gun rights activists. In so doing I was able to identify how typically unacknowledged social forces impact license holders' notions of criminal threat and the need for a concealed firearm. This became most evident when I realized that there is an important difference between the official, color-blind explanations of perceived threat offered by most of the instructors I interviewed and the ways license holders described times when they felt vulnerable. The primary way instructors explained threat was that it can happen "anytime, anywhere," but as I will show, license holders, including instructors, imagine criminal threat in more narrowly focused ways than is commonly acknowledged.

It was evident in the licensing course that I took with Bill that the color-blind discourses he uses to teach situational awareness in the classroom is belied by the way race actually factors into his perceptions of criminality. While instructing us on strategies that we could use to determine whether or not we were being followed in public, Bill told a story about an incident that had happened a few weeks before, when he was attending a large conference at a downtown convention center. Bill said that the expansive building was extremely crowded, which made it difficult to assess potential threats. As he was navigating the building, Bill realized that a group of three men had been walking behind him for what he thought was a suspicious amount of time. He decided that he needed more information, and so he kneeled down to retie one of his shoelaces, a tactic he recommended both because it allowed him to see how the men would respond and it offered him a chance to size them up. Bill stepped to the side, knelt down, and the men walked on, indicating that they were not following him.

Though this initially seemed like a fairly innocuous explanation of a useful self-defense strategy, as I rode with Bill to the gun range for the shooting portion of the class, I learned that there was more to the story: the three men in the convention center were black, a detail that he said he had left out because "people just aren't polite anymore." I was taken aback by this comment and admittedly failed to ask any follow-up questions that would have allowed me to plumb the meanings behind the story. And yet my familiarity with the criminalblackman trope leaves me confident that Bill was trying to let me know he had good reason to be suspicious. How else to explain his seeming need to ensure that I knew that the men were black? I presume the reason he did not disclose this bit of information earlier had less to do with good manners and more to do with the fact that two of his students were black men and he knew that this comment would sound bad, and maybe he even realized that a perception of intent based on race is in fact racist. Though he avoided talking about race in the classroom, when we were alone and in the all-white space of his pickup truck Bill acknowledged, however covertly, that race is a part of how he understands potential criminality. In the interviews I conducted for this study, I heard many similar stories that collectively suggest how central race is to the ways license holders imagine threat and vulnerability, and ultimately I discovered that race plays a key role in compelling some people to be armed in public.

Dangerous Neighborhoods

Nearly everyone I interviewed insisted that concealed firearms are critical for self-defense because crime can happen even when someone least expects it. In fact this "anytime, anywhere" perception of victimization is the primary maxim that justifies CHLs; if someone knew when and where a crime might occur, that person would not need a handgun, he or she could simply avoid the situation altogether. Nevertheless nearly all respondents admitted that they make decisions about whether to carry a gun, and in one case whether to carry more than one gun, based on where they are going. Common scenarios that evoked a desire to be armed include being somewhere new, traveling, and having to be in a part of town with a reputation for being dangerous. "Bad parts of town" were always marked as areas with high poverty and often, though not always explicitly, as predominantly black or Latino.

There was an assumption among respondents that some neighborhoods are so dangerous one should not venture into them without being armed. For example, when Krysti explained her initial desire to have a gun, she said, "I was living on my own, and I was living in a neighborhood that was a hit-or-miss neighborhood. So I just thought it would be a good idea to have a gun in the house and be familiar with it if I ever have to use it." Likewise Jackie said that traveling to Memphis to visit her sister-in-law is one of the primary reasons she has decided to obtain a CHL: "My sister-in-law lives in what can best be described as a transitional neighborhood. [*Laughs*.] Eighty-year-old house in a really nice neighborhood, but people are starting to carve them up and make condos and duplexes out of them and whatnot. It's not a bad neighborhood in the sense [that] it's not unsafe to walk down the street or walk your dog or anything like that. But her car gets broken into about twice a year; her house has been broken into about four times in the last few years. And I'm looking at this, going, 'I don't want to take my kids up there, I don't want to be driving around up there without being able to protect ourselves.'" Respondents' identification of particular neighborhoods or parts of town as places where a person would not want to travel without a gun was remarkable for its normalcy.

When Adam explained when and how he carries his firearm, he said that for a short while he kept a handgun in the glove box of his car; he liked having it handy "just in case" he might need it. When I asked if a specific threat led him to this tactic, he said:

> You hear about carjackings. Um [*pause*], let's say you pull up to
> a convenience store and there's some certain people outside that
> make you feel a little nervous, then you've got your gun there,
> you can slide it in the back of your pants or whatever, you know,
> to make yourself feel more comfortable or just to be able to defend
> yourself or protect yourself. Because growing up in Houston,
> like I said, I understand that there's people out there with guns.
> That's just the bottom line. So do you want to have one too? Or do
> you not? You know, I mean, do you want to defend yourself or
> do you not want to defend yourself? So, yeah, I guess, you know,
> worrying about carjackings and I drove, um, a really nice car,
> which kind of made me nervous. I had a little BMW sports car

convertible, and I would drive with the top down a lot and stuff like that. So it was really easy access if someone wanted to stick a gun in my face and tell me to get out of my car. It was really easy for them to do that.

Adam's description of a potential convenience store encounter with "certain people" was initially vague, and yet his later explanation of this scenario was a very telling example of how he imagines criminal threat.

Adam said that he does not regularly carry a gun because he now lives in a safe city, which he set in contrast to his experiences growing up in Houston, parts of which he described as a "war zone." Adam always carries a gun when he travels to Houston because, unlike his current city, where the "bad parts of town" are relegated to one side of the city and the "nice parts of town" are on the other, Houston isn't "zoned." He noted that his friends who live in Houston carry their firearms daily: "The gas station right down the street is totally different than the gas station one mile down the road. I mean you can have the one that's right by your house is fine and you've got no problems, there's no people hanging out there drinkin' beer and acting crazy. But you decide not to go to that one and you just drive down the street and all of a sudden it's like, you know, Compton down there." Adam invoked Compton as a euphemism for race; it is code for a space that he sees as predominantly poor, black, dangerous, and scary. It is because of Houston's uncertain racial landscape that Adam feels compelled to be armed.

Given that he had now mentioned the convenience store example twice, I asked Adam if it was a scenario that he had ever experienced. He said, "A couple of times, I think. Yeah." When I asked him to describe such a time, he said, "Um, late night, driving home from, I don't even know what, downtown, maybe? Or driving home from, uh, meeting with somebody and I needed gas or I needed to go the convenience store for something. And you pull up and there's, you know, three guys out there, gangster guys, just kind of hanging around at midnight in front of the convenience store. You know. So you make your decision. Do I leave? Or do I protect myself and, you know, so I needed gas, I think. So, getting out and you're vulnerable because you're pulling out your wallet and you're sticking your credit card in the gas machine. And you're sitting there pumping gas and what are you gonna do, you know, if they wanna come up and steal your car or steal your money or whatever? So when it's just you outside and them outside, um, you know, I would just kind of grab my gun and stick it in the back of my pants and pump my gas and be on my way." Given Adam's narrative style, it is not at all clear that this incident actually occurred. Adam begins by saying that it has happened "a couple of times, I think," and then he tells the story by going back and forth between relaying vague details of a specific time (e.g., "I was . . .") to suggesting a hypothetical event that could happen to anyone (e.g., "you pull up . . ."). The tendency to fall in and out of describing actual events and relaying imagined ones was not uncommon in my interviews, and it is something that I attribute to the way CHL holders are trained to think about potential threat. They are told by instructors to imagine scenarios in which criminals might attack them and to be vigilant when they encounter someone suspicious, regardless of the outcome. For example, Bill used his story about being at the convention center to explain that the men he had identified as potentially threatening could have been planning to assault him, and his use of evasive tactics might have been the reason he was not attacked. There is a tendency for the people I interviewed to explain any potentially threatening experience as a crime that could have been, no matter what actually happened, an interpretation that radically skews how license holders understand threat, as they are led to dramatically overstate the extent to which they are vulnerable in public spaces.

A second interesting thing about Adam's story is how race, class, and gender intersect in his perception of threat. Coupled with his description of the group of young men as "gangster guys" and his earlier reference to Compton, one can surmise that Adam is describing encountering a group of black men. He feels threatened by this group, unsure if he should get out of his car, something that he earlier identified as a status symbol that he believes made him a likely target of theft. Adam's willingness to rise to the occasion in a situation that he sees as intimidating is not just about personal safety; he acknowledged that driving away is an option. But instead of letting his fear of the criminal other restrict his behavior, he responds in a thoroughly masculine way, allowing him to assert—if only to himself—that he is not a coward. Gender and race are key elements not only in how he gauges threat; they are also central to how he sees himself and to the meanings embedded in the act of slipping a gun into his waistband. He is no longer a weak and vulnerable target for the black men he sees to prey upon; instead he is strong and prepared to fight back.

Jack explained that what and how he carries has changed as he has pursued more and more advanced firearm and self-defense training: "I've started carrying a backup weapon. And added a couple of knives. Cause as I go through training it just becomes very evident that equipment fails. And, uh, you can't afford for it to fail." Then he elaborated, "I don't always carry two guns. I'm only carrying one right now. Um, it just depends on what I'm wearing, where I'm going, and I realize that sounds stupid, because that's exactly the opposite of what I tell my students. You never know where it's going to happen. But, uh, I wanted to wear a T-shirt today and I can't wear two guns and a T-shirt." This explanation reveals how something as mundane as getting dressed can disrupt the self-defense strategy of even the most well-trained license holder. Moreover it indicates a fissure in the logic of concealed carry: despite the official "you never know where it's going to happen" line, Jack suggests that his perceptions of threat and his strategies for defense are tied to specific places. When I asked him to identify in which places he most feels the need to be armed, Jack said, "Well, all this crime you hear about in the bad side of town, that's criminal-on-criminal crime. Where they're hitting you is in your own neighborhood, they're going where the stuff is. They don't have that stuff in their own neighborhood." Jack extends the boundaries of "dangerous places" by asserting that the real threat is when criminals from those areas come looking for people of means. Notably Jack does not acknowledge that there might be crime victims in the "bad side of town," and instead he emphasizes that the *real* victim is "you," someone who presumably shares his status and my own (i.e., white, middle-class, suburban).

It seems clear that Jack tries to avoid the "bad side of town," but in at least one case he "got lost and ended up in a predominantly black neighborhood. [A man in] an old beat-up truck in front of me was driving around and he stops . . . in the middle of the road where I couldn't go around him. And he gets out, so I pulled my weapon out and put it right where he couldn't see it just below the door. Rolled my window down about an inch, and he comes back and he asks me some stupid question about how to get to the freeway and I told him, 'Don't know, can't help you.' And he's like, 'Thanks, God bless you,' or something, gets in his truck and leaves. I don't know if that was legitimate or what, but I wasn't going to take the chance." Rather than accepting the notion that the man who asked for directions was lost, just as he was, Jack maintains skepticism about the stranger who approached his car. Though he did not identify the man's race, the fact that he was in a black neighborhood is an important part of his story and indicates that Jack is drawing upon a "racialized fear of crime" (Davis 2007) whereby feelings of vulnerability are heightened when whites navigate predominantly black spaces.[3]

The men I interviewed were much more likely than the women to identify dangerous parts of town as a motivating force for why they carry a gun. I attribute this difference to two reasons: First, the men were much more likely than the women to report that they carry a firearm, and thus they have many more rationales for carrying than the women, who, with a few exceptions, were likely to have a gun with them only during specific times (e.g., when traveling out of town). The second explanation has to do with the way gender, race, and class intersect for license holders. Because they perceive that they are vulnerable to aggression by all men, women simply have a much larger pool of threatening people against whom they feel the need to be armed (making their lower rates of licensure and carry particularly significant and worthy of explanation).[4] By contrast, because the men I interviewed seemed to suggest that they are not regularly threatened in predominantly white spaces, they have a much more limited range of potential threats, a range that is more narrowly focused on spaces that they have racially defined as dangerous.

It is critical to note that when respondents suggest that poor and predominantly black neighborhoods are high-crime areas, they are not entirely inaccurate. While violent crime has been on the decline for decades, it remains stubbornly persistent in some areas, particularly those that are characterized by extreme economic disadvantage. Because of the "greater social and economic resources of whites and the greater investments made in areas where whites predominate," and because they experience few barriers to residential mobility, "whites have the power to escape problems that prevail in many other areas of a city" (Peterson and Krivo 2010, 116). Meanwhile racialized housing markets and economic inequality leave many blacks and Latinos to inhabit neighborhoods with relatively high rates of violent crime. But respondents' descriptions of dangerous neighborhoods suggest that they are not referring to these areas but instead are conflating any urban area with a potentially large black population or with some poor sections—places considered "hit or miss"—with risk. Such characterizations not only normalize crime in areas of extreme disadvantage (the implications of which are taken up in chapter 5); they also racialize and class crime by misattributing its causes: crime does not follow when areas are predominantly black or poor; instead black people who are poor are funneled into areas of extreme disadvantage, and these are places where violent crime is likely to emerge (Peterson and Krivo 2010).

The Visible Bad Guy

As was evident in Adam's description of encountering "gangster guys" outside of a gas station, dangerous neighborhoods are considered such because residents of those areas, particularly black men, are thought likely to be criminals. But how do respondents perceive criminal threat when they're not in high-crime areas? Mike and I met at a café in a predominantly white, upper-middle-class part of town. Despite claims that he carries wherever he can, Mike had left his gun in his truck, and as we talked he said, "I don't feel strange sitting here and not having it. I think if I did have it, it would probably make me a little bit more aware of my surroundings." I was taken aback by this comment, having assumed that the power a firearm bestows would allow a person to relax. Mike explained, "When I have it with me, I'm paying a lot more attention to people. . . . Somebody walks in, looks like they're lookin' for trouble. Somebody that doesn't fit. You know, not to play the, uh, race card or anything, but there aren't too many black people around here. So if you . . . walk into a place and you don't really fit in. Like if I went over to [a predominantly black part of town] and walked into Martin Luther King Jr. Church on Sunday morning, I'm betting I'd be one of the few white guys. And people would probably look at me and go, 'Well, what's this white guy doing here?'" Mike's explanation of how race factors into the way he imagines risk is cloaked in the discourse of "color-blind racism" (Bonilla-Silva 2001) as he seems initially unsure of how to relay this example. He self-consciously employs the term "race card," signifying that he knows explicitly identifying race is socially taboo, while at the same time admitting that he would identify a nonwhite patron as suspicious. Moreover he tries to avoid sounding racist by equating a black man being seen as a potential criminal with his being seen as out of place in a black church (marked as such by his use of Martin Luther King Jr.), yet race is central to how Mike understands potential criminalization. In this predominantly white space Mike feels safe enough not to bother with bringing his gun; however, this safety could be disrupted if a black man were to come into the café. Though he claims that this is just a matter of simple demographics, there is clearly an elaborate system of racialized meanings operating as subtext in his story. It is also apparent that race functions as a marker of class status, as Mike seemingly believes that it is unlikely that a black man would have a legitimate reason to enter a café in a wealthy part of town.

In another example wherein racialized perceptions of threat shaped a license holder's view of vulnerability, Ruth described a time when she and her husband pulled into a rest area while sightseeing in a national park in Colorado. Unlike Mike's description, this is an event that actually happened, though whether Ruth was really threatened is unclear:

> Well, there was this car with, like, four . . . um [pause] youth guys. They weren't white, Caucasian, they were various [pause], a little darker-skinned, I guess. Dressed in really baggy [clothes], casual like, with their shirt off and stuff like that. And they were, all of a sudden, they blocked the exit and two of them were out of the car. Luckily my husband had enough sense about him to say something's not right here. And he's yelling at me, "Ruth, get in the car, get in the car!" And, um, I'm like, "huh, huh?" And then I come back and he looks around at them and those guys are like trying to, I think they wanted to rob us or something. And so my husband had the wits about him to back up and back out the entrance. And, uh, that was scary. After I started registering in my mind what was happening, and he even started thinking more about what was happening. I wish we had a gun with us. Of course at that time you weren't allowed to carry in national parks. I think you are now. So we went to the visitors center and told the people, but they were probably gone by then. That was a time when I kind of wished, I would've felt better if I had had one. What if I couldn't get out the entrance or something, and they were confronting us? There was two of us and four of them.

Ruth struggled to explain this story as she tried to avoid explicitly mentioning race while at the same time making clear that it is central to why she believes the men she encountered harbored criminal intent. It is remarkable how often respondents simultaneously employed race in their descriptions of threat while at the same time trying to distance themselves from sounding racist.

Significantly in none of my interviews did a respondent identify a potentially threatening person as white, though presumably at least one of the respondents has felt threatened by someone who was not a person of color. Perhaps when respondents describe threatening situations and do not mention race, they are talking about white people who made them feel vulnerable. Though it is impossible to determine this with these data, their using race to identify threatening people only when they are not white is part of how crime is racialized; race is unmarked and apparently irrelevant when whites are confronted by other whites, but it is a central part of the narrative in stories involving black or Latino men.

The few people I interviewed who identified as racial or ethnic minorities did not differ dramatically from the rest of the sample in how they talked about the link between race and crime. For instance, Joseph, a forty-five-year-old CHL holder who identifies as white on forms but says that his father is Hispanic, explained that he used his "Hispanic appearance" to intimidate others when he lived in a high-crime neighborhood that was predominantly black and Latino, and he said that looking "pure white" would have made him a target. The only person in the sample who actively challenged racist constructions of threat was George, a forty-four-year-old CHL instructor who is Mexican American and lives in a predominantly Hispanic city along the Texas-Mexico border. George grew up with guys who are now involved in the drug trade, and he said that he tries not to have a "black and white" view of who is a threat: "Some of the nicest guys I know . . . have tattoos from [head to toe]. Some of the meanest guys I know are the stereotypical middle-aged . . . white male professionals [who are] hot-headed, hot-tempered, on edge, on the defense all the time." In the entire sample George was the only one who explicitly troubled the relationship between race, perceptions of criminality, and threat, and it is significant that he was one of two interviewees who was reared and currently lives in a region that is not predominantly white, suggesting that perhaps his perceptions of criminality were not developed according to the white racial frame (Feagin 2010).

Importantly, in none of these narratives of fear-inducing events does any respondent describe being overtly threatened by the black men they encountered. Instead they report that simply coming into contact with black men induces a desire to be armed and compels them to have their guns ready. The men I interviewed made clear that it is specifically black *males* that they identify as threatening. They project violence, aggression, and criminal intent onto black men, characterizations that are a form of "gendered racism," used to "validate inequality [and] also to contrast black masculinity with white masculinity as a hegemonic ideal"

(Wingfield 2007, 198). That is precisely what is at play when Adam imagines that the men he encounters are threatening to him; they are bad guys, and so he challenges himself to stand up to what he perceives as a threat, something he is able to do by grabbing his gun. Having constructed a sense of self that relies on identifying as a good guy, someone who *should* carry a gun, these men see their masculinity in contradistinction to what black masculinity represents to them: they presume that the black men they see are violent criminals, and so they are armed in defense. Thus CHL holders are able to associate themselves with hegemonic masculinity by defining themselves as good guys, a construct that clearly relies on whiteness. Given that CHL holders believe in the ever-present potential for criminal victimization, they regularly scan the public landscape looking for signs of trouble. It is in this context that black men and other, "not Caucasian, darker-skinned men," as Ruth described them, become hypervisible as potential criminals. Whiteness is critical to this dynamic not because white people with CHLs see their race as an evident marker of status but because (to them) whiteness signifies nothing at all. The privilege of not being seen as a potential criminal has profound effects, though by virtue of how this operates, they are difficult to measure.

Blurred Lines

While license holders convey fairly clear descriptions of who they imagine as bad guys, they did not address whether they might unwittingly create the circumstances that seem threatening to someone else or whether they might be considered bad guys. One clear case in which this emerged was in a story Mike told me in response to a question about whether he had ever felt threatened while armed. He became noticeably uncomfortable, gently laughed, and said that it was a long story but one he was willing to tell. Mike explained, "I'm comin' home from golf, I'm behind a guy on this road. . . . We pull onto a road [where] the speed limit is fifty-five. All right, well, he's goin' like forty, and when I come up to him, I get probably too close to him. My mistake. I thought he was gonna speed up, but he didn't. I'm driving this big F-250 and he's in some, sh—, you know, compact car. So I get too close to him, he taps his brakes, and I back off. And I'm like, okay. And then I start goin' up again thinking he's gonna speed up. He hits his brakes again, and I'm like, well, this is bullshit. Okay? So I went around him on the shoulder. I'm not gonna play this tapping the brake game. [I] go around him on the shoulder [and] come up to the light at the next intersection." At the intersection Mike was in the one lane of traffic that would go straight when the light turned green, and the man in the car had pulled into the lane over his right shoulder. He continued:

[I] pull up and stop and I look at traffic [to my left], and I look over [to my right], and I catch him in my mirror. I see him in my mirror. He's getting out of his car. All right? So in my mind . . . the conversation goes like this: Okay, people don't get out of their car at an intersection to come say hi. You know. If you get out of your car at an intersection, you're planning on doing something and it's gonna be trouble. So I better be ready. So I got my gun out. I hold it out and laid it, uh, center console was here. I had my hand across the seat like this, and I watched him come up, and he looks in my window and, you know, he starts saying something. I don't even know what he said, but I said, "I have a gun. You need to get away from my truck. Let me see your hands." That was my mantra, cause I practiced that. And if you don't think about what you're supposed to do in a situation, when the situation gets there you're not prepared, you just kind of go, "La la blah," you know? Flip out. So I had thought about this and what do you say to somebody if they're coming at you in a threatening manner. You need to let them know that you have a gun, you'll use it, and to get away. Right? And in this case I wanted to see his hands, because I'm in a big tall truck, I can't see his hands, I can see from [his chest] up. So I'm saying, "Let me see your hands! Get away from my truck." You know, "I have a gun, don't make me shoot you." The guy looks in my truck, looks at my gun, it's a freakin' .45. [It has] big bullets! I'm not pointing it at him, but he can see it. He goes, "You're not gonna shoot me." I'm like, "Dude! I have [*in a whisper*] a fuckin' gun! Get away from here, what are you doing?" And he, he was just like, "What's your name? What's your name? You're not gonna shoot me! What's your name?" I'm like, "You have got to be kidding me! Get away. Get away from here!" I'm like, "You're psycho." So . . . he got back in his truck, or he got back in his car, [the] light turned green, I went, he got back in his car, he followed me, called the cops.

I learned something here. If you're ever in a situation like that, call the cops. You need to be the first one. That was my mistake.

I should've called the cops. "Hey, this guy just tried to assault me at this intersection and I had to pull my gun out to defend myself. I didn't shoot him, but he saw my gun." If I had done that, it might've been a different situation. But it wasn't.

In my situation I said "Okay, it's done, I'm just goin home." And then I notice he's following me. I'm like, oh, this is bad. I can't go home, cause he will know where I live. So I took a right at, at an intersection, you know, about a mile before my house, cause I knew there was a neighborhood and I thought I'd see how far he'd follow me. Come in the back way. Well, by the time I got down to my turnoff, which was maybe, I don't know, a quarter of a mile down there, the cops were on me, man. They were, I told them after the fact, I said, "Hey, that was a great response time, by the way. [*Laughs*] Cause you guys were all over it." But yeah . . . they pulled me over. I'm pretty sure they had their weapons drawn. Uh, got me out of the truck, backed me up. Laid me down, cuffed me, put me in the back of their police cruiser until they could get their handle on the situation. So, yeah, I'm sitting handcuffed in the back of the car, thinking, "This is ridiculous."

Mike was not charged with a crime, and though the police officers confiscated his weapon, he was able to recover it two weeks later after it had been test-fired and put on file with the Department of Public Safety.

This story is remarkable for a number of reasons, but before those are analyzed, it must be stated that it is the only one of its kind that I heard during the research for this project, and I do not want to suggest that it is representative of how most license holders would act in a similar situation. I have little doubt that many of my respondents, particularly those who teach licensing courses, would have considered Mike's actions reckless and would likely note that his dangerous and aggressive driving provoked the situation and would thus leave him on very shaky legal ground when claiming that he acted only in self-defense.[5] Of course, had Mike killed the man, there would be only one version of events relayed to prosecutors, and so his story would be very difficult to refute. This "last person standing" component of Stand Your Ground legislation is one of the most problematic aspects of such laws.

Mike's story is remarkable largely because of what did not happen. He did not shoot the man who approached his truck, and the police did not arrest him or even cite him for brandishing his weapon, something he attributes to inexperience: "I think these guys were probably rookies and just didn't know what was going on. Cause they never booked me. They took my statement, they took his statement, [and] they let me go. They said, 'We're gonna pass it on to the D.A. and see what he wants to do about it.'" Whether because of inexperience or confusion, there is no debating that Mike was let off easily by the police. After all, he brandished a .45 semi-automatic handgun during an altercation that started because he was driving recklessly. Though one can only speculate, Mike's status as an upper-middle-class white man in a CHL-friendly part of Texas most certainly had some bearing on this outcome.

Given his actions, Mike could have been charged with second-degree assault for brandishing a weapon, something he insists would have been possible only if the events were "misconstrued." Mike believes that he was threatened when the man approached his vehicle and that this justi-fied his decision to draw his gun. When reflecting on whether he should have done anything differently, Mike said that he should have been less overt:

I'm going to be much more sure about a situation before I do it. Had I . . . kept my hand, like, on the side of my center console, instead of [draping over the console], [it would have been a] totally different situation. Okay, I'm still at a ready position, I can still defend myself, cause if he's walking up with a gun, I'm toast anyway. Cause even here he can just [put his hand up to the window], and I'm barely getting up. But if I'm here and he doesn't see it? And I say, "You need to get away. Do you know that Texas is a concealed handgun state?" You know? Be a little more veiled with it, instead of saying, "I have a gun." Probably got a little bit stronger defense against the prosecution. As long as he doesn't see it, though, what's he gonna do? That would be easy. The crappy part about this and what I learned is defense to prosecution's great, cause you don't go to jail, but you still have to go through all the crap. What's it the cops say? "You might beat the rap, but you won't beat the ride." You know, "You're going downtown, let the courts deal with it." I hate that attitude. There are some people out there like that. You know, it probably would've never gone anywhere. Uh, because in [this county], they're a little more into letting people defend themselves. And it was a clear case. I had no escape route. I mean, I could've gotten out of the car and abandoned it, I guess. But you tell me any, any cop or D.A. or whoever wouldn't do the same thing? I call 'em a liar.

Though he was not charged, Mike later sought legal advice as he strategized about how to deal with the potential fallout of this incident. He explained, "I happen to know a guy who used to work at the district attorney's office, so I called him for some advice about what to do. And he said, 'You need to get a lawyer. You need to get somebody in there arguing for you right now.' I'm like, 'Are you serious? I mean . . . I gave 'em my statement.' He goes, 'You did what? You gave 'em a statement?! [Mike]! Gah! . . . You never give a statement! They will turn that around on you.' He said, 'I know you, you probably did nothing wrong, you think you're perfectly innocent, but they'll take that statement and turn it around if they want to.' So I learned a lot through that experience." Though he now realizes that he should have been less overt and should have immediately hired an attorney, it seems that Mike learned nothing about whether pulling his gun was reasonable, or if his aggressive driving provoked the incident, or whether he might have been acting like a bad guy. Every step of the way, but particularly the tacit approval of police inaction, served only to confirm Mike's status as a good guy.

Had he needed to call on his connections or dip into the kind of resources available to a man who reported that he makes over $100,000 per year, Mike would clearly have benefited from his social position. But the most significant form of privilege in this incident is of the type that rarely leaves evidence of its having operated: his comfort with the responding officers, the fact that he was never charged with a weapons crime, indeed the fact that the officers who pulled their guns did not fire and instead waited to determine precisely what was going on during what was an undoubtedly stressful and confusing interaction. The benefit of Mike's race and class privilege is most clear when we consider how this incident might have unfolded were he not white. How would a black man who had brandished a .45-caliber handgun after tailing a motorist in a very large pickup truck and illegally passing him on the shoulder have been treated by the police? How many black men have been shot by police for much less aggressive behavior or when they are unarmed? These are experiences that Mike will likely never even consider; after all, he is a good guy.

Race, Class, Gender, and Threat

I employ the "good guys versus bad guys" language because that is what respondents used; as I have shown, it is a binary construct that relies on specific understandings of race, class, and gender. Masculinity is hegemonic in this framing, as the commonsense assumption is that good guys and bad guys are men. Men are much more likely than women to utilize "good guy" discourse in explaining their desires to be armed, and yet, as is true in the case of Mary, when they rise to the occasion, women can be good guys too. But they are almost never described as bad guys. The one exception is when Mary suggested that sophisticated criminals will sometimes use women as decoys because people are less likely to be vigilant when approached by a woman they do not know than when approached by a man. As I explained in an earlier chapter, men position women as dependent on them for protection, and what seems clear here is that it is impossible for women to be both vulnerable and threatening, in need of protection and a source of potential danger.

License holders justify their right to carry guns in public because as good guys they are the cream of the crop of our communities who embody the traits of the ideal gun user propagated by groups like the NRA. Their CHLs are seen as proof of their clean criminal history, something they use to justify their right to be armed. Good guys are also thought to represent a middle-class virtue related to beliefs about community engagement and dependability; however, there are clear limits to this construct. Most notably CHL holders are seen as people who would stop and render aid and who would be available should others need them, and yet these interviews suggest that this is true only in "good parts of town." In "bad parts of town," places that are considered dangerous, license holders assume that those who claim to need help are setting them up to be victimized; instead of reaching out a hand, they are likely to reach for their gun when they meet another person. Commonsense ideas about the need for self-protection in bad parts of town are seen by those I interviewed as a logical response to a dangerous situation, but my analysis suggests that danger is a social construction based largely on perceptions that are shaped by race, class, and gender rather than by an objective assessment of risk. This is evident in two ways: (1) if an area is thought to be poor and/or predominantly black (there is a tendency to conflate the two), it is presumed to be dangerous; (2) black and Latino men are seen as potential criminals even outside of such places. The implication of course is that poor areas, those places that most need the help and attention of people with resources, are not only ignored, they are vilified.

Though both men and women use race as a signifier of potential criminality, the women I interviewed referenced far fewer examples of specific moments in which they felt threatened by men of color they encountered.[6] While on the one hand I attribute this to the idea that women have a more diffuse sense of threat than men, it is also the case that, like all binary constructs, those who see themselves as good guys rely on bad guys to make sense of themselves; to that extent good guys need the racialized and classed specter of the bad guy. The men I interviewed ascribe a menacing masculinity to men of color and construct a sense of self in contradistinction to that. Because they assume the black men they encounter are likely armed and potentially dangerous, they want to carry a concealed handgun so they do not have to shrink from any threat. Rather than driving off when a group of black men at a gas station spells trouble, a white man with a gun and a CHL can get out of his car, stand his ground, and not back down, and thus he can be a "real man."

It has been established that gang members—and other marginal men—brandish and shoot guns in order to assert control and dominance over other men (Stretesky and Pogrebin 2007), and I would suggest that the men I interviewed use guns in a similar way but with profoundly different implications. When a gang member uses a gun, he may be empowered in that instance by his masculine performance of domination, but it is also a sign of his subordination. Indeed studies that examine how gang members use guns have focused on incarcerated populations (Stretesky and Pogrebin 2007). In contrast, the men in this study are among the most privileged in society and already have access to culturally celebrated versions of masculinity: most of them are white and middle or upper-middle class, and all of them are heterosexual. Their state-issued license to carry a concealed handgun, a license that is expensive and available only to those who can afford it and who are not legally restricted, gives them an added level of privilege: it offers them a symbol around which to construct an even more deeply empowered masculinity.

One of the most significant forms of privilege that the CHL holders I interviewed experience is that which comes by virtue of the meanings associated with whiteness, something that is most evident when one considers what can happen in the event that a CHL holder pulls his or her gun. Because a white person with a gun is not presumed to be a criminal, he or she can navigate the world with some confidence that other people with guns, most notably the police, will not presume that they are bad guys. In other words, the meanings associated with race, gender, and crime mean that white people enjoy the privilege of being innocent until proven guilty, while black people, particularly black men, are most often considered guilty until proven innocent. When the police officers pulled their guns on Mike and put him on the ground in handcuffs, he had confidence that they were doing so only because of a misunderstanding, and he knew that it would soon be cleared up and he would be vindicated. Even though it was his legally and ethically dubious actions that instigated the event, he could feel assured rather than threatened by the presence of police officers, and based on how the events unfolded, it seems he has every reason to believe that things will work out in his favor. There is perhaps no greater mark of privilege than for one to assume that social institutions—in this case the criminal justice system—will work to one's benefit. I use the term "privilege" intentionally here as Mike experienced a perk of whiteness insofar as he was able to evade an assault charge. But as Namoi Zack argues, privileges and rights should not be conflated. When white men's civil rights are upheld in interactions with police while black men and women's rights are routinely violated, the discourse of "white privilege" can obscure the injustices levied against blacks: "I hope we have not sunk so low in American society that plain, simple, justice according to the Constitution must be regarded as a perk" (Zack 2015, xiii).

In the next chapter I turn to an analysis of how license holders explain the political and economic underpinnings of criminal activity, and I describe how their understandings of the root causes of crime further entrench social inequality.

As part of the interview process I asked respondents if there had ever been a time they felt threatened and did not have a gun on them. What follows is Krysti's description of an experience she had while house-sitting. To contextualize her response I start with the question that I asked.

> *Angela*: Some of the people I've spoken with have said that they've really had to come to terms with the idea that if they're carrying a gun, someday they might have to shoot and kill someone. Have you gone through that process?
>
> *Krysti*: I have. I have no problem with that. You know, you asked me about a situation where I didn't have the gun, and this just came to me, because I have always said that I will shoot first and ask questions later. Um, one of the houses where I house-sit . . . she has a dog that barks incessantly. Well, anyway, . . . in her neighborhood, it's one of those hit-or-miss neighborhoods, [where] you can have a row of nice houses and then turn the corner and you'll have a crack house. So I always carry at her house, and if I have to go out to my car at night to get something, I take my gun with me just in case. Well, this particular incident, it was like two months ago, she had asked me at the last minute to house-sit. I packed in a hurry; I forgot [my gun] at home. I forgot her at home. And I came in late one night, it was about midnight. And I came in late and I let the dog out in the backyard for her business, and I thought, "Oh, shoot! I left my phone in my car." So I go out to my car to get my phone. And normally I would have taken my gun with me to this particular house. Well, now I thank God that I didn't take her because I reach into the passenger side, my door's open, I reach in, grab my phone, shut the door, and when I shut the door the neighbor, the man next door, is standing right there. Scared the hell out of me. My heart was in my throat. I gasped, you know, I panicked. I was just frozen. And . . . he goes, "Oh, I'm so sorry, I'm so sorry." I'm like, "What the hell! What are you

doing?!" And he said, "I'm so sorry, but could you bring your dog in? My wife is trying to sleep." And I said, "You have no idea how lucky you are. You have no idea how lucky you are." And he said, "Well, I'm so sorry." He didn't even have a clue. So he went back inside, and I got to thinking about that situation, of how I felt, and it was that sheer, it was that fear. And you are frozen. You freeze at that moment. And I got to thinking, would I have frozen and been able to compute, "Oh, neighbor"? Or would I have frozen at first and then had a knee-jerk reaction? What would I have done? I don't know. I don't know.

Angela: Does that scenario concern you?

Krysti: Yes, it does concern me, because I know the man. He's married and has two children and has a little bitty baby. And I could have shot him and I could have killed him, because she's loaded with hollow points. And he was so close. I could have killed him. You know? And yes, the gravity of the situation has really messed with me a little bit. But then again, I think, well, he was being a dumbass. He was coming up to a woman at twelve midnight. She was outside by herself, and he basically snuck up on me. He could have been walking up the driveway and [said], "Hello! Hello!" But instead, as soon as I shut the door, he was standing right there. That's *Friday the Thirteenth*–ish there. You know, that's, don't do that. So you gotta think, well, if he was dumb enough to put himself in a situation like that [*pause*], it's not my fault.

The man who approached Krysti had no intention of harming her, and yet, had she been armed, she may have shot him. While some may see this is as the perfect example of an event that could have turned unnecessarily violent, a cautionary tale of what can go wrong when someone carries a gun, arguably the most problematic aspect of this scenario is not contained in the specific events but is instead the cultural meanings that inform and are reinforced by this story. Specifically, Krysti's description of the neighbor she encountered in the driveway—he was married, had a baby, and so on—marks him as a "good man," in sharp contrast to the people who might wander over from the "crack houses" down the street. While the good man should not be shot, Krysti believes that her gun is necessary for those who she constructs as potentially dangerous. What does such a distinction say about how we understand others, whether they live in "nice" neighborhoods or among "crack houses"? Moreover, while the events of that night "messed [her] up for a little bit," Krysti has found a way to explain the incident such that the man who approached her is the one culpable: given the setting, the time, and the fact that she was a woman alone, she believes that the neighbor would have been responsible if she were to have shot him. How does this focus on personal responsibility absolve Krysti, and what are the implications for how we understand handgun carry more broadly?

The Criminal Other

In chapter 4 I examined how license holders utilize discourses of race, class, and gender in understanding threat and safety in public places. Here I explore how those I interviewed understand the forces that motivate criminals, something I have identified as a key element in understanding both the appeal of CHLs and their consequences for society. Beyond perceptions of vulnerability and safety, the social construction of good guys and bad guys is also tied to the ways society utilizes criminals to define and affirm its values. Criminals are not simply guilty of breaking the law; they are seen as irresponsible and immoral and thus must be controlled by the state, even after they have served their time. To this extent they are labeled strangers, and as Patricia Hill Collins (2000, 70) explains, "As the 'Others' of society who can never really belong, strangers threaten the moral and social order. But they are simultaneously essential for its survival because those individuals who stand at the margins of society clarify its boundaries."

As I have shown, my respondents believe neighborhoods that are poor and predominantly black or Latino are dangerous places. While there is evidence that neighborhoods of extreme disadvantage have higher rates of violent crime than ones that are economically privileged (Peterson and Krivo 2010), it is not the case that the poor are thus more likely to commit crimes. And yet the link between perceptions of criminality and poverty runs so deep in U.S. culture that there is a tendency for some to believe that criminals are poor and the poor are criminal. Reiman and Leighton (2010, 174) argue that this is not an accident, that the image of "the common criminal" as impoverished serves to "narrow the public's conception of what is dangerous to acts of the poor and to present a convincing embodiment of this danger." Utilizing a Marxist analysis, the authors say that this focus keeps attention away from individuals and organizations with power as people come to believe that "the threat to law-abiding Middle America comes from below them on the economic ladder, not above them" (175). Not only do those with power avoid scrutiny, but the relationship between privilege and inequality is obscured. If the poor are likely to be criminal, then they are "morally defective, and thus their poverty is their own fault, not a symptom of social or economic injustice" (175). Consequently one of the primary ways criminals affirm society's values is in the reproduction of ideas about "personal responsibility," something made even more plausible via the social construction of black criminality that I discussed in chapter 4.

The idea that the poor are more likely to be criminal is one facet of a larger "culture of poverty" discourse that is commonly used to explain economic inequality. According to this logic, "opportunities in the United States are available for anyone motivated to succeed, economic outcomes are a function of ability and effort, and existing inequalities are fair and inevitable" (Royce 2009 159). These sentiments are an outgrowth of neoliberalism, a political-economic philosophy that "places overwhelming emphasis on individualism, self-reliance and the free market as organizer of all aspects of life" (DeGoede 1996, 351). Neoliberal discourses make the *structural* inequality that is one consequence of the free market invisible and explain *individual* choices as the primary reason social problems exist, particularly poverty and its attendant social ills (Royce 2009). According to neoliberalism, the market has provided everything we might need, and as a result the only explanation for poverty is a refusal to do what it takes to succeed. In this way poverty itself is the crime. Loïc Wacquant (2009) argues that by focusing on the poor, the public becomes so concerned about crime and the need for elaborate crime control that it fails to realize the various ways our economy and, through its complicity, our government are failing us.

Jennifer Carlson (2012) suggests that we must consider the neoliberal context in which gun carry has unfolded if we are to understand what motivates license holders. In her study of concealed carry holders in Michigan, Carlson finds that there is a distinction between license holders who want to be armed because they believe that the state has failed to protect them (those who hold "neo-liberal gun politics") and those who feel that they must protect themselves from the state (those whose politics she describes as "neo-radical"). In a clear utilization of neoliberal discourse, Carlson finds that for many of her respondents, "their embrace of firearms was simultaneously a means of *repudiating dependency* on the state and *assuming personal responsibility*" (1121). She explains that in the face of the police's inability to adequately protect citizens, some gun advocates take matters into their own hands, a tactic that is particularly attractive to men who may feel emasculated by the state's capacity to dominate. Given its ubiquity in NRA rhetoric, it is no surprise that gun advocates would utilize neoliberal discourses to explain their desire to carry guns. The NRA has long associated gun ownership with self-reliance and rugged individualism, meanings that are key to its ability to mobilize its largely white, male membership (Melzer 2009). Thus as symbols of individual freedom, guns are perhaps the quintessential neoliberal tool.

While Carlson's explanation of the appeal of concealed carry in neoliberal times elucidates why people want to carry firearms, she fails to examine the implications of this self-defense strategy for society more broadly. It is important not only to ask what motivates license holders, we must also understand what the normalization of this worldview might mean for society. I argue that respondents utilize neoliberal discourses of the underclass and personal responsibility that not only justify why people need to be armed but also rationalize inequality and obscure the social reproduction of race, class, and gender privilege.

Creating Criminals

Most of my respondents said that they need to be armed because of the type of criminal threats described in chapter 4 (e.g., carjackings, robberies, violent assaults by strangers); however, some suggested that people who are emotionally unstable or mentally ill are also potentially threatening. The three people in this study who work in schools, all women who are teachers, said they wish they could carry their firearms at work because of the threat of school shootings perpetrated by mentally ill young people. For example, Krysti said, "There [are] too many situations that have happened to where, you know, you get some crazy kid that wants to come in and shoot up the school, and he comes to shoot me and I'm defenseless." What makes the distinction between common criminals and the mentally ill significant is the way these two groups are parsed.

Susan said that people need to take more responsibility for their self-defense because, she believes, there is a growing number of mentally ill children and adults who have access to firearms. Because she had used the term at various points in our interview, I asked her to clarify who she meant when she referred to "bad guys." She said:

You have your gang members. Who . . . for whatever reason, culturally that's what they do. Now you can say it was because they were poor, you can say it's because they live, you know, . . . on the East Side, you can say, you know, whatever. But at some point it's a choice. At some point it's culturally acceptable, because it's happening in those communities. I mean there are white, Hispanic, and black gang members out there, you can't, you know, Chinese whatever. You can't just say it's one race that's doing all of it. There's corruption among all of it because you've got the drugs, you've got the money, you've got low self-esteem, you know, whatever they didn't do in school, whatever. But you have a momma come on the TV and say, "Oh, my kid was so good," when he has a rap sheet this long [*holds up her fingers indicating over two inches*], I'm sorry, is bullshit. And you as a parent at some point have to take responsibility for not moving, not doing better, not whatever. You know, I'm not going to say that I know the situation for all those people and why they don't move to the better areas. We all do the best we can, but you know what, there's people like me in middle-class America that go out and shoot up schools. And that are not gang members, you know, so you've got some level of, wherever they are, the social standing, they're hearing I'm not good enough, I'm not smart enough, I don't have opportunity. At every level kids are hearing the same thing.

Susan's explanation is a useful example of how race and class combine in perceptions of criminality for many of the people I interviewed. First, Susan split threatening groups into poor gang members and middle-class kids responsible for school shootings. (It seems that in both instances she is referring to young adults.) Considering the comments that precede this quotation, Susan assumes that the kids responsible for school shootings have a mental illness. Indeed she went on to explain that her son has autism and is often depressed about his inability to make friends; she feels that as a parent it is her responsibility to ensure that he does not ever get hold of her guns, lest he consider taking them to school.

Though she framed her answer in color-blind language, Susan's description of criminality in poor neighborhoods draws upon racialized discourses. She said that gangs can include members from any racial category, yet she identified a part of town that is known for being predominantly black and Latino to make her point. Furthermore when she said that "it's culturally acceptable because it's happening in *those* communities," she sets herself in contrast to an other, a point reinforced by the ostensibly antiracist *"even middle-class people like me* shoot up schools." The way she distinguished the mentally ill from gang members is also notable: she assumed that a gang member from a poor area is representative of a cultural deficiency—the entire community is to blame for his failing—whereas a mentally ill middle-class kid has a personal struggle. Indeed Susan said, "You can't go out and blame these kids or these people when they do things out of mental illness if nobody has stepped up to help them." She does not blame *middle-class culture* for the school shootings, and she does not mark the areas of town where those *types of kids* usually come from. And perhaps most significant, she does not suggest that the black kid from the poor part of town—to say nothing of his mother—might need help too. In this construct blackness and Latinoness are implied and vilified while whiteness remains an unmarked category.

When I asked Lisa if she has a sense of what motivates criminals, she said, "Entitlement" and then elaborated: "We've almost glamorized . . . criminal activity." Then in a mocking voice, "I'm a big-time criminal. . . . I'm a gangsta." I asked if she was referring to representations in popular culture, and she said, "Absolutely! Absolutely, totally in pop culture. It's cool you know!" She continued, "You've got kids all over the place that they think they can just pick up a gun. It's part of being in a gang. . . . They're entitled and they get to use it however, whenever, to commit [a] crime. There's a complete lack of respect for the law." Though Lisa never explicitly mentioned race, her explanation is loaded with racialized discourses of black criminality, including her use of the term "gangsta." Importantly, while Lisa criticized popular culture representations for "glamorizing" criminals, she too seemed to draw upon constructions of blackness in popular culture; in her description the representation and the real are indistinguishable.

As Lisa's explanation of what motivates criminals continued, she said that she believes that crime is "a societal problem" and that "it would stop . . . if we eliminated entitlements. If we truly prosecuted criminals and held them accountable and did not make it, you know, an easy thing, if you will." Lisa said that entitlements make people believe that "you owe me and I deserve that. And, you know, who are you, you're privileged; I get to take from you. And there is that whole mentality of distribution. You've got it; I'm going to take it." Though Lisa is the only one who directly linked criminality to entitlements, many respondents explained that crime is primarily perpetrated by people who prefer not to work to get what they want. For example, when I asked Caroline to explain why people turn to crime, she said, "I think they're lazy. [*Laughs.*] Get off your ass and get a job!" For these respondents crime is motivated by an unwillingness to work and is an issue of morality and character.

Though these discourses are not inevitably tied to race, for some respondents they are clearly racialized. While Lisa traced criminal behavior to unspecified government entitlement programs, she also explained that it is rooted in the breakdown of the American family: "We have lost, especially in some of the minority cultures, we don't have that father figure. We don't have family values that raise responsible adults. And when you don't raise responsible adults, they're susceptible to gangs, to other influences." This emphasis on "minority cultures" makes it clear that Lisa links race, class, and crime in a "culture of poverty" discourse to explain what she sees as the connection between poverty, family structure, welfare dependency, and criminal behavior. According to Edward Royce (2009, 52), proponents of the "culture of poverty" thesis believe "the welfare system rewards the poor for not working, for not marrying, and for having babies out of wedlock." Moreover "it undermines personal responsibility, saps individual initiative, and fosters an ethos of dependency." Such characterizations of the "undeserving poor" are highly racialized in the United States; this is precisely how many white Americans characterize African American poverty (Gilens 1999). Lisa sees criminal behavior as one consequence of the culture of poverty, a problem that she believes is concentrated in minority communities.

Lisa also said that this situation is made worse by a criminal justice system that is overburdened and does not adequately prosecute criminals, something that "creates an 'I can get away with it' attitude and so their crimes tend to escalate, I believe. I really do. Whether it starts with the petty theft or drugs or what have you. Um, but I do think they have the upper hand because we're not enforcing the law, and when you can get away with it, guess what you're going to keep doing? Doing it!" Lisa said that we have "allowed lawlessness to rule." She explained, "There's a complete lack of respect for the law. I mean it's evident in everything we do. . . . For example illegal immigration, which is off-topic, but it's a perfect analysis of [this]. What part of 'illegal' don't you understand?"

Lisa was not the only person to argue that society is dangerously permissive of criminal behavior. June, sixty-seven, recalled the famous Houston-area case of Joe Horn, whom she described as "the guy that saw some Mexicans breaking into his neighbor's house."[1] Horn dialed 911 and then grabbed his loaded shotgun before confronting the two men, despite the operator's plea that he remain in his own house and wait for police to arrive. Horn shot and killed the robbers, and though evidence showed that they were shot in the back, he was not indicted because they had ventured onto his property and thus he was covered under Texas's castle law. June said she feels bad for all of the problems that the case caused Horn: "He had to get rid of his house and move, and he was a grandpa." June is outraged that he should experience any trouble over the events: "They were Mexican nationals, you know. They were wanted for crimes! So in a way, why should he get in trouble over it? Of course, you get me on another subject there about the illegals."

A belief that lawlessness is allowed to rule was something I heard in many of my interviews. For example, Paul said that society has become more lax in enforcing laws because people excuse criminal behavior. In a mocking tone he said, "Oh, but they had a hard life." He elaborated, "It doesn't mean the guy down the street didn't have just as hard a life, but he's working four jobs to make it work. This guy decides to take from somebody else because that is what was easiest for him. Not because they couldn't work. It was just because that was easier in his mind than it was to actually work. You know, if the punishment was great enough, if the punishment was such a deterrent, then there wouldn't be a [belief] of 'Oh yeah, maybe I should just go rob this place instead of goin' out and getting four jobs.'"

The notion that society contributes to the crime problem by discouraging personal responsibility is by no means universal among the people I interviewed; however, it is what some identified as one part of a constellation of factors that make CHLs important. Paul, Lisa, Caroline, June, and others who utilize "culture of poverty" discourses see social problems in a fairly simple way: as a morality tale in which the government meddles in people's lives and thus creates a dysfunctional underclass. While they see their own lives as determined by individual effort, they believe that this underclass is conditioned—by welfare dependency and an enabling culture—to refuse personal responsibility. When Paul said "having a hard life" is no excuse for theft when someone can just get four jobs to make ends meet, he was making a claim about unbridled agency, a fundamental tenet of neoliberalism. However, an underlying deficiency of the free market is embedded in his argument: if a person must have four jobs to "make it work," there is arguably something severely dysfunctional about our economic structure. Moreover, should one be able to find four jobs, how might one be expected to balance competing work schedules? And what of the other responsibilities that many adults must find time to balance, including child care? Such claims associate crime with poverty; criminals are assumed to be poor, and the poor are assumed to be criminals. This is a racialized and classed view of crime that both justifies doing nothing to address chronic poverty and that renders privileged criminals (e.g., those responsible for white-collar crime), who arguably commit the most consequential and socially damaging of all crimes and who are disproportionately likely to be white, invisible (Reiman and Leighton 2010).

Those respondents who believe that society is contributing to a culture of dependency and lawlessness also believe that the more law-abiding people arm themselves, the better off society will be. Respondents invoke "the government"—a term that is never specified—as a stand-in for "the social." Programs perceived to be in the interest of society and legislation that restricts individual freedoms are seen as oppressive threats to liberty, while "freedom" and "personal responsibility" are used interchangeably, discourses that echo the sentiments found in neoliberal rhetoric. Implicit in such characterizations is that being financially secure, even gainfully employed, is a product of hard work, smart planning, and savvy choices. CHLs are an extension of this ethos in that they symbolize for those who have a license that they are the embodiment of personal responsibility.

Among those I interviewed only one person seemed to have some ambivalence about the way she sees criminals. Earlier I explained that Catherine was threatened and stalked by a contractor and decided to get a CHL after many months of feeling helpless. When I asked Catherine what compelled this shift, she said, "When I decided that even though I didn't think that killing someone was the right thing to do, I realized that [*pause*] we're all animals at the most basic level. Like we all really want to survive. You know? So whatever ethical, religious, moral, spiritual, societal convictions we have, I mean, even the most passive person, even the person who claims to be a pacifist, if you were to hold their head under water would fight back . . . to try to get a breath." Later Catherine elaborated: "I don't want someone else who is a criminal to be able to deprive me of, you know, life, liberty, pursuit of happiness, all that good stuff, as cheesy as it sounds." She said that when she was younger, she thought of her life and the lives of others as equally important: "I'm not sure that I feel that way now. Because to me? My life is most important." She said that her view of criminals has changed significantly: "I've just become extremely intolerant of people who are criminals." But then after a long pause she added, "Although, I say that, but I have a kid in this class that's in [a drug cartel] and we're buddies. I don't know. He hangs out after school to talk to me about what he should do with his life. And, so . . . [*laughs*] I guess I'm intolerant of it unless I [*pause*], really, I don't know. I don't know how to describe that. It's, it's, I don't know." Catherine's feelings are unresolved; while her general view of potential criminals has fundamentally changed, when discussing her student she is deeply ambivalent. It is as though Catherine finds it impossible to simultaneously hold an image of the criminal other, a figure that after many years she has decided to arm herself against, with a real-life person who is involved with crime but with whom she feels a strong connection. When she imagined a criminal as the person who threatened her, she felt sure she wanted to be armed; however, when that image was replaced with someone she knows and cares about who is also involved in criminal activity, her sense of conviction about a criminal as an abstract figure starts to fade.

CHLs and Personal Responsibility

Control and personal responsibility are at the heart of how the people I interviewed explain the appeal of carrying a concealed firearm. As Gil explained, "See, everybody's conditioned by society to believe that you call 911 and they're gonna help you." He said that when you ask people why they call 911, they often say it is because police have guns and can respond to threatening situations. "But," Gil asked, "what are you gonna do in the seven to nine minutes it's gonna take them to get there? . . . [Are] you gonna say to the robber, 'Hey Mr. Robber, hold on a second. Take a time-out. The cops will be here in seven to nine minutes, and then we'll get back to this.' Or are you gonna be dead by the time the cops get there?" Gil's explanation is partly tied to the commonsense understanding that many CHL holders have that average response times are much too slow to rely on the police for help in stopping a violent crime. Evidence bears this out. Though response times vary by region, national data compiled by the Bureau of Justice suggest that responses to level-1 priority calls (violent assaults and homicides) are likely not quick enough to stop a crime in action. In 25 percent of cases police reach the scene within one to five minutes; in 28.5 percent of cases it takes six to ten minutes; and in 37.6 percent of cases it takes police eleven minutes to one hour to reach a crime scene (Klaus and Maston 2000). To cite one example, police in Milwaukee, Wisconsin, arrive on the scene of priority-1 calls an average of fourteen minutes after a call is placed to 911 (Poston 2011).

And yet my analysis suggests that the focus on personal responsibility is not limited to concerns about response time. Instead respondents emphasize the more general significance of being self-reliant. As Gil said, "I think you . . . either adopt an attitude of, 'I'm gonna depend on society; I'm gonna depend on the government to make sure I'm cool' or 'I'm gonna take responsibility for my own safety and my family's safety.'" Many respondents reported that they believe U.S. culture has been corrupted by dependency on the government. For example, John explained that recent events, including flooding and terrorism, have shown many Americans that we all need to be prepared to take care of ourselves: "People have kind of come back around to the idea that, you know, 'Gee, I shouldn't just sit on my ass and wait for the people in the uniforms to do stuff. Because they may not get there in time or may not be there.' So it comes back around to this mind-set that I need to take care of myself. I need to have the skills and the equipment, and that's not just guns. First aid, fire, emergency preparation . . . It's a different mind-set in America, which is the way it used to be, [in the] 1940s, 1950s . . . World War II. You know, that changed a generation. . . . Now we've come back around to a certain amount of self-reliance." Self-reliance was a recurring theme in nearly every interview I conducted, and it was not only mentioned with respect to self-defense. In most cases concealed handgun licensing was explained as one facet of a larger self-sufficiency ethos that respondents believe is less prevalent now than it was in the past.

Many of the people interviewed for this project believe that there is a tendency for too many people to rely on the government during crisis. Wendy, who works for her county's emergency management preparedness agency, said, "I get so frustrated! [Laughs.] In my job we really, really, really get frustrated. And . . . we walk a fine line because we don't want to turn our backs on people, but at what point do you, do people have to start thinking for themselves? And doing for themselves? Just how much do people expect the government to do for them?" Wendy said that too many people believe that "they're here, they're alive, and government and someone else is responsible for everything that they do. And the more I see that view, the more I don't want to be that person. Ever." Wendy explained that she has taken various measures to ensure that she is self-reliant, including storing reserves of food and obtaining a CHL. She loved taking the CHL class: "I was really jazzed to be in a room with like-minded people who were all thinking about self reliance, self defense, personal defense, handguns, that sort of thing."

When I asked Wendy if she has always been like that or if it is something she has developed over time, she said, "We were just raised as, that's what you do. That's what you're supposed to do. That's what's right. And if, you know, God granted you favor and you have extra, you share it with those that don't. But you don't, you're not a codependent, you're not an enabler. You know, being generous didn't mean that you gave to the point where that person didn't want to work. You gave to people who were willing to help themselves but were just down on their luck." Wendy makes clear that she is not dismissing the importance of charity—so long as it is reserved for the deserving poor—but she believes that systematic assistance can lead to dysfunction.

Similarly Susan believes that government policies are fostering a culture of dependency that creates a populace that wants to be "taken care of." She explained, "You know, it just seems like everybody wants this health care, everybody wants government handouts, everybody wants [government] to pay for everything, you know, if you notice, there's free programs for everything and there's complete dependency where people are just complacent to be dependent instead of being self-sufficient. And then they complain when what they're being dependent on isn't good enough!" This framing is part of the "welfare discourse" according to which government aid undermines personal responsibility and corrupts people's character (Fraser and Gordon 1994; Misra, Moller, and Karides 2003). Health care reform (a topic that was regularly in the news at the time of these interviews) was mentioned by a number of respondents who felt that President Obama's policies were partly intended to increase people's dependency on government. Notably Susan's comments about the threat of government were offered spontaneously in the context of talking about the importance of CHLs. She and other respondents who emphasized the importance of self-reliance seamlessly wove explanations of government policies (or perceptions of government policies) into their explanations for why they want the ability to carry a gun in public and their advocacy of gun rights.

For example, when I asked June if she felt gun rights where threatened in this country, she said that she did and that she was concerned about government in general. She explained, "Obama is trying to cram everything that he wants down everybody's throats. . . . If he could make this country like Hitler did, he would do it." June said her biggest concern is that the government wants "to take over everything." She continued, "I think it's really sad, I mean, even seatbelts. Okay, yeah, I think . . . it's a shame that they have to make a law that you have to wear them. At the same time, if you don't wear 'em and you get hurt, it's going to be 'Too bad, so sad; you take care of yourself.' The government shouldn't have to pay to give you, what do you call it, disability or anything. If you're stupid enough not to put on a seatbelt and you get hurt, it's your own fault. And yeah, you can feel sorry for people, but at the same time, you know, you [have] got to take responsibility for yourself." A focus on government control and government-facilitated irresponsibility as a threat to individual liberty was identified by respondents as a cultural problem that manifests in a wide variety of social ills.

Adam explained his disdain for how the government interferes with personal liberties when he described his view that it is illogical to bar CHL holders from carrying their firearms into gun-free zones because someone who is intent on committing a crime will have no regard for whether guns are legally allowed. What is telling about how he explained his animosity toward gun-carrying restrictions was the way he linked this infringement on his freedom to what he sees as other forms of governmentally enforced injustice:

[Gun-free zones] work against the people who care, and this society in general is really starting to lean towards that whole mentality of "Punish the righteous." I mean, it's like with the mortgage deal, and I'm in the real estate business so you know I have some strong beliefs on it. You're rewarding bad behavior and punishing good behavior. I pay my mortgage on time. I've never been late. I always make sure I pay it. Yet I can't get a reduction in my mortgage rate. But people who don't pay their mortgage, the government says, "Well, okay, you really can't pay your mortgage, so here's what we're gonna do. We're gonna give you a 3 percent interest rate." Well, I'm still paying 11 because I pay my bills on time. It doesn't make any sense! You know. "Hey guys, you can't bring your guns in here, but the guys who don't care about that are able to." So when someone stands up in that restaurant and says, "Hey everybody, empty your wallets, I've got a gun!," the people with CHLs don't have guns. So they can't do anything about it.

As Adam explained his views, he became visibly agitated and was clearly upset. But curiously Adam does not regularly carry his firearm in public. While "24/7 carriers" might feel vulnerable when they are unable to legally carry their guns into businesses where guns are not allowed, Adam is not one of those people. Instead he feels a sense of moral outrage about what he sees as a societywide tendency to "punish the righteous," whom he defines as those who value personal responsibility and self-reliance. This discrepancy suggests that in addition to being a tool of self-defense, Adam's CHL serves as a symbol of his worldview, a totem that expresses his commitment to values that he holds dear, values he believes have been the key to his success in life.

The extent to which moral outrage is a part of CHL licensing was evident in a different point in my interview with Adam, when he said that there is a tendency for some people to suggest that crime is not a huge concern if it is only property crime. He said that while to a certain extent he agrees because his family's safety is his biggest priority, he also said that there should be a strong reaction against criminals because "it's not right for somebody to . . . rob you or hurt you or, you know, any of those, it's just, it's not, it's not right." Adam feels that what he refers to as "liberal" social policies and a tendency to dismiss nonviolent crime have created a cultural climate that excuses bad behavior and "punishes the righteous." For many respondents the government is a central part of the problem in this dynamic because it breeds a lack of personal responsibility and threatens individual freedom, particularly for people who are doing "the right thing." Adam feels embattled against a government and a larger society that is helping the wrong people while leaving responsible people like him to fend for themselves.

Concealed handgun licensing is described as a practice that allows people to exercise their individual right to self-defense, but it is also a reaction to what some see as a cultural shift toward dependency and government control. Susan said that personal responsibility is directly tied to firearms because guns are one of the main ways people are able to ensure that the government will not dictate every facet of their lives: "There's a big divide of people who want to be taken care of and people who don't want to be taken care of. And the people who don't want to be taken care of are the same people who want to keep their guns. . . . And so there's a whole breakdown, and it just seems like somehow guns are right in the middle of keeping you separate from which side are you on?" Susan said this isn't simply about self-defense: "It's about who we are as citizens." Susan clearly sees personal responsibility and irresponsibility as existing in a binary opposition, to which she has attached many other values, including independence/dependence, empowered/powerless, and free/enslaved.

Mike shares the view that the government encourages dependency so that it can control the population. He said, "There are two, in my mind, if you were to divide the American people into two groups, personal accountability and responsibility and the government is supposed to take care of it. All right? These guys are gonna get funneled into concentration camps and put to work at whatever the government wants them to do. These guys are hopefully going to fight that tyranny. Cause it's not, that's not what our founding fathers wanted out of government. You know?"

Nearly every respondent believed gun rights were threatened, and those who were most concerned made claims rooted in the fear that guns are the only thing standing in the way of government control of our lives. This, they believe, is why those politicians who advocate for social programs like a government-backed change to health care are the same ones who propose gun control. Such beliefs explain the overwhelming opposition to Obama's candidacy in the 2008 and 2012 elections among gun advocates. Not only was he on record supporting gun restrictions as an Illinois senator, but his advocacy for health care reform and other social programs made him an extremely dangerous figure for those gun rights advocates steeped in a neoliberal worldview (Carlson 2012). Because they believe that self-reliance is the opposite of government intervention, they feel that personal freedom is hampered by an insistence on social welfare programs. Consequently "the government" is used as an umbrella term that encompasses any threat to personal liberty, whether gun restrictions or welfare dependency. Even if only as a symbol of freedom, handgun licensing is seen as one step toward rejecting such constraints and reaffirming the importance of the individual.

The idea that guns are the only guarantors of freedom is circulated widely in NRA discourse (Melzer 2009). Horwitz and Anderson (2009, 3) refer to this rhetoric as "insurrectionism," a belief "that the government should be kept in a condition of weakness because collective approaches to social problems are wasteful at best and more often constitute an insidious threat to individual liberty." While concealed firearms are an important step toward self-protection from the dysfunctions bred by too much social interference and too little personal responsibility, these meanings extend beyond preparedness for interpersonal crime and reach their apex among respondents who plan for much graver calamities

Living beyond Society

Susan was the second person I interviewed for this project, and toward the end of our interview she asked me, "I don't know if you've found [this]. But do you notice that more of the people you are talking to with guns are also more on the survival prep page?" At the time I had not considered the connection between concealed handgun licensing and survival preparation, but as I would come to discover, for many respondents there is a clear connection between the two. Mary explained the link as follows: "I think anybody that recognizes their mortality and that their mortality can come from outside of their health has got to recognize the fact that your way of life, what you've got going, can be taken from you from outside forces. Whether it's natural or man-made is irrelevant. And most people, once you recognize that, tend to plan for other things as well."

Among my respondents perspectives on the need for survival preparedness range from elaborate plans (including owning remote tracts of land, having connections to larger survivalist networks, and storing nonperishable food to last many months) to minimal planning (including having a location in mind to meet up with one's spouse and a store of food and water to last a few days). While those with elaborate plans tend to believe that the threat of societal collapse is a real possibility, those with more modest plans tend to prepare for natural disasters. For example, John is concerned only about having enough food and water for about a week. He lives in the Houston area and said that sometimes, after severe hurricanes, basic infrastructure (electricity, water, etc.) is down for a few days.

Those with more extensive planning cite a range of potential calamities that could lead to societal collapse. When I told Mike that some of the people I had spoken with had discussed their self-reliance plans, he smirked and seemed somewhat embarrassed. He said that he and his wife have a plan, including stockpiled food and water, that they refer to it as their "SHTF Kit" or "Shit Hits the Fan Kit." Mike explained, "I'm not really dreamin' up any horrible scenario. I mean if it goes real bad to that extent, I mean, we all might be dead anyway. Freakin' nuke or something. But if it's just having to stay home because the, uh, World Health

Organization declares a level-6 pandemic and you're quarantined to your house for three weeks, well, we've got enough supplies to get us through that." Though Mike said he does not have any specific threats in mind, it is clear he has contemplated a range of potential forces that could lead to social upheaval. He explained, "It's very interesting to look at the level of authority that the World Health Organization has over us, U.S. citizens, once the pandemic has been established. It's kind of scary. So yeah, that's one of the things that we talked about last year, when this swine flu first started coming out." Later Mike said that he and his wife do not have "specific triggers" in mind, and then he elaborated, "[It's] more like, if things get sideways. And we don't really sit around and define what that means. Let's put it this way: if something like what happened on September 11, 2001, was to happen again? You can bet that I'm not gonna sit around my office and ask my boss if I can leave. All right? I'm hitting the road, because I know that my wife is on the way home, we're gonna meet there, get the kids, get our provisions, and get out of the neighborhood. And, uh, depending on if the roads are still available and not blocked, I'm either gonna go south to my friend's land or north to family land."

Despite the seeming ease with which he explained his plans, Mike was clearly uncomfortable and embarrassed with this discussion and said, "I'm gonna sound like a freakin' conspiracy theorist when we start talking about this." Sensing his discomfort, I said, "You know, you sound reluctant to talk about it, but you'd be surprised; this is very common." He replied, "Yeah? Among, among the people that you're talking to?" I nodded, and he continued, "Yeah. It doesn't surprise me. It's just [*pause*], it's just kind of [*pause*]. I don't know. I'm conflicted with the whole thing. I would love to be able to believe in my heart that my government is here to do the right thing. But as I get older and learn more about what goes on, I don't believe that anymore. I think our government is fundamentally flawed. We don't, we can't hold elected officials accountable anymore. [*Pause*] Look at what's goin on with health care. Don't get me started on that! [*Laughs*.] Just look at what's goin' on and, and, our country is in rapid decline. Which saddens me because we're gonna hand off a world to my kids that's gonna be [*pause*] crap." Though Mike's elaborate survivalist plans can be read as a fairly radical lack of faith in society, his explanation also indicates that he feels a great sense of loss, pain, and concern about the state of our democracy.

Susan was the first to bring up the importance of survival prep, and she proved to have the most elaborate plans of any of the people I interviewed for this project. She and her husband have a large cache of weapons and ammunition, grains, canned goods, and powdered milk in the event that community infrastructure breaks down, but these provisions are not what set her apart from the others. When I asked her to describe what types of events she imagines could unfold that would require that she utilize her resources, Susan explained that it could be anything: weather-related catastrophes, terrorism, government insurrections, or foreign military invasions. When Susan explained her family's plans she said, "I don't think we're extremists. I think we know people who are extremists. I think we are aware and we are listening. I think we're doing what's responsible, you know. If something bad was to happen, like even, say, weather-wise, we're not dependent on the government. And that goes hand in hand with having our guns. If we need to shoot our own food, we can. Or protect what we have. We have what people want. So if something goes bad, like [Hurricane] Rita, could we protect what we have? You know. Yes, we could. Our neighbors? Not so much. You know, so it's, it kind of takes that step too, why guns are so important is to protect what we've acquired, not to let somebody else come in and take our food supply."

When I asked Susan if she feels responsible for protecting other people, for example her neighbors, she explained, "You know what, it comes down to that there's people that we have prepared for. My parents, who . . . don't understand, who kind of, I think, know we're doing this but haven't taken any steps at all. My husband's parents, that's who he learned it from . . . through the cold war [*laughs*]. You know, this was my in-laws' thirty years ago or whatever. We have a social network of people that we know that is each collecting things, their portion, so we come together in a central location. So we already have a community. Now we know that, like, my parents and maybe my husband's brother who is not able to . . . his wife's not on board. But you can't leave your brother and his wife out, and his kids." While Susan said that she and her husband feel a responsibility to provide for their immediate family (and here she includes her husband's brother), her next-door neighbors would be a different story. She said you have to consider, "What can they offer? Unfortunately the husband doesn't offer anything. The wife would offer [something] because she can cook and she can do certain things. She'd be somebody we'd consider taking along. Now let's say worst-case scenario, end of the world–

type stuff, where, like, we have to rebuild. You know? They would be good because they have two daughters, I have two sons."

Though Susan's plans and ideas about societal collapse may seem extreme, I would suggest that they fit with the logic of individualism and emphasis on personal responsibility offered by the CHL holders I interviewed. In many ways disaster preparedness simply takes the CHL ethos to its logical conclusion: though individuals arm themselves for self-defense because of potential interpersonal crime, the worldview that shapes this practice can easily translate into much larger plans for much larger calamities.

It is important to emphasize that levels of preparedness and ideas about what might be an impetus for crisis vary widely among the CHL holders I interviewed. Some respondents have no plans at all, while others seem ready for society to collapse. It is also important to stress that it is not the case that all respondents believe in the most extreme forms of disaster, though nearly everyone I interviewed is familiar with someone who thinks this way. George said, "I'm not waiting for Armageddon. I'm not waiting for the world to come to an end. The zombies aren't coming over the hill. The Chinese aren't going to be at our borders. I'm not worried about that. I don't have a bunker down in the floor. I don't have three months of food stashed away somewhere buried. But I do know people that think that way."

For many respondents CHLs are connected to survival preparation in a more simple way, as John explained:

We're not talking about hordes of zombies. We're not talking about Y2K, a total societal collapse. We're talking about natural disasters, wildfires, floods, tornadoes, hurricanes, earthquakes, et cetera. There have been dozens of situations in the past ten years where communities have had to go, you know, people in the community have had to go off the grid for . . . three to five to seven days. And even the government's own website, the ready .gov has some good stuff on there about emergency preparedness. And yeah, personal defense is certainly a factor in that, because people get desperate. . . . If you're poor and you've got eight children and they're hungry and you need stuff, maybe you're not normally willing to do certain things. But when you get desperate, you know, survival instincts are what they are. And unfortunately, then it becomes a bit more of an aggressive competition for resources for survival. And those that have planned ahead are going to have what they need. And those that have not are gonna be desperate.

John said, "I'm not there with the Alex Jones people that, you know, the dollar's gonna collapse and we're gonna have total social unrest.[2] I don't think that's gonna happen." He continued, "We would all like to believe we live in this wonderful, civilized world where nothing could possibly ever go wrong like that and situations couldn't break down." But there have been too many recent examples—particularly hurricanes and 9/11— that show people need to be prepared. And anyway, John believes, "there's never any harm done by being cautious. There's always harm, there's always risk for harm if you're reckless."

I include this information in my analysis because it is clear to me that there is a strong connection between ideas about social disaster and the need for concealed handgun licensing that go beyond respondents' realizations of their own mortality. Susan made this link clear when she explained that a large-scale disaster is "basically gonna be God's way of thinning the herd. You know, those who choose reality and those who want the government to take care of them." Susan believes that self-reliance comes in many forms and that it is the ultimate measure of a person's value in society. These ideas are based in the same sort of social Darwinist rhetoric that justifies neoliberalism: the strongest, savviest, most capable will survive, and those who do not have the moral fortitude, those who have been content to let others take care of them will not make it. According to this worldview, individuals who are completely responsible for themselves are the embodiment of what is just and right. Meanwhile the government is not simply a constraint on personal freedom; it is among our greatest existential threats, and anyone who relies on it is irredeemably broken.

"Good Guys" and the Myth of Individualism

This chapter shows the extent to which race and class are central to the social construction of good guys and bad guys. First, the distinction that respondents made between gang members and mentally ill school shooters is important for what it says about the ways race shapes ideas about culpability and responsibility. While the school shooters need help, the gang members need greater involvement in the criminal justice system;

though school shooters are seen as tragic deviations from what is normal for middle-class white males, gang members are seen as representing the cultural values of their communities. This rhetoric relies on ideas about a pathologized version of blackness steeped in a culture of poverty (Royce 2009) that serves to naturalize crime in impoverished black and Latino neighborhoods in a way that makes the link between structural inequality and criminality invisible. Respondents avoid overtly racist language by employing the rhetorical shield of color blindness (Bonilla-Silva 2001), yet this does not mean that race does not weigh heavily in their understandings of criminality. Many respondents draw a clear line connecting racialized poverty and social problems, and they do so in a way that obscures the causal relationship between the two. My respondents, like many white Americans (Gilens 1999), believe it is the inferior morality of the poor that explains both their poverty and the higher crime rates that plague many of their neighborhoods.

One of the most alarming consequences of this discourse is the very disparate ways that shootings are treated in this country. The vast majority of perpetrators and victims of school shootings are white, middle-class children, and in the wake of these events the outpouring of grief, media coverage, and calls for reform (no matter how short-lived) consume the public's attention. And yet the most common victims of gun violence are not middle-class, white, suburban schoolchildren but African Americans. According to the Pew Research Center, despite making up only 12 percent of the population, blacks represented 55 percent of all gun homicide victims in 2010, while whites, at 65 percent of the population, represented only 25 percent of victims (Cohn et al. 2013). Using white gun deaths as a baseline, this means that 4,763 more African Americans died from gun violence in 2010 (not including suicides and accidents) than would be expected based on population. The disproportionality of these statistics is astounding, but what is perhaps even more alarming is the lack of attention given to black homicide victims.

There are likely two reasons African Americans are largely ignored as victims. The first might be that there is simply a lack awareness of data on criminal victimization. As is clear in the crime literature, most people's attitudes about crime are based almost exclusively on perceptions of reality and not on empirical evidence (Warr 2000). Perhaps most people simply do not know the astronomically high rate of homicides plaguing black communities. Yet my analysis suggests that there is something else at work. Beyond mere ignorance, as was made evident in chapter 4 and affirmed here, blacks, and specifically black men, are regularly imagined as criminals, and so they are thought to have brought their victimization on themselves and are unsympathetic victims. Given the homicide rates of black males, this can only be viewed as case of white racial apathy (Forman and Lewis 2006).

In general, respondents have elaborate ideas about criminality. They imagine that the poor are too content to wait around for "handouts" or for the government to solve their problems and thus are overdetermined by the social, while the respondents are unfettered individuals. In sharp contrast to dependency, those I interviewed see themselves as self-reliant, and they understand their place in society to be a product of their commitment to personal responsibility. This focus on individualism is a characteristic discourse of whiteness (Bonilla-Silva 2001), and it obscures white privilege (Lewis 2004) by denying the various ways many white Americans benefit from their social location. Thus whiteness matters not because of the meanings that adhere to the racial category "white" but because racial categories are said not to matter at all. By explaining their successes as a product of individual effort, people who are privileged are able to use the "underclass" as a foil against which their own status can be explained. According to this construction, there is no such thing as privilege, and if there is no such thing as privilege, there is no such thing as inequality; we all get what we deserve. In other words, just as the social construction of gender requires the contrast between masculinity and femininity for meaning, impoverished criminality is a central component in the narrative of middle-class success in neoliberal discourse. This "othering" is facilitated by a racialized and classed understanding of crime that allows many white Americans to imagine that most crimes are committed by poor people of color who are compelled by their weak character and suspect morality, two things that my respondents believe will only be made worse if the government misguidedly tries to help the poor. In sharp contrast to these moralistic explanations of criminality, a structural analysis makes it clear that "crime rates are higher on average in African American than in other neighborhoods, not because members of this group are more criminally oriented, but because African American communities have the highest average levels of disadvantaged social conditions owing to the role of race in structuring opportunity and community access" (Peterson and Krivo 2010, 6). In other words, our lives are not determined simply by our character but also by the social conditions in which we live.

The refusal to take seriously the existence of systematic inequality rests on a set of "sincere fictions"—"personal and group constructions that reproduce societal myths at the individual and group level" (Feagin, Vera, and Batur 2001, 26)—that many whites, particularly those who are middle class, hold about how society operates. These are sincere fictions because those who believe in these narratives think that they hold the key to a successful life and a healthy society: their hard work and responsibility have paid off, and so it must be that the poor are simply refusing to play by society's rules. By denying the significance of social structure and the inherent interdependence of society, individualism operates as the ultimate sincere fiction of whiteness, a discourse that reaches its zenith in the fantasies of hyperindividualism contained in disaster preparedness. According to this logic, if society as we know it were to disappear, the only people capable of survival would be those who have the wherewithal—and enough firepower—to survive.

Conclusion

The Social Implications of an Armed Citizenry

· ·

Jack said that one of the reasons he decided to pursue a CHL and advanced training was what happened after Hurricane Katrina struck New Orleans. According to his ex-wife's Louisiana-based family, there were "bands of people" roaming evacuated areas and ransacking houses. One cousin was reportedly shot and robbed of his gas tanks and a generator, and so other family members sat on their front porches with shotguns to keep the looters at bay. Jack said these stories taught him "there's a thin membrane that separates society and civilization and anarchy, and it's imaginary. All it takes is we lose our infrastructure for just a few days and it's gone. And we become animals." When I asked Jack how he sees the nature of criminals, he explained, "I think you just have some people who are just bad people and they're just waiting for an excuse to be bad. And they're going to be the first ones to start erupting when something like this happens. Criminals are going to continue to be criminals, they'll just be amplified. Other people will probably devolve and do what's necessary to survive. I'm not going to go take anybody's stuff or anything like that. I'll protect myself. I'll protect my family. But I'm not going to go out and shoot people for a generator or something, but a lot of other people will." As is true of other respondents, Jack constructs an other who lacks control and morality, while he insists that he would remain calm, rational, and law-abiding.

I asked Jack whether he thinks there is something about CHL holders that makes them more likely to take steps toward disaster planning, and he replied, "I think they're only starting to scratch the surface of taking care of themselves. . . . I think they've got just a glimpse of it, and some of them take it a little further. But the reality is, only about 1 percent of CHL holders really pursue their training and really get to the point where it starts to become evident what could actually happen and what position they could find themselves in and how they might have to exercise this right. I think most of them are just kind of on the fence, where they go, you know, 'I carry a gun, I carry it when I need it.' And they'll probably never use it. In fact most of them probably won't even have it with them when they need it. I think for a lot of people it's a novelty. And for some of them, it gives them a false sense of security. Cause they don't know what they don't know."

Jack said that as an instructor, he tries very hard to get them to see that they need more advanced training:

> The first thing I tell them [is that] this class is not enough. I am not going to help you survive a gunfight. We can talk about scenarios, I can give you an understanding of the laws and where you can carry and where you can't carry, and I can give you tips on this and that, but what it comes down to to survive that gunfight is conditioning. What's going to help you survive are the actions that you have repeated over and over again that you have committed to habit. Where when your adrenaline is shooting out your ears, your heart rate's going, and who knows what's running down your legs, you have no ability to think rationally, and it just happens because you've done it so many times. That's what's going to make you survive that gunfight. You're not going to remember two words I say today. Some of 'em, I think it sinks in. Most of 'em, I think it doesn't.

In his admonition to his students to seek more training, Jack admits that they learn a minimal amount in the CHL course, and he questions whether it will help at all should they feel the need to draw their firearm. While Jack is the only respondent who suggested that some might seek a license because of the sheer novelty of having one and who said that a CHL might provide a person with a "false sense of security," most of the instructors I interviewed questioned whether a licensing course sufficiently prepares one to carry a gun in public, and yet most also insisted that the state should not require any additional training, a tension that reveals both the potential inadequacies of the licensing process and a key source of resistance to changing it.

In this conclusion I provide a direct critique of concealed carry as social policy, including the process by which one becomes licensed to carry a gun in public. Some readers might imagine that the most important thing about handgun licensing is that it introduces the possibility of more gun violence. While this is not an insignificant point, and may become increasingly so as more and more people obtain licenses, calculating how much risk an armed citizenry introduces to the public is not only beyond the scope of this project, as I will argue, potential gun violence might not be the most consequential aspect of licensing. Instead as I will show, handgun licensing is most important because of its effect on the culture.

Licensing Instruction

When I asked respondents if they felt that the licensing course prepares people to carry guns in public, their responses reflected an ambivalence rooted in both a deep distrust of government regulation and a tepid acknowledgment that it is rather easy to obtain a CHL. Views on regulations ranged from Chris's belief that all gun ownership should include a training requirement to Mary's view that there should not be any restrictions. Chris admitted that his politics represent a "middle of the road" that many gun owners would find objectionable. Nevertheless he explained, "When you drive a car, you have to learn how to drive the car itself, plus you have to know all the laws and rules of the road. Not so with a handgun. Anybody can go to a gun shop and buy a gun, just pass a quick computer background check, and there's no training at all with the law. So a lot of people have guns and they just don't have the training, and I think they should." Chris believes that a CHL course is representative of the kind of instruction that all gun owners should receive.

Licensing courses in Texas include information on gun laws, safe storage of firearms, and basic gun-handling techniques, but the fact is that it is a very basic introduction to firearm safety, and it includes very little in the way of preparing people for what to do if they feel they must pull their guns from concealment. Many respondents expressed at least some apprehension about this, and yet while the majority admitted that the CHL course is simple and does not require a great deal of skill in shooting, they were also opposed to any more state regulation. John said that the CHL course teaches license holders how to stay out of jail and that the shooting portion allows people to "demonstrate that they are proficient enough with their handgun that they're not going to be a danger to others around them if they draw their gun in public." But, he said, "that does not teach them what they need to know to actually have good chances of winning should they be in a real situation." John believes that CHL holders need to know a range of skills that are not taught in the licensing course, including drawing a handgun from concealment, shooting at night, and practice in engaging a threatening person. A typical licensing course simply cannot provide this level of instruction because public shooting ranges are not willing to risk the liability. John said, "Because the problem is that if they allow somebody like me to go in there and draw from concealment and shoot very quickly, then the guy three stalls down who has no idea what he's doing is gonna say, 'Well, that guy gets to do that, how come I can't do that?' And then he'll try to do it and shoot himself in the leg and put a hole in the ceiling." He emphasized that though it is prudent for license holders to seek advanced instruction—which they can get from training facilities like the one he runs—he believes it should be voluntary and supplemental to the licensing process, not mandated by the state. Joseph said that anyone who carries a gun should do the training required to be able to handle a threatening situation: "Cause if not, you're just another idiot with a gun." But he does not think the government should interfere with individual rights and he resents the fact that he had to obtain a government-issued license to carry a gun legally.

Early in this project I wondered whether CHL training should not be as rigorous as what police officers go through when they learn to handle firearms, but I soon learned from instructors that many CHL holders receive nearly as much training, and some are much better trained than the typical officer. Mary said, "The average number of shots any person with a CHL fires annually is ten. Because they shoot fifty [when testing], and they have to renew every five years." But "the average number of annual shots a police officer shoots is one hundred because they have to qualify a hundred rounds, [and] they usually do it once a year. It's the only time they get the gun out. These are the people I'm gonna have protecting me? They're more likely to shoot me than the bad guy. I've had more police officers tell me that they'd rather have my husband or me as their backup than their partner because they'd feel safer. It's pretty pathetic! [Laughs.]" Notably Mary and her husband are competitive shooters who spend a great deal of time practicing marksmanship. But by her own admission, a typical CHL holder does not have to shoot more than an average of ten shots per year to be legally allowed to carry a gun in public. While conceding that he and many CHL holders he knows are much better shots than most police officers (and he hosts many at his facility), John had a more sympathetic view of police training. He explained that police officers have such broad duties and responsibilities that they have to be competent at a wide range of skills, whereas civilians—like Mary and her husband—can specialize in specific tasks: "I'm not saying police officers are bad. I'm just saying that they have to be masters at a lot of skills, and there's simply not enough hours in the year and dollars in the training budget for them to be expert, master-class level in every single thing that they have to do in their job, because there are so many pieces of it." Still the fact remains that the kind of training John and Mary participate in is not at all typical of most CHL holders.[1] Without anything required beyond the CHL course, what would compel a person to seek more advanced instruction? As Mary admits, most CHL holders have very little experience with shooting guns, and few have any training at all. The shooting requirements for obtaining a CHL are so minimal that one can easily qualify for a license even if the licensing class is the first time one has ever seen a gun, much less fired one. Claiming that police officers have only slightly more training than a typical license holder is not a sound argument for CHL advocacy; it only calls into question whether all police should be armed or whether more training might be necessary for anyone with the state-sanctioned right to be armed in public, something that seems particularly necessary given the attention to officer-involved shootings in recent years.

The deep antigovernment ideology to which many license holders ascribe shapes their views of the role of the state in mandating gun restrictions, including CHL training. Mary said that not only are the licensing requirements adequate, but she advocates for complete deregulation: "I have no issue with the states that require nothing. You can carry if you want. You can open-carry if you want. You can conceal-carry if you want. It is a right given by the Constitution, and you can have your guns and you can carry them. You will find that they have no more crime, no more statistics that are out of whack than any other state. They are just fine. Normal, responsible people are going to act like normal, responsible people." Mary is right that there are few studies that show the impact of specific gun carry legislation on shooting outcomes; however, this is more of an issue with a lack of reliable data than proof that gun policies have no effect. While Mary said that anyone who is not legally restricted should be able to carry a gun because "normal, responsible people" are fundamentally trustworthy, this begs the question of who is a "normal, responsible person." Is a felony criminal record, a record of domestic violence, or admission to a psychiatric hospital (among the disqualifiers for gun purchases and CHLs) the only proofs that someone is not normal or responsible? Take the case of my respondent June, who admitted that the reason she first obtained a license was that her late husband, who had just been diagnosed with Alzheimer's, wanted one and she felt it would be prudent if she went along. She said, "I was surprised at how easy it was for him to get it, not being well. I don't think the tests are all that hard, do you?"[2] While the instructors I interviewed said they would not pass someone if they felt he or she were a danger to society, how would they determine this during a one-day training that can be as short as four hours?

A recent analysis by Jeffrey Swanson and coauthors (2015) found that an estimated 8.9 percent of the general population has a gun in the home and also has a history of impulsive angry behaviors, including outbursts, fighting, and breaking things out of anger, and that approximately 1.5 percent of the general population that exhibits angry behaviors regularly carries a gun outside of the home (a number that has likely increased given that these data were collected between 2001 and 2003 and CHLs have since dramatically expanded). Not only is impulsive anger associated with a propensity for violence, but those who both exhibited angry behaviors and carried a gun outside the home "were significantly more likely to meet diagnostic criteria for a wide range of mental disorders including depression, bipolar and anxiety disorders, PTSD, [and] intermittent explosive disorder" than the general population. While these disorders do not disqualify a person from owning a firearm, they would make someone ineligible to obtain a CHL in Texas if they had a diagnosis; however, the process relies on the applicant's voluntary disclosure.[3]

Pro-gun advocates who want few if any restrictions on gun purchasing and carrying argue that it is not fair to restrict the rights of the vast majority of gun owners, who are "normal, responsible people," simply because a small proportion of the population might someday use their guns to commit violence. But how can it be that these types of incidents are too uncommon to justify restrictions on gun purchases but so common that the general population should be armed and ready to defend themselves?

It is true that acts of random gun violence are rare: in a congressional report detailing mass public shootings from 1999 to 2013 (Krouse and Richardson 2015), researchers, utilizing the federal definition of "mass killing" as any event in which four or more people were killed (excluding the perpetrator), found that there was an average of twenty-one cases per year. However, most of those involved familicides (murder of family members) or murders that occurred in the course of other felonies (e.g., drug deals or gang wars). When looking only at those shootings that were of the random type described by respondents as reasons to carry a concealed firearm—for example the Virginia Tech shooting—the numbers are much smaller. From 1999 to 2013 there were just over four public mass shootings per year with an average of twenty-nine people killed and approximately twenty-two people wounded.

Though the probability of finding oneself in a mass shooting is already low, it would be lower still if stronger safeguards were implemented that restricted those with known violence-related mental illness from purchasing and possessing firearms, and if there was a more thorough process to ensure that people with restraining orders and histories of domestic violence do not possess firearms.[4] Many of the people I interviewed would argue that any restriction would represent a slippery slope toward confiscation, but this is conspiratorial rhetoric that is often used to justify doing nothing when it comes to gun violence. There are already categorical restrictions on firearms based on age and criminal history, and though there are many existing issues to resolve, it is well within the capacity of the state to strengthen policies that prevent people with histories of violent behaviors from having firearms.[5]

While some of my respondents resent the fact that they are forced to endure a bureaucratic process while criminals can just pick up a gun and carry it, the fact is that illegal carry is fundamentally different from carrying with a state-issued license. Not only are criminals always at risk of being discovered (and given this, do they actually carry firearms in public to the extent that my respondents assume?), but a CHL serves as a form of endorsement that may embolden license holders, as though completing a background check and licensing course proves they are capable of sound judgment and skillful marksmanship. One can see this clearly in the "good guy" discourse I analyzed in previous chapters. But, put simply, the sense of validation that comes with the license is unwarranted given how easy it is to obtain one. Chris compares it to getting a driver's license, but Texas law requires anyone under the age of twenty-five to complete a driver's education course, which is in fact much more rigorous than what is required to become licensed to carry a gun in public, something that anyone who is twenty-one or older can do, assuming they have passed the CHL course and are not restricted.

The licensing process differs by state, but in Texas one is required to sit for four to six hours of instruction, prove that one can hit a target from three, seven, and fifteen yards, and pass a simple state-issued exam. The shooting test requirements are minimal (most shots happen from within seven yards; a shooter can be wildly inaccurate and still get credit for hitting the target; and a shooter is given three chances to pass), and the written test includes questions and answers that are covered verbatim in the course. This does not prepare a person to have sound judgment in a hostile confrontation, nor does it provide any evidence that one is capable of drawing one's gun and safely engaging a target. Moreover shooting a gun on a range with a firearms expert walking you through every step, showing you precisely how to work your gun, and even reloading your gun for you (as I saw happen in my course) is not at all like shooting a gun when you are alone on a range, much less in a high-pressure situation. This is not to say that some civilians would not make excellent candidates to carry guns in public. I feel confident that Mary, John, Bill, and others have the training and the dispositions necessary to be armed, but they are not typical license holders; they have dedicated a great many hours to training at very high levels, and still there is nothing to guarantee that they will always make the right decision with their guns. Of course there is nothing to guarantee that anyone will.

Though the CHL requirements are minimal, one section of the Texas course that should be replicated by other states is its focus on nonviolent conflict resolution. As the instructors I interviewed maintained, using a handgun should be a person's last resort; one must first do everything in one's power to de-escalate a situation. Despite this emphasis it was clear from interviews that instructors are sometimes met with resistance from students who find it boring or unnecessary. Susan said, "I think women take the nonviolent dispute resolution class to heart a little bit more, [and] men, I think, kind of roll their eyes just to get through it. I hate teaching that class, but I try to teach it as effectively as I can. I tell everybody, 'Now, okay, no rolling eyeballs at me. . . . I have to tell you these things. I have to tell you to be nicey nice.' And you know, I try to make it reality-based, you know, give scenarios on how every day we have an opportunity to make a situation go bad or good." This explanation reveals not only the masculine bias evident in Susan's course but also the possibilities and the constraints of licensing instruction. Though training in nonviolent conflict resolution could go a long way toward teaching license holders to refrain from using their firearms, it has a slim chance of being effective if the instruction is minimal and if applicants can still qualify for a CHL even if they do not take it seriously. As is true in any form of education, not all training is equal, and even the best training can leave license holders uncertain about what to do at the moment they feel they might need to reach for their gun.

One area of training that should be added to licensing courses is attention to how biases shape our ideas about crime. As was clear in chapters 3 and 4, many of the license holders I interviewed use racialized perceptions in determining potential threats. But, as in the culture more broadly, there is a remarkable lack of direct engagement with that fact in CHL instruction. I saw this in my own course when Bill actively avoided discussing race while in the classroom but later privately admitted that it plays a role in how he thinks about crime, and also in the various ways that license holders simultaneously tried to avoid talking about race while signaling to me that race is an important part of how they think about danger. A growing body of research in psychology shows not only that racial biases are widespread and that they lead people to associate black males with danger but that implicit biases can be controlled if people work to undo stereotypes.[6] By not dealing with what seems to be a pervasive underlying anxiety about race and crime, CHL instructors are not only contributing to discourses that help to maintain racial inequality, they are also missing an opportunity to invite students to interrogate how their ideas might lead them to misjudge threats.

It is easy to obtain a CHL to carry a concealed firearm in Texas, and any discussion about this policy should include an acknowledgment of that fact. While the course contains minimal instruction, and many of my respondents suggest that further training is prudent, it became clear in my analysis that this might very well have unanticipated consequences.

The Costs and Benefits of Situational Awareness

According to licensing instructors, spotting trouble before it happens and having a plan for responding to danger are the keys to staying safe, and so they teach their students situational awareness, the practice of being alert to potential danger in public places. Someone who is situationally aware will routinely scan areas for potential threat, position himself or herself in strategically chosen spots, and always have a plan for responding to any dangerous scenario. Chris explained the importance of situational awareness as follows: "It does no good to have a concealed handgun if you're not aware of your surroundings. Criminals like the element of surprise. If they know you're not paying any attention to them, they will take advantage of that, and you will become a victim and your gun [is] not going to help you." Most important, situational awareness can keep a person from having to pull his or her gun—an action that everyone I interviewed agreed should be avoided if at all possible.

In addition to what they've learned from their CHL courses, many respondents explained that they watch television shows and read magazines and books devoted to self-defense. Ruth said that she and her husband have learned a lot about safety techniques this way: "I think going through the class and all and those shows, I tell anybody, you learn, even if you don't want to carry a gun, you need to be aware of these personal defense things that you can think of ahead of time. Where are you going to sit? Where are you going to look? What are you going to see? If somebody's acting funny, walking funny, you know. Maybe I should leave now."

Respondents reported that the more firearm self-defense training they receive and the more exposure they have to self-defense discourse, the more they become aware of their vulnerability. This is an important point to consider as it troubles what might otherwise be interpreted as a selection effect. In other words, while a range of concerns might compel a person to consider obtaining a license to be armed—for my respondents, this included becoming a father, traveling to unfamiliar areas, and living in a pro-gun political climate—my analysis suggests that the process of being immersed in CHL culture fundamentally alters how one thinks about threat, violence, and self-defense. I experienced this myself in the process of researching this book, as I began to see potential threat in all kinds of places. Once when I was teaching a course at the University of Texas, an unfamiliar student walked into the class and sat in the back of the room. As I lectured, I looked to see what size bag he carried, and I made a plan for what to do if he had a gun. Given the layout of the room and the fact that he sat near the door, I realized that my only option was to quickly exit through the emergency door near the stage and to call campus police. This sort of thought had never crossed my mind before conducting this research, and yet I had started to imagine all sorts of potential violence. Late-night walks to my car included much more alert scanning than I had previously done (though, like most women, I had always been vigilant when walking alone at night), and entering parking lots now involved getting a read on all the people in my vicinity. I was, in the situational awareness lingo, routinely operating in "code yellow," a state of attentiveness to threat that is a level above the obliviousness of white but not quite at level orange—something one reaches when a potential threat is identified, a plan is needed, and evasive techniques are required. The highest level—red—is reserved for a clear and present danger (e.g., an active shooter).[7]

Learning to be aware of potential threats is a beneficial skill that anyone can use to keep obliviousness from getting him or her into trouble, and it is something I am happy to have learned in the course of this research. But the CHL worldview does not stop at awareness of basic threats; it teaches license holders to think through how they would respond to a violent confrontation with their firearms, which then compels them to become reliant on their guns to feel secure. While I heard this from people who said they felt "naked" without their guns when they were forced to go without them and from others who said they simply could not fully relax unless they were armed, one of the clearest examples is Susan, who said that since becoming a CHL holder, she has realized that "a lot of us kind of walk around, you know, with blinders on. We don't really pay attention to what's going on around us. Since doing this now for two years, I don't want to say I'm on a heightened level of paranoia, but I'm very aware of what's happening around me. You know, almost like somebody who's been raped or attacked, they're always looking behind them, or they're just much more aware of where they go and what they do. So I find myself always, you know, just taking account of where I'm at." Despite this new approach to navigating public spaces, Susan does not always have her gun with her. She described a time when she realized what a mistake going unarmed could be:

> I was at Wal-Mart at Christmastime at like 11:30 with my neighbor
> one night, and I'm thinking to myself, "Man, I'm out this late,
> and I didn't bring my gun with me. And wouldn't you know, tonight
> would just be the night that I'd have that bad luck." And I saw a
> man walk in from one of the doors and alls I saw was this figure
> [*holds her right hand up with her elbow bent at a 90-degree angle*],
> and he was walking with a couple of other people and I, like, fell
> down [*laughs*], up against the soda machine for like a second,
> because here I was just thinking about my situational awareness
> and then I see this [*sticks arm up again*], and it was a price gun
> that he had in his hand. And I thought, "Now I didn't have my
> gun with me tonight. What if?" Cause you never know when
> and where it's gonna happen. And I don't want to say that was
> paranoia. I want to say I was maybe overlook—or looking into it
> too much, but it just reinforced that if this is what you believe,
> if you are prepared to take those actions, then, yes, you carry your
> gun with you everywhere you go, and you choose not to go to

certain places or businesses that don't allow you to have your gun. And I tell people that if you are that committed to keeping your gun with you all the time, then you need to reevaluate how you live your life. Where you shop, where you go, how you do business. Because you can't take it everywhere you go. And some people are just that serious.

Here again is an incident that could have made Susan realize that she is in fact more secure than she imagines but instead became a lesson that she should have had her gun with her, and it serves to reinforce her belief that there is no such thing as a safe place. While she believes it was a coincidence that she had just been thinking about situational awareness when she imagined that a man had a gun, I would suggest that she saw a firearm where only a price gun was present *because* she was thinking about her vulnerability. The heightened vigilance that CHL training encourages has led her to see crime even where none exists. Because the premise of CHLs is that violent crime can be unpredictable, the only way to stay safe is to be ever alert and always prepared, and since the most powerful response is the most comforting, CHL holders become increasingly dependent on their guns to feel secure. Though this makes them feel safer when armed, it also seems to increase feelings of vulnerability when they do not have their firearms with them, something that may be particularly consequential for women, who, as I described in chapter 3, are socialized to see themselves as inherently weak, "natural" victims. While Susan said she is grateful for her newfound attention to safety, as we sat at a small table in a Starbucks with few other customers, her edge was clearly evident when at one point an employee who was cleaning the coffee bar behind her banged a sugar canister against the countertop. Susan jumped and quickly turned around; the employee apologized and Susan laughed.

Mark too has developed an awareness of vulnerability that he did not have prior to becoming a CHL holder. In his case it was in advanced firearm training that Mark realized he did not have the skills required to protect himself and his family from harm, a realization that he said made him feel "stupid": "You know, I went eleven years. If I could have all that time back to train the right way? You know, it would be night and day." Nothing happened to Mark or his family before he received this training, but he has reinterpreted the past as a time when they were vulnerable, and he is now prepared for a wide range of scenarios: "You know, I've had the carjacking situation. You know, somebody sticks a gun in my face, I'm gonna push them away." He tells his wife that "she shouldn't lean forward, she should lean back. It's, if it's gonna [fire, it will go] right into the dash. That kind of a thing. If there's more than one, we're getting out of the car, period, we're not gonna fight. They can have the car. You know."

According to psychologist Joseph LeDoux (1998), anxiety exists when a fear stimulus is not present but is anticipated, something that it is most likely to occur when people feel that their life is in danger. Any behavior that resolves the anxiety is likely to be maintained given the sense of relief that one feels. With respect to concealed firearm training, threat scenarios are intended to prepare a person to know how to respond to danger, but in so doing they produce a momentary flash of anxiety that is resolved by the self-defense strategy. Thus CHL holders who see threat lurking in places they never did before manage to feel simultaneously safer (due to the possession of a gun) and more vulnerable. This was clear in the case of Ruth, who told the following story about how her perception of potential victimization has grown since becoming licensed:

One time I was pumping gas and my gun was in the car. I lock all the doors and I only unlock my door, see, because I know, and I've seen videos where someone will come up and open the passenger door and steal your purse. So I lock all my doors except for my door. Well this guy, him and this other lady, they were standing around the gas station. Apparently the gas station let them try to sell a cleaner or something like that. So he walks up to me and he starts to ask me about this, and I said, "Get away from me! Leave me alone!" Normally I might not have done that, but being that I'm a little more aware of what's going on around me, "I don't know you from anybody and I don't need somebody selling me something when I'm pumping gas." And I just want to be straightforward and bold and say that. And he said "Okay, ma'am," and he just walked away. And now I don't care if I hurt his feelings or [pause]. I was looking out for me. I wasn't trying to be rude, but I really don't need to be really nice to everybody. You know, some of those parents are teaching their kids to be nice. They need to teach you to be aware, and sometimes there's a time when you don't need to be nice. Not nasty, but, you know, "Get away from me. I don't need to talk to you. Leave me alone."

Ruth's vigilance is clear, and she feels validated by and secure in what she has learned in her self-defense training. In fact she so values this new worldview that she looks forward to teaching it to her granddaughters: "One, she's not even five yet, and the other is two and a half, but I want to teach them that. Because you see these people who are oblivious, and they could walk right into a convenience store being robbed and not even know it because they're talking on the phone." Ruth is describing people who, according to Mary's terms, are sheep. Now that Ruth sees the world through the eyes of someone who is prepared to respond to danger, a sheepdog, she realizes that potential threats are everywhere, something that must be terrifying for a grandmother who is worried that her granddaughters will become victims.

For those respondents who already have a high degree of situational awareness, obtaining a license to carry a gun will likely not increase their feelings of vulnerability but will allow them to feel a new sense of security in public places. The phrase "once a cop, always a cop" speaks to the tendency for police officers to be unable to let go of the situational awareness training they learn on the job even long after they leave the profession, as evidenced in the cases of Joseph and Leo. The same is true of military veterans, particularly those who have served in combat, and for anyone who has been a victim of violent crime. Who would argue that Caroline, who was abducted and raped in a parking garage, was not better off once she started carrying a handgun and could venture into public places without feeling vulnerable? Or Catherine, who was afraid every time she left her house that the man who was stalking and threatening her would eventually find her alone and she would be unable to defend herself? In these cases license holders do not develop a sense that they are potentially vulnerable; they already feel it, and carrying a concealed firearm can allow them to quell the anxiety that might already be a part of their everyday lives.

CHL proponents argue that concealed firearms are necessary to prevent victimization. But what if the gun carrier comes to see the world as a person who has already been victimized? In such cases, do the benefits of being armed for a low-probability, high-consequence event outweigh the costs? Is Susan, whose vigilance leaves her on edge, who said she navigates public spaces like someone who has been attacked or raped, better off than someone who is unarmed? Is Mark, who carries a gun everywhere whether or not it is legal because his training has taught him that he is always potentially vulnerable, measurably safer now? According to the

National Crime Victimization Survey, 1.2 percent of the U.S. population twelve years and older experienced a violent crime in 2013, a number that declines significantly if a person is thirty-five or older, white, and married (Truman and Langton 2014). The same demographic that is most likely to obtain a CHL is the least likely to be a victim of violent crime, calling into question whether the effect on a license holder's worldview is worth the risk.[8] It is critical to realize that our perceptions of truth become our reality: it is not that society becomes more dangerous when we believe that there are threats lurking at every turn but that our individual lives can come to feel more dangerous, no matter what the crime rate or our actual risk of victimization. And to the extent that we change our lives to accommodate our ideas about vulnerability and threat, we can be victimized by our own perceptions.[9] A concealed firearm in one's waistband or a loaded handgun by one's bedside is a symbol of both safety and risk; a reminder that one is always able to respond to threat is also a reminder of always being threatened. It is important that those who are contemplating obtaining a license consider these potential effects.

And what of the social costs of this worldview? When gun carriers come to dread the approach of strangers or answer the door with a loaded gun, they are inhabiting a psychological world in which few can be trusted and social bonds are weak. This is particularly problematic because, as is already clear, perceptions of threat are not neutral; they are constructed via race, class, and gender.

At its worst, these dynamics can play out in tragic ways, as happened on February 26, 2013, when George Zimmerman, a white CHL holder and self-appointed neighborhood watch captain, shot and killed Trayvon Martin, a seventeen-year-old African American who was walking from a nearby 7-Eleven to his father's girlfriend's house. As is clear from 911 recordings, Zimmerman thought Martin was acting suspiciously and assumed that he might be connected to the rash of break-ins that his neighborhood had experienced. Zimmerman called 911, then followed Martin, first in his truck and then on foot. A fight broke out, and according to his defense, Zimmerman shot Martin only after fearing for his life.

My respondents were split on whether a license holder should intervene in circumstances like this. While John said he would never confront someone he thought was engaged in property crime, Bill, who is his neighborhood's watch captain, said he sees himself as a "shepherd," protecting the flock of sheep that is his community. He, like Zimmerman, wants to be the good guy, to fight back against crime. The gun lobby and larger cultural characterizations of heroes fighting bad guys represent an idealized version of masculinity that likely influenced Zimmerman's desire to obtain a CHL, carry a firearm, and patrol his neighborhood. Had Zimmerman been unarmed, he might have been less likely to approach Martin and might instead have waited for the police to arrive. Without the capacity to dominate another person, he might have felt less emboldened and more cautious. And perhaps most important, had Zimmerman not occupied the role of the good guy, he might not have been so quick to see Martin as a bad guy. Of course this does not mean that the police would have used better discretion, but they would have been more likely to use rules of engagement that are intended to mitigate the potential for unnecessary use of force. Moreover their role as police officers would have made the situation clearer, though perhaps no less fraught with danger for a young black male.

While Martin likely would not have been shot if CHLs were not legal, one of the most important laws that shaped the case was Florida's Stand Your Ground (SYG) law. SYG laws have not only extended the "no duty to retreat" provisions of the castle doctrine into the public sphere, but in most cases they have also provided a remarkable degree of legal cover to those involved in lethal confrontations.[10] Most states with SYG laws allow the use of deadly force in defense of property and when the assailant is retreating, and many protect people who act in self-defense not only from criminal prosecution but from civil suit (Lave 2013). The evidence on SYG suggests not only that the law has contributed to an increase in homicides (Cheng and Hoekstra 2013) but also that it is utilized in ways that exacerbate racial disparities. According to one study, when the shooting victim is black and the shooter is white, the case is 281 percent more likely to be ruled a justifiable homicide than when the people are of the same race. Moreover when the victim is white and the shooter is black, the case is half as likely to be ruled a justifiable homicide than when the people are of the same race (Roman 2013). While the legal right to carry a concealed firearm may not in itself contribute to racial inequality, evidence suggests that laws invoked in the event that a firearm is used do.

Though Zimmerman's attorneys did not argue a Stand Your Ground defense, Florida's SYG law played a role in at least two ways: not only did the judge in the case instruct the jury to consider SYG when determining whether Zimmerman was guilty (Coates 2013), but the use of SYG in such cases reflects and reinforces the cultural normalization and therefore acceptance of the idea of shooting in self-defense. Legal scholars refer to the connection between legislation and norms as law's "expressive impact." According to Louis N. Schulze, Jr. (2012, 37), "Legal expressivism holds that law exerts power not only in its ability to change citizens' actions through direct sanctions, but also through its ability to convey messages about the shared beliefs of the community as communicated by a legal authority." In other words, law can justify social arrangements by endorsing ways of relating. In combination, SYG laws and CHLs are important in shaping how we see one another and in how we imagine reasonable responses to threat. Given the cover of whiteness and the power of the fear of crime, there is grave risk that the racialized dynamics exacerbated by these laws, with all of their dire consequences for black men, will be seen as natural, normal, and "just the way it is."

While the Trayvon Martin case shows what can go horribly wrong when race, class, and gender converge in shaping perceptions of good guys and bad guys, such instances are not likely to happen with regularity. The fact is that because there are relatively few CHL holders (4.8 percent of the Texas population that is twenty-one or older) and violent crime that victimizes people twenty-one and older is rare, the odds are slim that a CHL holder will use his or her firearm in self-defense. But beyond the individual and interpersonal consequences, CHLs are important to understand on a much larger level, and that is in the relationship between culture and structure. Concealed handgun licensing is not simply a contained practice that affects only individuals. Like all practices, the meanings that contribute to and stem from CHL policy play a role in shaping the larger culture, which may well be its most significant impact.

Good Guys and the Reproduction of Inequality

Insofar as it represents a measurable violation of law, crime is a fairly straightforward phenomenon: a person who breaks a law is a criminal, and in the interest of social order, crimes must be prosecuted and consequences must be meted out. But crime also occupies a place of fantasy, where mythic stories about human nature and morality run wild. From this analysis I have come to believe that what society thinks about crime, and particularly that slice of society to whom politicians are most responsive—the white middle to upper-middle class—is more consequential than actual crime. After all, when one considers how perceptions of criminality have been used to justify policies that ruin black lives and communities, it is clear that more people are victimized by the social construction of criminality than by crime itself. This is seen not only in the oppressive War on Drugs policies that Michele Alexander (2012) refers to as "the new Jim Crow" but also in the social neglect that has allowed many poor black neighborhoods to languish in a state of unrelenting deprivation.

Gun users' framing high-crime areas as dangerous neighborhoods to be avoided at all costs, and particularly so when armed, obscures what we should be asking: not "Should I carry one or two guns," but "How is it that there are cities in the United States that can be described (accurately or not) as 'war zones'?" Structural inequality is reproduced thus: white fear of black neighborhoods makes them undesirable places for white people to live and do business in, which drives down property values for black homeowners and ensures that black-owned businesses are less likely than white ones to thrive. License holders naturalize such spaces as dangerous when they explain that no one should ever go to these neighborhoods without being armed, a characterization that allows them to ignore the reality that a wide array of people who are not involved in crime—including children—live there.

Crime happens, and it is sometimes violent and horrific, but it is important to put criminalization into context, to understand how much crime happens, where it happens, and to whom. One of the most problematic aspects of handgun licensing is that it focuses a disproportionate amount of attention on white men and women in suburban areas as potential victims when victimization rates for those groups are very low, while victimization rates for black men and women is relatively high. To take homicide as an example, from 2002 to 2011 the homicide rate for white males peaked at age twenty with 11.4 per 100,000 in the population, while the rate for white females peaked in the first year of life with 4.5 per 100,000. For black men the peak rate occurred at age twenty-three with 100.3 homicides per 100,000, while the rate for black women peaked at twenty-two with 11.8 per 100,000 (Smith and Cooper 2013). Given this remarkable disparity, the question for those committed to social justice is this: How is black male *victimization* not our most pressing social issue? Whether or not black victims of homicide are involved in crime should take a back seat to the reality that far too many young black men are dying by violence. Victimization is a sign of marginalization, and it is a condition made worse by the fact that black victimization is often invisible in American culture. Instead of seeing the relatively low victimization rate that exists in predominantly white, suburban communities as a sign of social privilege, we are living in a cultural moment wherein people in those areas are being encouraged to take up arms. The discourse around handgun licensing ignores dynamics of social privilege and inequality and instead focuses on ways to arm those who are the least likely to be victims of violent crime against the criminal other. While this characterization is not unique to CHL holders, what is unique is that concealed firearms are being offered as a "good guy" response to crime, while doing nothing to challenge the social dynamics that contribute to crime in the first place. To this extent the underlying structures that foster social problems are not only ignored; they are potentially worsened. This is not to say that the act of carrying a concealed handgun is responsible for making social conditions what they are, but concealed handgun licensing is an extension of a more general privatized response to social problems that has come to dominate political discourse: rather than funding vibrant public schools, vouchers are on the rise; instead of expanding publicly subsidized medical care, there has been a deepening reliance on for-profit care; even security forces in international conflicts are increasingly run by private corporations. Neoliberal discourses of individualism suggest that social responses undermine individual initiative; the more entrenched this worldview, the more difficult it becomes to confront. Instead of considering the structural conditions that create disproportionate levels of crime and violence in some spaces and imagining structural solutions to these problems (e.g., mixed-income housing initiatives, government-backed job creation, sufficiently funded schools, universal and high-quality preschool), individuals are increasingly encouraged by discourses of personal responsibility to fend for themselves. If this individual solution was offered alongside large-scale social investments, perhaps handgun licensing would be less consequential, but it is not. Moreover the cultural focus is on those who wander into high-crime neighborhoods only when they miss their exit on the interstate—the focus is *their fear* rather than the individuals and families who live, work, and play in those spaces. This does nothing to change the lives of those who exist under conditions of extreme disadvantage, and to the extent that it rationalizes neglect, it only makes matters worse.

Of course CHL holders want to be armed not only for the sorts of crimes that are imagined as typically occurring in poor, predominantly black neighborhoods but also for those moments when violence strikes closer to home, as it did on December 14, 2012, when twenty-year-old Adam Lanza shot his way through the front doors of Sandy Hook Elementary

School in Newtown, Connecticut. Armed with a Bushmaster XM-15 and two 9mm handguns, Lanza killed twenty children and six adults before killing himself. It was a horrific event that led to an outpouring of grief and, in some corners, mobilization to tighten gun laws. In a press conference one week after the shooting, NRA vice president Wayne LaPierre said that these types of tragic events should push us all to determine how best to "protect our children" from the "monsters and predators of the world." According to LaPierre, until every school has armed security, children will continue to be vulnerable, because ultimately "the only thing that stops a bad guy with a gun is a good guy with a gun." Though this statement made waves at the time, it was simply an explicit declaration of what the NRA had been implicitly telling its members for decades.

The Newtown shooting provides yet another example of how gun violence becomes news only when it strikes in a place where it is "not supposed to happen," where white middle-class children are positioned as uniquely tragic; it also shows how the construction of good guys and bad guys is used to obscure our understanding of social dynamics by reducing complexity to a simple morality tale. The discursive contrast that LaPierre makes between monsters and predators is likely one of intent: monsters cannot help who they are, while predators seek out their victims. This is the same sort of discourse that Susan used when she distinguished school shooters from gang members. Instead of asking how an emotionally disturbed young man had access to any gun, much less multiple semi-automatic ones, Lanza is painted as a monster, so that social context is stripped away and all that is left is the embodiment of evil. And as anyone familiar with children's stories knows, the only way to kill a monster is if a hero saves the day.

Mass public shootings are also terrifying because of their seemingly random nature, and perhaps this is why they are covered so extensively by news media, an institution that is notorious for its tendency to focus on (and thereby help to create) spectacles of fear (Schudson 2011). The last mass shooting incident that occurred as I was completing this book happened in San Bernardino, California, on December 2, 2015, when Syed Farook and Tashfeen Malik, each armed with a .223 semiautomatic rifle and a 9mm semiautomatic handgun, opened fire at an office holiday party. In the end twelve people were killed and twenty-two wounded. Not unlike what happens with most mass public shootings, the media firestorm that followed this event suggested that the country is gripped by gun violence that seems to get worse by the day. One *New York Times* headline read, "How Often Do Mass Shootings Happen? On Average, Every Day, Records Show," and in the first few paragraphs the authors claimed that many mass shootings occurred "on streets or in public settings" (LaFraniere, Cohen, and Oppel 2015). A terrifying prospect to be sure, but how does it actually line up with the data?

The article relies on an analysis of news accounts compiled by shootingtracker.com, a website that documents any shooting in which four or more people are killed *or* injured. Yet as Richardson and Krouse (2015) argue, it is much more in line with traditional criminological research only to consider an incident a "mass shooting" if four or more people are *killed* (not including the shooter); this is not intended to minimize gun violence but to create consistent measurements so that we can accurately gauge whether or not it is actually getting worse. My analysis of the data used in the *New York Times* article ("Mass Shooting Tracker" 2015) suggests that of the 330 shootings that happened in 2015, approximately twenty could be defined as mass shootings, and a closer look at the news reports that are linked shows that eleven of those happened in the context of family violence, four seemed to be related to other felony crimes, and four were of the random, public sort including a shooting at an Oregon community college and a shooting at a black church in Charleston, South Carolina, that left nine people dead.[11] Not only does twenty mass shootings in one year fall in line with the national average dating back to 1999 (Krouse and Richardson 2015), but the one figure that is an increase over previous years is the number of mass shootings happening among family members, a fact that is entirely left out of the national media spotlight.

Reimagining the "Good Guy"

The "good guys versus bad guys" story is timeless because it has great appeal. Not only does it simplify a complex reality, but it reinforces our individualistic culture and tells us that if we want to be successful, all we need is the right character and values. If we are privileged, if we live in safe communities, have access to the spoils of the economy, and know that the police are on our side, we must be good guys too, or at least we can be if we have the courage and the conviction to be prepared to respond when called, to be a sheepdog protecting sheep from wolves. Of course crime does happen; it would be naïve to suggest otherwise. But sociological explanations make it clear that violent crime is patterned, not random, and if we examine those patterns, we can see that individualistic explanations are inadequate, no matter how intoxicating they may be.

If we want to reduce crime, we have to address the conditions that foster crime, which means creating stronger communities and doing what we can to keep guns out of the hands of people who should not have them. The government will have to play a role in both of these issues, and so the insurrectionist, antigovernment bent of much pro-gun discourse is a barrier to meaningful change. This is not to say that there is no cause to be concerned about government overreach or threats to liberty. But we cannot forget that we live in a democracy and that it will be only as functional as we demand. This is as true for those committed to social justice as it is for those concerned about losing individual freedoms. Rather than giving up on government, we should be invested in making it work effectively for all of us. In the words of Desmond and Emirbayer (2011, 537), "We must refuse to become victims in a democratic society," which we do through political apathy and through antigovernment discourse.

To actually reduce crime will require a degree of mutual sacrifice and a willingness to turn toward unknown others and not away from them—a difficult endeavor given that outsiders define society's boundaries and provide us with the contrasts that tell us who we are (Collins 2000). This is precisely why good guys need bad guys: they are the reminder of what not to be and how not to live. That the bad guys who receive most of the attention in crime discourse are often poor only supports the dominant culture's idea that they are morally defective. Perhaps this is another reason school shootings are so unsettling. Not only are our children not supposed to be victims, but they are also not supposed to be perpetrators, and while calling them "monsters" instead of "our children" is an attempt to deny that fact, it should be remembered that Lanza too was once a first-grader at Sandy Hook. Was he a monster then?

I don't believe we have to completely throw out the idea of the good guy. As in every other age, there are countless social problems that need the attention of people willing to fight for change. But it seems that we do need to reimagine what a good guy is, because as this analysis has shown, to the extent that the good guy identity rests on opposition (to femininity, to the poor, to racial others, etc.), it will not fundamentally challenge the terms by which inequality is reproduced. Instead of crafting their identity in contrast to others, what if good guys battled the conditions that create suffering? What if they were willing to sacrifice a measure of their freedom to make our gun laws safer? What if they fought social injustice instead of only arming themselves against its byproducts? What if they were willing to interrogate why patriarchal gender norms make violence so appealing? I think my respondents would be willing to consider these ideas; after all, most of them carry guns out of a conviction that they can thereby participate in creating a safer world. This analysis is not intended as an argument against concealed carry. It is rational for well-trained people to want to be armed in case of a low-probability, high-consequence event. But it is my hope that they could do so without also possessing an individualistic worldview and a cynical approach to the social. As Zygmunt Bauman (2000, 287) writes, this worldview carries a grave risk: "If individuals behave *as if* their experience and fate had no collective ramifications, that assumption tends to become true in its consequences. First the collectivity disappears from view, and then, as solidarity fades, it vanishes from living reality." There is a certain amount of trust required to live in society, and to have it we must give up the constant suspicion of others and perception of perpetual threat that loom so large in self-defense rhetoric and, increasingly, in the culture more broadly.

What this will take is an active resistance to the forces that compel us to be afraid of each other, which we must be vigilant about, as I learned during the course of this research, since they are quite seductive. Fear is a powerful emotion, and no matter how it enters into our thinking— whether via media that report so regularly on mass shootings that we might come to believe that they are common when they are in fact rare, or from the firearms industry and its lobby (who are among the greatest beneficiaries of our distrust)—we must realize that our fear can distort our ability to understand what is actually happening in the world and it can drive us further and further from solving social problems. I wanted to study concealed handgun licensing because I thought it was important to understand why someone would want to carry a gun in public, but I have to admit that I already had a strong sense of the answer. I already knew the impulse to be ready to respond to danger, to feel like one has control over any situation. My degree of attachment to the good guy identity started when I was young and would act out Chuck Norris and Jean-Claude Van Damme movie scenes with my friend Simon. I insisted on always being the good guy and assigned him the role of the bad guy, and naturally I always got to win. In many ways I haven't grown out of this drive, and I understand why my respondents want to be armed. But what I learned in this research is that the good guy status comes at a cost. Not only can it exacerbate feelings of distrust that make peaceably living among others difficult, but in its individualism it denies a structural account of social inequality that perpetuates injustice. And that is something that no good guy should stand for.

Appendix I

Demographic Characteristics of Respondents

Name*	Sex	Age	Race/ Ethnicity	Highest Level of Education Completed	Estimated Income
Adam	M	36	White	High school	$61–80,000
Alex	M	26	White	High school	$21–40,000
Allison	F	30	White	Advanced degree	$61–80,000
Ashley	F	30	Hispanic	High school	$81–100,000
Bill	M	38	White	Technical school	$101,000+
Caroline	F	67	White	College degree	$81–100,000
Catherine	F	35	White	College degree	$41–60,000
Chris	M	63	White	College degree	$41–60,000
Cindy	F	39	White	College degree	$41–60,000
David	M	66	White	Advanced degree	$21–40,000
George	M	40	Hispanic	College degree	$101,000+
Gil	M	65	White	High school	$101,000+
Greg	M	57	White	High school	$101,000+
Jack	M	46	White	College degree	$101,000+
Jackie	F	53	White	College degree	$101,000+
Jeff	M	48	Latino & White	College degree	$81–100,000
John	M	44	White	Advanced degree	NA
Joseph	M	45	White & Hispanic	Associate's degree	$81–100,000
June	F	67	White	High school	$61–80,000
Krysti	F	37	White	College degree	$41–60,000
Larry	M	54	White	Associate's degree	NA
Leo	M	52	Hispanic	Advanced degree	$101,000+
Lisa	F	44	White	High school	$61–80,000
Mark	M	34	White	High school	$61–80,000
Mary	F	53	White	College degree	NA
Matt	M	46	White	Trade school	$81–100,000
Mike	M	36	White	College degree	$101,000+
Molly	F	36	White	College degree	$81–100,000
Paul	M	34	White	Technical School	$61–80,000
Rachel	F	41	White	Advanced degree	$41–60,000

Name*	Sex	Age	Race/ Ethnicity	Highest Level of Education Completed	Estimated Income
Richard	M	38	White	College degree	$101,000+
Ruth	F	53	White	High school	$101,000+
Steven	M	30	White	Advanced degree	$101,000+
Susan	F	33	White	High school	$81–100,000
Tina	F	47	American Indian	College degree	NA
Wendy	F	50	White	High school	$41–60,000

* All names are pseudonyms.

Appendix II

Texas Handgun License Law

As of January 1, 2016, a CHL license holder is legally allowed to carry a handgun "on or about his person" either concealed or in the open, but there are some places where carrying weapons is prohibited. These gun-free zones include primary and secondary schools (unless the license holder has received express written consent), polling places, race tracks, court houses, correctional facilities, and secured areas within airports. Hospitals, nursing homes, amusement parks, and any establishment that receives 51 percent or more of its revenue from the sale of alcohol are also off limits, provided the establishment posts a clear sign that fits the requirements of the law. Private property owners and business owners can determine whether or not they will allow concealed guns on their property. In most cases and unless specifically prohibited, gun-free zones apply only to buildings, and gun carriers can leave their weapons concealed in their cars. Anyone who is found carrying a handgun on his or her person without a valid CHL license has committed a "weapons crime," a class A misdemeanor punishable by a fine of up to $4,000 and one year in jail.

Every state in the United States has some form of concealed handgun licensing. The vast majority are "shall issue" states, wherein if an applicant meets the state's terms and remits a fee, the licensing entity *must* issue a license. In a "may issue" state, licensing agencies have discretion with respect to who does and does not qualify for a license. Four states—Alaska, Arizona, Vermont, and Wyoming—do not require residents to obtain permits to carry concealed handguns. Most "may issue" states have very restrictive licensing procedures; some are so severe that they are effectively "no issue" states, such as Hawaii. In California applicants for a license must show good cause and have a compelling reason to fear for their personal safety. Additionally applicants for a CHL must be deemed to have a "good moral character" by their relevant licensing agency (either the local sheriff or police department).

Most "shall issue" states have a much more objective licensing process. For example, to be eligible for a concealed handgun license in Texas, applicants must (among other things):

- Be at least twenty-one years old and a Texas resident for no fewer than six months (though active-duty members of the military are eligible if they are eighteen or older).
- Not have a felony conviction or a class A or B misdemeanor conviction in the five years prior to their application.

- Not be delinquent on any child support payment collected or processed by the attorney general's office or delinquent on any local, state, or federal taxes.
- Not have a court order or restraining order against them.
- Not be found to be incapable of sound judgment in the proper use and storage of a firearm. (*Texas Concealed Handguns License Laws* 2014)

Certain conditions qualify someone as being incapable of sound judgment: a psychiatric disorder including schizophrenia, bipolar, chronic dementia, dissociative identity disorder, intermittent explosive disorder, or antisocial personality disorder (unless a licensed psychiatrist testifies that the condition is likely not to reappear); a disorder that has resulted in psychiatric hospitalization and/or inpatient or residential substance abuse treatment in the previous five years; or a diagnosis of chemical dependency. If an applicant successfully completes a firearms training course, remits a fee (typically $140), and is not disqualified on any of the above measures, he or she must be issued a license to carry a concealed handgun. Licenses are good for a period of five years, after which time a renewal fee and an updated criminal background check must be submitted.

Notes

Chapter 1

1. All respondents are identified with pseudonyms, and further steps have been made to ensure confidentiality, including secure storage of identifying information and vague references to details that might allow a reader to ascertain where respondents live.

2. It is important to note that as of January 1, 2016, anyone in Texas with a valid CHL will be legally allowed to openly carry a firearm. No additional training is required.

3. There were 4.7 homicides per 100,000 people in 2011, the lowest rate since 1963 (Smith and Cooper 2013).

4. "Dr. Suzanna Hupp Testimony before Congress on the 2nd Amendment," YouTube, 1 June 2010, http://www.youtube.com/watch?v=DEJFAvA-ZUE.

5. Studies that focus on the causes of crime fears have examined how they are shaped by fictional crime dramas and news coverage of actual criminal events (Eschholz, Chiricos, and Gertz 2003; Kort-Butler and Hartshorn 2011; Weitzer and Kubrin 2004). Analyses of consequences have focused on the extent to which fear of crime negatively impacts health (Humpel, Owen, and Leslie 2002; Warr 2000), contributes to the deterioration of community life (Box, Hale, and Andrews 1988; Hale 1996), and increases residential segregation (Liska and Bellair 1995).

6. Researchers caution that self-reports of gun ownership may be inaccurate because some gun owners fear that reporting might lead to government confiscation (Saad 2011).

7. For a thorough examination of state-level laws see News21 (2015).

8. Tellingly, although it is unclear whether there are more gun owners in the United States now than in the 1970s, what is clear is that there are many more guns; there are now nearly as many firearms in the United States as there are people (Cohn et al. 2013).

9. "NRA Refuse to Be a Victim Seminar Info," YouTube, 6 July 2009, https://www.youtube.com/watch?v=cLBdT9D_iOE.

10. This number reflects those who sat for a formal, recorded interview. While I informally interviewed people during ethnographic work the bulk of this analysis focuses on the in-depth interviews.

11. It impossible to know whether the income of the respondents reflects the population of CHL holders in Texas. According to one analysis, the distribution of CHLs in Texas suggests that residents in high-income zip codes are more likely

than those in low-income areas to obtain a license (Grissom, Stiles, and Tedesco 2010). Because the total costs associated with getting a CHL are typically between $200 and $250, it is likely prohibitive for those with low incomes.

Chapter 2

1. See appendix II for a description of other licensing requirements.

2. For a recent discussion of the connection between hunting, fathers, sons, and masculinity see Messner (2011).

3. For more on the police as a masculinist institution see Prokos and Padavic (2002), and for the military see Hinojosa (2010).

4. Steven described two separate incidents when men he had prosecuted confronted him in public, and on both occasions he was unarmed. One of the incidents happened when he stopped at a Wal-Mart on his way home from the gym: "I hear, 'What's up, fucking DA?' And so, [I] turn around [and] there's this dude who's pissed off and he's a known drug dealer. . . . We had custody of his kids is how he knows me. And uh, last time in court I really tore into him, so he's pissed off at me. And he starts threatening me and asking me if I'm married, you know, and all this stuff." As a prosecutor, Steven's motivation to be armed is quite distinct from those who are not engaged in his line of work.

Chapter 3

1. According to the Bureau of Justice Statistics, in 2011 the violent crime rate for men was 25.4 per 1,000 males twelve years and older, while the violent crime rate for women was 19.8 per 1,000 females twelve years or older (Truman and Planty 2012).

2. For example, Sutton and Farrall (2005) suggest that men report low fear levels because cultural norms make it impossible for men to both be seen as masculine and admit to feeling fear. They argue that when careful attention is paid to how questions are asked, men "are actually more afraid of crime, but are unwilling to admit it" (221). Similarly, in interviews with heterosexual married men, Nicole Rader (2010) found that many men feel they cannot admit to fearing crime because they are expected to be their wives' protectors. These studies suggest that responses to questions about crime fears are a form of "doing gender" (West and Zimmerman 1987) and that men are doing masculinity when they perform fearlessness—in interviews or with their spouse—and women are doing femininity when they perform fearfulness.

3. Caroline's presumption that the men she encountered were members of a "Mexican gang" is a topic taken up in chapter 4.

4. The relationship between Obama's election, fear of crime, and the rate of CHL distribution is addressed in chapter 5.

5. The definition of a mass shooting is any shooting that resulted in four or more homicide victims (excluding the perpetrator). It should also be noted that

domestic violence was a factor in fully 20 percent of all mass public shootings (Krouse and Richardson 2015).

Chapter 4

1. As of 2011, an employer cannot prohibit an employee who is legally allowed to have a CHL from storing a gun in his or her locked vehicle on employer-provided property. Exceptions include when an employee drives an employer-owned vehicle and if they work for a school (and do not have express written consent).

2. Only one person in this sample was caught while carrying a gun illegally, but her prior experience with a judge allowed her to get out of a weapon's charge. For more, see chapter 3 on women and guns.

3. I included this story in a presentation for a group of criminology graduate students at The Ohio State University's Criminal Justice Research Center's Speaker Series. One audience member, who was a military veteran, said that soldiers are trained to assume that a car that stops in front of a military vehicle is likely part of a coordinated attack. I reminded him that Jack was not in Iraq, he was lost on a street in Houston, Texas.

4. See chapter 2 on men and guns and chapter 3 on women and guns for a gendered analysis of licensing rates and carrying practices.

5. A license holder's use of his or her gun would not be considered justifiable if he or she provoked the altercation in which their gun was used.

6. Many more women than were highlighted in this chapter explain abstract perceptions of threat, including factors that shape criminality in the "black community" in highly racialized ways. An analysis of those findings can be found in chapter 5.

Chapter 5

1. The men killed by Joe Horn were indeed undocumented immigrants but were Colombian, not Mexican.

2. Alex Jones is a radio host known for being antigovernment and believing in global conspiracies of a small group of powerful people.

Conclusion

1. John said he shoots a couple of times a week now, but at the peak of his competition days he shot tens of thousands of rounds per year. In one year alone he reportedly shot 50,000 rounds.

2. Given his illness, June's husband should not have qualified for a CHL, but as his case shows, voluntary reporting means that people can easily slip through the cracks.

3. See appendix II for more on specific licensing requirements.

4. Though I am focused on self-defense, solutions to address gun violence should also include the number of suicides that occur each year with firearms. See Swanson (2013) for the relationship between suicide and firearm access.

5. See Luo and McIntire (2013) for a report on the limits of state level laws, and Krouse and Richardson (2015) for more specific recommendations that Congress should consider.

6. See Payne (2006) and Plant, Peruche, and Butz (2005) on racial bias in simulated decisions to shoot or not to shoot.

7. See Baum (2013) for an excellent journalistic description of how a concealed firearm worldview can change one's perception of threat.

8. Estimates of defensive gun uses vary widely, from 600,000 to 2.5 million (Cook and Ludwig 1998). Kleck and Gertz (1995, 180) argue that there is "little legitimate scholarly reason to doubt that defensive gun use is very common in the U.S.," and yet many other scholars provide compelling evidence that does just that. Cook and Ludwig (1998) argue that reported incidents of DGUs are methodologically unsound, and McDowall, Loftin, and Presser (2000) say that most reported DGUs contain ambiguous information and cannot prove that the presence of a gun stopped a criminal act. While the rate of DGUs that occur during typical violent crimes is unknown, according to Krouse and Richardson (2015, 3), "Out of the 317 incidents of mass shootings from 1999–2013, [our research] found one incident in which a mass murderer was killed by a civilian in a justifiable homicide with a firearm."

9. Not everyone will experience learning to anticipate threat in the same way. Recall from chapter 1 that Mary feared I would represent her as someone who is "an incredibly paranoid person" when she is actually calm and rational about her desire to be armed in public. She did not become paranoid from learning situational awareness though others did. This could be because she has much more extensive training than other respondents, or perhaps it is merely dispositional.

10. For most of U.S. history, English common law required that a person retreat from any hostile confrontation or provocation, whether in public or inside one's own home. However, in 1921 the Supreme Court ruled in Brown v. United States that inside of one's home one is free of the duty to retreat, a policy that became known as the castle doctrine (Levin 2010).

11. Two of the other mass shootings are of unclear type but the victims seemed to be targeted and were likely shootings that happened in the commission of other felony crimes, indicating they should not be considered mass public shootings.

Bibliography

Alexander, Michelle. 2012. *The New Jim Crow: Mass Incarceration in the Age of Colorblindness*. New York: New Press.

Anderson, Elijah. 2008. *Against the Wall: Poor, Young, Black, and Male*. Philadelphia: University of Pennsylvania Press.

Bailey, James E., et al. 1997. "Risk Factors for Violent Death of Women in the Home." *Archives of Internal Medicine* 157 (May): 777–82.

Barrett, Paul M. 2012. *Glock: The Rise of America's Gun*. New York: Crown.

Baum, Dan. 2013. *Gun Guys: A Road Trip*. New York: Vintage.

Bauman, Zygmunt. 2000. "Ethics of Individuals." *Canadian Journal of Sociology* 25: 83–96.

Black, M. C., K. C. Basile, M. J. Breiding, S. G. Smith, M. L. Walters, M. T. Merrick, J. Chen, and M. R. Stevens. 2011. "The National Intimate Partner and Sexual Violence Survey (NISVS): 2010 Summary Report." Atlanta, GA: National Center for Injury Prevention and Control, Centers for Disease Control and Prevention.

Blair, Elizabeth, and Eva Hyatt. 1995. "The Marketing of Guns to Women: Factors Influencing Gun-Related Attitudes and Gun Ownership by Women." *Journal of Public Policy and Marketing* 14: 117–27.

Blee, Kathleen M. 1998. "White-Knuckle Research: Emotional Dynamics in Fieldwork with Racist Activists." *Qualitative Sociology* 21, no. 4 (December): 381–99.

Bonilla-Silva, Eduardo. 2001. *White Supremacy and Racism in the Post–Civil Rights Era*. Boulder, Colo.: Lynne Rienner.

Box, Steven, Chris Hale, and Glen Andrews. 1988. "Explaining Fear of Crime." *British Journal of Criminology* 28: 340–56.

Britton, Dana. 2011. *The Gender of Crime*. Lanham, Md.: AltaMira Press.

Browder, Laura. 2006. *Her Best Shot: Women and Guns in America*. Chapel Hill: University of North Carolina Press.

Burbick, Joan. 2007. *Gun Show Nation: Gun Culture and American Democracy*. New York: New Press.

Carlson, Jennifer. 2012. "I Don't Dial 911! American Gun Politics and the Problem of Policing." *British Journal of Criminology* 52: 1113–32.

———. 2015. *Citizen Protectors: The Everyday Politics of Guns in an Age of Decline*. Oxford, UK: Oxford University Press.

Centers for Disease Control and Prevention. 2015. National Violent Death Reporting System, 13 June, https://wisqars.cdc.gov:8443/nvdrs /nvdrsDisplay.jsp.

Centers for Disease Control and Prevention, Injury Prevention and Control: Division of Violence Prevention. 2010. *The National Intimate Partner and Sexual Violence Survey (NISVS): 2010 Summary Report.* Atlanta, GA: National Center for Injury Prevention and Control, Centers for Disease Control and Prevention.

Cheng, Cheng, and Mark Hoekstra. 2013. "Does Strengthening Self-Defense Law Deter Crime or Escalate Violence? Evidence from Expansions to Castle Doctrine." *Journal of Human Resources* 48, no. 3 (Summer): 821–45.

Chiricos, Ted, Ranee McEntire, and Marc Gertz. 2001. "Perceived Racial and Ethnic Composition of Neighborhood and Perceived Risk of Crime." *Social Problems* 48: 322–40.

Clay-Warner, J. 2002. "Avoiding Rape: The Effects of Protective Actions and Situational Factors on Rape Outcome." *Violence and Victims* 17: 691–705.

Coates, Ta-Nehisi. 2013. "How Stand Your Ground Relates to George Zimmerman." *Atlantic*, 16 July.

Cohn, D'Vera, et al. 2013. "Gun Homicide Rate Down 49% Since 1993 Peak; Public Unaware: Pace of Decline Slows in Past Decade." Pew Research Center, 7 May, http://www.pewsocialtrends.org/files/2013/05/firearms_final _05-2013.pdf.

Collins, Patricia H. 2000. *Black Feminist Thought.* New York: Routledge.

———. 2006. "A Telling Difference: Dominance Strength and Black Masculinities." In *Progressive Black Masculinities?* edited by A. Mutua. New York: Routledge.

Connell, R. W. 1995. *Masculinities.* Cambridge, UK: Polity.

Connell, R. W., and J. W. Messerschmidt. 2005. "Hegemonic Masculinity: Rethinking the Concept." *Gender & Society* 19: 829–59.

Cook, Phillip J., and Jens Ludwig. 1998. "Defensive Gun Uses: New Evidence from a National Survey." *Journal of Quantitative Criminology* 14: 111–31.

Cooper, Alexia, and Erica L. Smith. 2011. "Homicide Trends in the United States, 1980–2008." Washington, D.C.: Bureau of Justice Statistics.

Cramer, Clayton E. 1999. *Concealed Weapons Laws of the Early Republic: Dueling, Southern Violence, and Moral Reform.* Westport, Conn.: Praeger.

Crawley, Sara L., Lara J. Foley, and Constance L. Shehan. 2008. *Gendering Bodies.* Lanham, Md.: Rowman and Littlefield.

Davis, Angela. 2007. *Race, Ethnicity, and Gender.* 2nd ed. Edited by Joseph F. Healey and Eileen O'Brien. Thousand Oaks, Calif.: Pine Forge Press.

DeGoede, Marieke. 1996. "Ideology in the US Welfare Debate: Neoliberal Representations of Poverty." *Discourse & Society* 7: 317–57.

Desmond, Matthew, and Mustafa Emirbayer. 2010. *Racial Domination, Racial Progress: The Sociology of Race in America.* New York: McGraw-Hill.

Donovan, Barna William. 2010. *Blood, Guns, and Testosterone: Action Films, Audiences and a Thirst for Violence*. Lanham, Md.: Scarecrow Press.

Douglas, Mary. 1994. *Risk and Blame: Essays in Cultural Theory*. New York: Routledge.

Elizondo, Juan B. 1996. "Report on the State's Concealed Gun Law Lists 4 Deaths Overall." *Houston Chronicle*, 17 July.

Eschholz, Sarah, Ted Chiricos, and Marc Gertz. 2003. "Television and Fear of Crime: Program Types, Audience Traits, and the Mediating Effect of Perceived Neighborhood Racial Composition." *Social Problems* 50: 395–415.

Eskenazi, Stuart, and Suzanne Gamboa. 1996. "Concealed Gun Holder Shoots, Kills Man in Dallas." *Austin American-Statesman*, 22 February.

Feagin, Joe, Hernán Vera, and Pinar Batur. 2001. *White Racism: The Basics*. New York: Routledge.

Feagin, Joe R. 2010. *Racist America: Roots, Current Realities, and Future Reparations*. Hoboken, N.J.: Taylor & Francis.

Ferraro, Kenneth F. 1996. "Women's Fear of Victimization: Shadow of Sexual Assault?" *Social Forces* 75: 667–90.

Forman, Tyrone A., and Amanda E. Lewis. 2006. "Racial Apathy and Hurricane Katrina: The Social Anatomy of Prejudice in the Post–Civil Rights Era." *Du Bois Review* 3: 175–202.

Franklin, Cortney A., and Travis W. Franklin. 2009. "Predicting Fear of Crime: Considering Differences across Gender." *Feminist Criminology* 4: 83–106.

Fraser, Nancy, and Linda Gordon. 1994. "A Genealogy of Dependency: Tracing a Keyword of the U.S. Welfare State." *Signs* 19: 309–36.

Gay, Malcolm. 2010. "More States Allowing Guns in Bars." *New York Times*, 3 October.

Gibson, James. 1994. *Warrior Dreams: Paramilitary Culture in Post-Vietnam America*. New York: Hill and Wang.

Gilens, Martin. 1999. *Why Americans Hate Welfare*. Chicago: University of Chicago Press.

Goldstein, Jeffrey. 2005. "Violent Video Games." In *Handbook of Computer Game Studies*, edited by Joost Raessens and Jeffrey Goldstein. Cambridge, Mass.: MIT Press.

Grissom, Brandi, Matt Stiles, and John Tedesco. 2010. "Wealthier, More Conservative Texans Have Gun Permits." *Texas Tribune*, 3 October.

Griswold, Wendy. 1994. *Cultures and Societies in a Changing World*. Thousand Oaks, Calif.: Pine Forge Press.

Hale, C. 1996. "Fear of Crime: A Review of the Literature." *International Review of Victimology* 4: 79–150.

Hartigan, John. 2005. *Odd Tribes*. Durham, N.C.: Duke University Press.

Hartmann, Tilo, and Peter Vorderer. 2010. "It's Okay to Shoot a Character: Moral Disengagement in Violent Video Games." *Journal of Communication* 60: 94–119.

Hinojosa, Ramon. 2010. "Doing Hegemony: Military, Men, and Constructing a Hegemonic Masculinity." *Journal of Men's Studies* 18, no. 2: 179–94.

Hollander, Joceyln. 2001. "Vulnerability and Dangerousness: The Construction of Gender through Conversations about Violence." *Gender & Society* 15: 83–109.

———. 2004. "'I Can Take Care of Myself': The Impact of Self-Defense Training on Women's Lives." *Violence against Women* 10: 205–35.

———. 2009. "The Roots of Resistance to Women's Self-Defense." *Violence against Women* 15, no. 5: 574–94.

Holloway, Wendy, and Tony Jefferson. 1997. "The Risk Society in an Age of Anxiety: Situating Fear of Crime." *British Journal of Sociology* 48 (June): 255–66.

Homsher, Deborah. 2001. *Women and Guns: Politics and the Culture of Firearms in America.* Armonk, N.Y.: M. E. Sharpe.

Horwitz, Joshua, and Casey Anderson. 2009. *Guns, Democracy and the Insurrectionist Idea.* Ann Arbor: University of Michigan Press.

Humpel, Nancy, Neville Owen, and Eva Leslie. 2002. "Environmental Factors Associated with Adults' Participation in Physical Activity." *American Journal of Preventive Medicine* 22: 188–99.

Hupp, Suzana Gratia. 2010. *From Luby's to the Legislature.* San Antonio, Tex.: Privateer.

Jeffords, Susan. 1994. *Hard Bodies: Hollywood Masculinity in the Reagan Era.* New Brunswick, N.J.: Rutgers University Press.

Johnson, Kirk. 2008. "On Concerns over Gun Control, Gun Sales Are Up." *New York Times,* 6 November.

Jones, Ann. 1994. "Living with Guns, Playing with Fire." *Ms.*, May/June.

Jones, Jeffrey M. 2005. "Public Wary about Broad Concealed Firearm Privileges." Gallup Poll, 14 June. http://www.gallup.com/poll/16822/Public-Wary-About-Broad-Concealed-Firearm-Privileges.aspx.

———. 2009. "In U.S., Record-Low Support for Stricter Gun Laws." Gallup Poll, 9 October. http://www.gallup.com/poll/123596/in-u.s.-record-low-support-stricter-gun-laws.aspx.

———. 2011. "Record-Low 26% in U.S. Favor Handgun Ban." Gallup Poll, 26 October. http://www.gallup.com/poll/150341/record-low-favor-handgun-ban.aspx.

———. 2013. "Men, Married, Southerners Most Likely to Be Gun Owners." Gallup Poll, 1 February. http://www.gallup.com/poll/160223/men-married-southerners-likely-gun-owners.aspx.

Jones, Nikki. 2009. *Between Good and Ghetto: African-American Girls and Inner City Violence.* New Brunswick, N.J.: Rutgers Press.

Keene, David. A. 2012. "We Must Stand Together to Fight Attacks on Our Rights." *American Rifleman.* http://webwonks.org/Extra/NRA/nraarchive/2012/feb.html.

Kelly, Caitlin. 2004. *Blown Away: American Women and Guns.* New York: Gallery Books.

Kimmel, M., and M. Mahler. 2003. "Adolescent Masculinity, Homophobia, and Violence: Random School Shootings, 1982–2001." *American Behavioral Scientist* 46: 1439–58.

Kimmel, Michael. 1996. *Manhood in America: A Cultural History.* New York: Free Press.

———. 2010. "Masculinity as Homophobia: Fear, Shame, and Silence in the Construction of Gender Identity." In *Privilege*, edited by Michael S. Kimmel and Abby L. Ferber. Boulder, Colo.: Westview Press.

Klaus, Patsy, and Cathy Maston. 2000. "Criminal Victimization in the Unites States, 1995." Washington D.C.: Bureau of Justice Statistics.

Kleck, Gary, and Marc Gertz. 1995. "Armed Resistance to Crime: The Prevalence and Nature of Self-Defense with a Gun." *Journal of Criminal Law and Criminology* 86: 150–87.

Koppel, Herbert. 1987. "Lifetime Likelihood of Victimization." Washington, D.C.: U.S. Department of Justice, Bureau of Justice Statistics.

Kort-Butler, Lisa A., and Kelley J. Sittner Hartshorn. 2011. "Watching the Detectives: Crime Programming, Fear of Crime and Attitudes about the Criminal Justice System." *Sociological Quarterly* 52: 36–55.

Krouse, William J., and Daniel J. Richardson. 2015. "Mass Murder with Firearms: Incidents and Victims, 1999–2013." Washington D.C.: Congressional Research Service.

LaFraniere, Sharon, Sarah Cohen, and Richar A. Oppel Jr. 2015. "How Often Do Mass Shootings Occur? On Average, Every Day, Records Show." *New York Times*, 2 December.

LaGrange, Randy L., and Kenneth F. Ferraro. 1989. "Assessing Age and Gender Differences in Perceived Risk and Fear of Crime." *Criminology* 27: 697–720.

LaPierre, Wayne. 2012. "All or Nothing Election for the Second Amendment." *American Rifleman.* http://webwonks.org/Extra/NRA/nraarchive/2012/feb.html.

Lave, Tamara Rice. 2013. "Shoot to Kill: A Critical Look at Stand Your Ground Laws." *University of Miami Law Review* 67: 827–60.

LeDoux, Joseph. 1998. *The Emotional Brain: The Mysterious Underpinnings of Emotional Life.* New York: Simon & Schuster.

Leonard, David J. 2010. "Jumping the Gun: Sporting Cultures and the Criminalization of Black Masculinity." *Journal of Sport and Social Issues* 34: 252–62.

Leonardatos, Cynthia. 1999. "California's Attempt to Disarm the Black Panthers." *San Diego Law Review* 36: 947–96.

Levin, Benjamin. 2010. "A Defensible Defense? Reexamining Castle Doctrine Statuses." *Harvard Journal on Legislation* 47: 523–53.

Lewis, Amanda. 2004. " 'What Group?' Studying Whites and Whiteness in the Era of 'Color-Blindness.' " *Sociological Theory* 22: 623–46.

Liska, Allen E., and Paul E. Bellair. 1995. "Violent-Crime Rates and Racial Composition: Convergence over Time." *American Journal of Sociology* 101: 578–610.

Lott, John. 1998. *More Guns, Less Crime.* Chicago: University of Chicago Press.

Luo, Michael, and Mike McIntire. 2013. "When the Right to Bear Arms Includes the Mentally Ill." *New York Times,* 21 December.

Lupton, Deborah, and John Tulloch. 1999. "Theorizing Fear of Crime beyond the Rational/Irrational Opposition." *British Journal of Sociology* 50: 507–23.

Madriz, Esther. 1997. *Nothing Bad Happens to Good Girls: Fear of Crime in Women's Lives.* Berkeley: University of California Press.

Mass Shooting Tracker. 2015. "Mass Shootings in 2015." 17 December, http://www.shootingtracker.com/wiki/Mass_Shootings_in_2015.

McCaughey, Martha. 1997. *Real Knockouts: The Physical Feminism of Women's Self-Defense.* New York: NYU Press.

McDowall, David, Colin Loftin, and Stanley Presser. 2000. "Measuring Civilian Defensive Firearm Use: A Methodological Experiment." *Journal of Quantitative Criminology* 16: 1–19.

Melzer, Scott. 2009. *Gun Crusaders: The NRA's Culture War.* New York: NYU Press.

Messerschmidt, James W. 1993. *Masculinities and Crime: Critique and Reconceptualization of Theory.* Lanham, Md.: Rowman and Littlefield.

———. 2000. *Nine Lives: Adolescent Masculinities, the Body, and Violence.* Boulder, Colo.: Westview Press.

Messner, Michael. 1992. *Power at Play: Sports and the Problem of Masculinity.* Boston: Beacon Press.

———. 2011. *King of the Wild Suburb.* Austin, Tex.: Plainview Press.

Mifflin, Lawrie. 1999. "Many Researchers Say Link Is Already Clear on Media and Youth Violence." *New York Times,* 9 May.

Miller, Jody. 2008. *Getting Played: African American Girls, Urban Inequality, and Gendered Violence.* New York: NYU Press.

Misra, Joya, Stephanie Moller, and Mrina Karides. 2003. "Envisioning Dependency: Changing Media Depictions of Welfare in the 20th Century." *Social Problems* 50: 482–504.

Mitchell, Lee Clark. 1998. *Westerns: Making the Man in Fiction and Film.* Chicago: University of Chicago Press.

News21. 2015. "Public Records and Data." *Gun Wars,* 12 June, http://gunwars.news21.com/data/.

O'Connor, Anahad. 2011. "Head Injuries on the Football Field." *New York Times,* 8 September.

O'Keefe, Ed. 2010. "Federal Government to Lift Restrictions on Guns in National Parks." *Washington Post,* 19 February.

Omi, Michael, and Howard Winant. 1994. *Racial Formation in the United States.* New York: Routledge.

O'Neill, Kevin Lewis. 2007. "Armed Citizens and the Stories They Tell: The National Rifle Association's Achievement of Terror and Masculinity." *Men and Masculinities* 9: 457–75.

Pascoe, C. J. 2007. *Dude You're a Fag: Masculinity and Sexuality in High School.* Berkeley: University of California Press.

Payne, Keith. 2006. "Weapon Bias: Split-Second Decisions and Unintended Stereotyping." *Current Directions in Psychological Science* 15 (December): 287–91.

Peterson, Ruth D., and Lauren J. Krivo. 2010. *Divergent Social Worlds: Neighborhood Crime and the Racial-Spatial Divide.* New York: Russell Sage Foundation.

Plant, E. Ashby, B. Michele Peruche, and David Butz. 2005. "Elimination of Automatic Racial Bias: Making Race Non-diagnostic for Responses to Criminal Suspects." *Journal of Experimental Social Psychology* 41: 141–56.

Poston, Ben. 2011. "Police Response Times Lag as Patrol Strategy Shifts." *Milwaukee Journal Sentinel*, 6 August.

Power, Marcus. 2007. "Digitized Virtuosity: Video War Games and Post-9/11 Cyber-Deterrence." *Security Dialogue* 38: 271–88.

Prokos, Anastasia, and Irene Padavic. 2002. "'There Oughtta Be a Law against Bitches': Masculinity Lessons in Police Academy Training." *Gender, Work, and Organization* 9: 439–59.

Quigley, Paxton. 1989. *Armed and Female.* New York: St. Martin's Paperback.

———. 2012. "Who Is Paxton Quigley." Paxton Quigley, 10 May, http://www.paxtonquigley.com/?page_id=9.

Quillian, Lincoln, and Devah Pager. 2001. "Black Neighbors, Higher Crime? The Role of Racial Stereotypes in Evaluations of Neighborhood Crime." *American Journal of Sociology* 107: 717–67.

Rader, Nicole E. 2010. "Until Death Do Us Part? Husband Perceptions and Responses to Fear of Crime." *Deviant Behavior* 31: 33–59.

Reiman, Jeffrey, and Paul Leighton. 2010. *The Rich Get Richer and the Poor Get Prison: Ideology, Class, and Criminal Justice.* New York: Allyn & Bacon.

Reinarman, Craig, and Harry G. Levine. 1997. *Crack in America: Demon Drugs and Social Justice.* Berkeley: University of California Press.

Robison, Clay. 1993a. "Handgun Plan Wins Approval by Senate Panel." *Houston Chronicle*, 15 May.

———. 1993b. "Police Applaud as Richards Vetoes Gun Bill." *Houston Chronicle*, 4 June.

Roman, John K. 2013. "Race, Justifiable Homicide, and Stand Your Ground Laws: Analysis of FBI Supplementary Homicide Report Data." Urban Institute, July, http://www.urban.org/sites/default/files/alfresco/publication-pdfs/412873-Race-Justifiable-Homicide-and-Stand-Your-Ground-Laws.PDF.

Royce, Edward R. 2009. *Poverty and Power: The Problem of Structural Inequality.* Lanham, Md.: Rowman & Littlefield.

Russell-Brown, Katherine. 2009. *The Color of Crime.* 2nd ed. New York: NYU Press.

Saad, Lydia. 2011. "Self-Reported Gun Ownership in U.S. Is Highest Since 1993." Gallup Poll, 26 October. http://www.gallup.com/poll/150353/Self-Reported -Gun-Ownership-Highest-1993.aspx.

———. 2013. "U.S. Remains Divided over Passing Stricter Gun Laws." Gallup Poll, 25 October, http://www.gallup.com/poll/150353/self-reported-gun -ownership-highest-1993.aspx.

Schreier, Philip, and Frank Horak. 2010. "NRA & BSA: 100 Years of Partnership," 19 November, http://www.americanrifleman.org/articles/2010 /11/19/nra-bsa-100-years-of-partnership/.

Schrock, Douglas, and Michael Schwalbe. 2009. "Men, Masculinity, and Manhood Acts." *Annual Review of Sociology* 35: 277–95.

Schudson, Michael. 2011. *The Sociology of the News.* 2nd ed. New York: W.W. Norton & Company.

Schulze, Louis N., Jr. 2012. "Of Trayvon Martin, George Zimmerman, and Legal Expressivism: Why Massachusetts Should Stand Its Ground on 'Stand Your Ground.'" *New England Law Review on Remand* 47: 34–41.

Schwalbe, Michael. 2014. *Manhood Acts: Gender and the Practices of Domination.* New York: Paradigm.

Sigler, John C. 2009a. "The Time to Act." *American Rifleman.* http://webwonks .org/Extra/NRA/nraarchive/2009/feb.html.

———. 2009b. "Grassroots Activism is a Powerful Force." *American Rifleman.* http://webwonks.org/Extra/NRA/nraarchive/2009/mar.html.

Smith, Erica L., and Alexia Cooper. 2013. "Homicide in the U.S. Known to Law Enforcement, 2011." Washington, D.C.: U.S. Department of Justice, Office of Justice Programs.

Smith, Tom W., and Robert J. Smith. 1995. "Changes in Firearms Ownership among Women, 1980–1994." *Journal of Criminal Law and Criminology* 86: 133–49.

South, Jeff. 1996. "In the Concealed Handgun Law's First Year, 115,000 Texans Apply." *Austin American-Statesman*, 31 December.

Spitzer, Robert J. 2011. *The Politics of Gun Control.* 5th ed. Washington, D.C.: Paradigm.

Sprague, Joey. 2005. *Feminist Methodologies for Critical Researchers.* Walnut Creek, Calif.: AltaMira Press.

Stacey, Judith. 1988. "Can There Be a Feminist Ethnography?" *Women's Studies International Forum* 11: 21–27.

Stange, Mary Zeiss, and Carol K. Oyster. 2000. *Gun Women: Firearms and Feminism in Contemporary America.* New York: NYU Press.

Stanko, Elizabeth. 1995. "Women, Crime, and Fear." *Annals of the American Academy of Political Science* 539: 46–58.

Stein, Arlene. 2010. "Sex, Truths, and Audiotape: Anonymity and the Ethics of Exposure in Public Ethnography." *Journal of Contemporary Ethnography* 39: 554–68.

Stretesky, P. B., and M. R. Pogrebin. 2007. "Gang-Related Gun Violence: Socialization, Identity, and Self." *Journal of Contemporary Ethnography* 36: 85–114.

Stroud, Angela. 2012. "Good Guys with Guns: Hegemonic Masculinity and Concealed Handguns." *Gender & Society* 26: 216–38.

Sutton, Robbie M., and Stephen Farrall. 2005. "Gender, Socially Desirable Responding and the Fear of Crime: Are Women Really More Anxious about Crime?" *British Journal of Criminology* 45: 212–24.

Swanson, J. 2013. "Mental Illness and New Gun Law Reforms: The Promise and Peril of Crisis-Driven Policy." *Journal of the American Medical Association* 309: 1233–34.

Swanson, Jeffrey W., et al. 2015. "Guns, Impulsive Angry Behavior, and Mental Disorders: Results from the National Comorbidity Survey Replication (NCS-R)." *Behavioral Sciences & the Law* 33. http://nmcgv.org/wp-content/uploads/2015/04/swanson-guns-impulsive-angry.pdf.

Swarns, Rachel L. 2004. "Hispanics Resist Racial Grouping by Census." *New York Times*, 25 October.

Tavernise, Sabrina, and Robert Gebeloff. 2013. "Share of Homes with Guns Shows 4-Decade Decline." *New York Times*, 9 March.

Taylor, Kate. 2012. "Stop-and-Frisk Opponents Set Sights on Mayoral Race." *New York Times*, 12 February.

Texas Concealed Handguns License Laws, 2013–2014. 2014. Austin: Texas Department of Public Safety. https://www.txdps.state.tx.us/internetforms/Forms/CHL-16.pdf.

Texas Department of Public Safety. 1996–2015. "Demographic Information by Race/Sex: License Applications: Issued." http://txdps.state.tx.us/rsd/chl/reports/demoreportscy14.htm.

——. 2015. "Active License/Certified Instructor Counts, as of December 31, 2014." https://www.txdps.state.tx.us/rsd/chl/reports/ActLicAndInstr/ActiveLicandInstr2014.pdf.

Truman, Jennifer L. 2011. "Criminal Victimization, 2010." Washington, D.C.: National Crime Victimization Survey, Bureau of Justice Statistics.

Truman, Jennifer L., and Lynn Langton. 2014. "Criminal Victimization, 2013." Washington, D.C.: National Crime Victimization Survey, Bureau of Justice Statistics.

Truman, Jennifer L., Lynn Langton, and Michael Planty. 2013. "Criminal Victimization, 2012." Washington, D.C.: National Crime Victimization Survey, Bureau of Justice Statistics.

Truman, Jennifer L., and Michael Planty. 2012. "Criminal Victimization, 2011." Washington, D.C.: National Crime Victimization Survey, Bureau of Justice Statistics.

Ullman, Sarah E. 2007. "A 10-Year Update of 'Review and Critique of Empirical Studies of Rape Avoidance.' " *Criminal Justice and Behavior* 34: 1–19

U.S. Bureau of the Census. 2010. "Race and Hispanic or Latino Origin: 2010, Texas." http://factfinder.census.gov/faces/tableservices/jsf/pages /productview.xhtml?src=CF.

U.S. Bureau of the Census. 2010–2014. "American Community Survey 5-Year Estimates." http://factfinder.census.gov/faces/tableservices/jsf/pages /productview.xhtml?src=bkmk.

U.S. Department of Justice, Federal Bureau of Investigation. 2013. *A Study of Active Shooter between 2000 and 2013*. Washington, D.C.: Federal Bureau of Investigation.

U.S. Department of Justice, Office of Justice Programs. 1995. *Criminal Victimizations in the United States, 1995*. Washington, D.C.: Office of Justice Programs.

U.S. Government Accountability Office. 2012. *Gun Control: States' Laws and Requirements for Concealed Carry Permits Vary across the Nation*. Washington, D.C.: GAO.

Wacquant, Loïc. 1995. "The Pugilistic Point of View: How Boxers Think and Feel about Their Trade." *Theory and Society* 24: 489–535.

———. 2009. *Prisons of Poverty*. Minneapolis: University of Minnesota Press.

Warr, Mark. 1984. "Fear of Victimization: Why Are Women and the Elderly More Afraid?" *Social Science Quarterly* 65: 681–702.

———. 2000. "Fear of Crime in the United States: Avenues for Research and Policy." In *Criminal Justice 2000*, vol. 4: *Measurement and Analysis of Crime and Justice*, edited by D. Duffee. Washington, D.C.: National Institute of Justice.

Watkins, Craig. 2005. *Hip Hop Matters: Politics, Pop Culture, and the Struggle for the Soul of a Movement*. Boston: Beacon Press.

Weitzer, Ronald, and Charis E. Kubrin. 2004. "Breaking News: How Local TV News and Real-World Conditions Affect Fear of Crime." *Justice Quarterly* 21: 497–520.

Wellford, Charles, John Pepper, and Carol Petrie, eds. 2004. *Firearms and Violence: A Critical Review*. Committee on Law and Justice, National Research Council. Washington, D.C.: National Academic Press.

West, Candace, and Don H. Zimmerman. 1987. "Doing Gender." *Gender & Society* 1: 125–51.

Wingfield, Adia Harvey. 2007. "The Modern Mammy and the Angry Black Man: African American Professionals' Experience with Gendered Racism in the Workplace." *Race, Gender, and Class* 14: 196–212.

———. 2009. "Racializing the Glass Escalator: Reconsidering Men's Experiences with Women's Work." *Gender and Society* 23: 5–26.

Winkler, Adam. 2011. *Gunfight: The Battle over the Right to Bear Arms in America*. New York: Norton.

Wintemute, Garen J. 2006. "Guns and Gun Violence." In *The Crime Drop in America*, edited by Alfred Blumstein and Joel Wallman, 2nd ed. Cambridge, UK: Cambridge University Press.

Wolf, Naomi. 1994. *Fire with Fire: The New Female Power and How to Use It.* New York: Ballantine Books.

Zack, Naomi. 2015. *White Privilege and Black Rights: The Injustice of U.S. Police Racial Profiling and Homicide.* Lanham, Md.: Rowman & Littlefield.

Index